International Studies of the

Committee on International Relations

University of Notre Dame

Peru and the

United States, 1900-1962

Peru and the United States, 1900-1962

By JAMES C. CAREY

UNIVERSITY OF NOTRE DAME PRESS 1964

Library of Congress Catalog Card Number: 64-23666
Manufactured in the United States

TO
WENONAH, LEONA,
WENONAH MAY

PREFACE

It is an illusion to think that there is, or ever can be under the present conditions, anything which realistically approximates "A United States Policy for Latin America." How can there be one definite course of action designed for dealing with twenty nations as diverse as these twenty? Paraguay and Uruguay, side by side, are as different as Switzerland and Spain, or as different as Great Britain and Greece. Costa Rica and neighboring Nicaragua are as unsimilar as Sweden and France or Italy and Denmark. Yet the United States has tried to apply some will-o-the-wisp "Latin-American Policy" without seriously attempting to build a common market or a common monetary unit.

If one country were to be selected as a cross-section reference for studying both private and public (official and nonofficial) interchanges between United States and Latin America, it would be difficult to find one more representative of the many cross-currents than Peru. The dominant position of the United States over pre-1959 Cuba or the slight influence of the United States in Uruguay is met half way in our dealing with Peru. Peru affords us a good specimen study of the complex pattern with its multiplicity of lines and positions in that something which we call "The Latin-American Policy of the United States." This writer does not claim that Peru has been the anvil of American foreign policy as much as has Mexico. Neither has it been as far removed from United States international interest

as has Paraguay. But here again, Lima has often been more of a middle ground sounding board than have most capitals of the Western
Hemisphere. United States-Peruvian relations may have been overlooked by scholars because the relationships have usually been "normal" and not of such an immoderate nature as to draw special
attention or to distort the general picture.

It is important to note that this study is not merely an attempt to
analyze policies, relations, or activities of the respective governments.
Private United States enterprise and private aid, as well as public
enterprise and aid, will be traced and examined. The traditional
emphasis upon boundary negotiations and formal treaties between
nations will not be made. With the social revolution now stirring
Peru, the particular distinction of Peruvian (or non-United States)
politics should be noted. It appears that the majority of Peruvians
have often been disappointed and unhappy with their government
over the past 140 years. They may have loved their country at the same
time that they disliked, and even distrusted, their government. This
being the case, it is evident that the traditional diplomatic-history
approach would not be as significantly pertinent as citizens of the
United States might at first assume. Relationships which may have
pleased the government of Peru did not necessarily please the people
of Peru.

There are various other reasons why a general diplomatic historical
approach fails to explain significantly the status of relationships between Peru and the United States. For one thing, Peruvian official
documents as well as most materials published in Peru before 1940,
are not particularly meaningful for an understanding of the Peruvian
points of view up to that time. Dictatorial handling of public documents and close governmental control of printed materials have left
us with a paucity of reliable sources on the attitudes of the Peruvian
citizenry. The near-disastrous fire which destroyed part of the National
Library in 1943 further reduced the availability of general source materials. However, periodicals stored there are of considerable help.
Materials from the periods of the dictatorial governments are quite
limited, simply because the editors could not have reflected popular
sentiment even if they had so desired. For over half the time from
1900 to 1958, three dictators governed Peru without permitting freedom of expression. This explains why it is necessary to use writings
done in exile, and supplemented by United States sources, to uncover
Peruvian criticism, at the time, of unpopular relationships between

the two nations. In United States official documents, as well as in unofficial accounts, there has often been some reflection of Peruvian points of view as expressed by United States writers. This is not only helpful to the scholar but it is also a tribute to the sense of justice and integrity north of the border. A freer press and a more responsible government, especially during 1945-1948 and since 1956, have opened the door to wider and better balanced expressions of Peruvians, both publicly and privately.

An effort has been made here to study the private United States activities in Peru at the same time that public relationships are being examined. The official interexchanges between Lima and Washington which dealt with hemispheric and world matters have usually been quite harmonious. No prolonged, serious controversy in the last thirty-five years has stood in the way of Peruvian-United States co-operation at either the Inter-American Conferences or at the Meetings of Foreign Ministers. However, in the undertow near the surface, various unofficial or quasi-official exchanges relative to private commerce, industry, and finance have caused serious rifts between the peoples of the two nations. Private United States capital investment has been particularly significant in Peru, and the result has not always worked for good relations between Peruvians and the United States. The outburst against Vice-President Nixon—even when allowing for some professional rabble-rousing activity—revealed that the traditional policies and decisions of the two countries had not been acceptable to a good many Peruvians.

In examination of United States activities in Peru, it soon became evident that there was not a distinct line between the unofficial and the official, nor between the private and the public, nor even between the individual and the national. Particularly was this true when the dollar was involved. Loyalties of United States diplomats and businessmen have been divided, confused, or both, on many occasions. It is a problem of dual allegiance—loyalty to the dollar and to the nation at the same time. Often, there is a compatibility in this double allegiance. But, on occasion, the two loyalties are not compatible, and then the problem is as old as time; what is good for the dollar is not always good for the United States as a nation.

Research for this study involved the use in Peru of the Ministry of Foreign Affairs, the National Library, all the Ministries of the national government, San Marcos University, the Catholic University, the Callao Municipal Library, the *Instituto Cultural Peruano-Norte-*

americano, and the United States Embassy in Lima. The principal fact-finding in the United States was carried out at the Library of Congress, the National Archives, and various offices of the Department of Commerce. Six United States libraries, as well as the Harry S Truman Library at Independence, Missouri, were visited. A sample survey of Peruvian public opinion, conducted in 1962 in Lima and Callao, has helped with interpretations of the more current developments, but only time can show the validity or fallacy of those interpretations. The opinions as to whether United States private efforts have supplemented or hampered United States public efforts in relations with Peru, and *vice versa,* must be categorized as rumination and conclusion-drawing at one and the same time.

Early in the course of this work, Professor Fritz L. Hoffmann and Professor Arthur P. Whitaker gave me inspiration and valuable assistance. Since that time, many people (too many to mention here) have aided me with this study. Interviews with twenty-six Peruvians proved to be of great value, and I thank those kind people who took time from busy schedules to help me. This aid was appreciated more than might be thought. My sons, Steve and Jim, missed out on many fishing trips while I worked on the manuscript. My father, F. L. Carey, and my father-in-law, S. A. Moline, helped out on the "fish-pole duties" in various ways. I believe that all of them, cabinet minister, library attendant, and would-be fishermen, join with me in the hope that this study will work for better relations between Peru and the United States.

Kansas State University   James C. Carey
Manhattan, Kansas

CONTENTS

1: HISTORICAL OUTLINES OF PERU

THE POLITICAL OUTLINE

As adequate background for this study, it was important that the broad lines of development in Peru's history be examined, with stress upon its twentieth-century relationships with the United States. Peru arrived on the twentieth-century scene a weak nation of three nearly isolated regions (coast, mountains, jungle). Descendants of the cultures of ancient Peru have not been drawn into the modern, European-based national political system which struggled along through the nineteenth century, scarcely maintaining more than its own self-survival.

The national life of Peru from its beginning had been torn by disturbances. Many of these disrupting factors have had their source in soil foreign to Peru: Spanish domination; war with Bolivia and the turmoil of the Santa Cruz Confederation; Spain's war against Peru, Chile, Ecuador, and Bolivia; the War of the Pacific and the consequent Chilean occupation of Lima; boundary disputes; and financial dependence upon foreign powers—all these make up a partial list of outside disruptive forces.

Peru, center of Hispanic-Catholic conservatism in the New World, was one of the last segments of Spanish colonial society to aspire to and achieve independence. Lima was the stronghold of Spanish rule in South America. When patriots arose there, few indeed in comparison to the rest of America, they found the viceroyalty securely cemented to Spain. Outside movements, that of San Martín from the south and of Bolívar from the north, were needed to wrest this area from the grasp of the Old World. These two movements for emancipation left Peru with "two fathers" and divided loyalties; neither José de San Martín nor Simón Bolívar could unite the Peruvians under one government. To the present day there is difference of opinion as to the relative importance of these two movements for independence, although San Martín seems to hold the most prestige.

Peruvians lacked the necessary unity to establish their own govern-

1

ment as they struggled for independence from Spain. San Martín[1] bowed out of the picture and left Peru in 1822 after realizing that his forces were not strong enough to drive the Spanish out of the country, and—after his meeting with Bolívar at Guayaquil—that it was for the best interests of Peru that he leave. Bolívar and Antonio José de Sucre led the patriots to victory over the Spaniards in the last two important battles, Junín and Ayacucho, in 1824, but they did not leave the Peruvians united behind one government. When Bolívar returned to Bogotá in 1826, Peru was again thrown into confusion over an attempt to work out a plan of government.

Victory for the patriots at Junín and Ayacucho had not sufficiently broken the powerful grip of Spanish rule in Peru. Colonial institutions prevailed under the control of clerics, military officials, and a small but powerful landed aristocracy. This closely knit, conservative oligarchy desired little change in the social, economic, and cultural patterns which Spain had maintained. The early years of the young republic's life were very unsettled, mainly because of a general lack of experience in self-rule. The absence of clearly determined boundaries also brought difficulties with other nations. The aftermath of the severe wars for independence had left Peru in a troubled situation. Hardship, distrust, and hatred thrived under the existing conditions of poverty, illiteracy, and the inflexibility of the social system.

Civil strife followed in Peru when the Peruvians lost a short war (1828-1829) over territorial claims with Colombia. The resulting civil war in Peru made it possible for General Andrés Santa Cruz to subdue Peruvian forces and combine Peru and Bolivia in the *Confederación Peru-Boliviana* (1836-1839). Many Peruvians welcomed the Confederation and a period of rest under the dictatorship of Santa Cruz, but his enemies joined Chilean forces to bring about his downfall. Argentina, as well as Chile, strongly opposed the confederation.

Peru had its share of *caudillos*, confusion, and conflict in the period following the confederation when Peru and Bolivia were again sepa-

[1] San Martín freed Lima (July 12, 1821) and held it against the Spanish forces; the latter entrenched themselves in a fort at Callao and at various points in the central highlands. On July 28, a *cabildo abierto* declared Peru's independence from Spain. San Martín proclaimed himself dictator, "Protector of Peru," and promised to give up his position once Peru's independence was insured. For a recent critical interpretation of San Martín's actions (or rather inaction) see James C. Carey, "Lord Cochrane: Critic of San Martín's Peruvian Campaign," *The Americas*, XVIII (April 1962), pp. 340-351.

rate nations. Political anarchy, however, finally brought forth dic-tatorial rule. Fortunately for Peru a mild dictator appeared on the scene to establish a moderate and progressive government. Under Ramón Castilla, 1844-1850 and 1856-1862, a military figure who proved to be tolerent, energetic and honest, Peru moved ahead. But Castilla's government was "strong arm" rule, and a decade of chaos and corruption followed it.

Friction with Spain and subsequent war (1866-1879) climaxed this dismal period of early national history.[2] Bolivia, Chile, and Ecuador joined Peru in the fight against the mother country. Only brief sporadic struggles ensued, and Spain abandoned its aggressive moves in South America after having failed to make permanent gains. Dur-ing this conflict between Spain and the four South American coun-tries, Washington informed the Spanish government that Spanish occupation of Peruvian territory would disturb relations between Spain and the United States.

In the late 1860's, Peru made a series of contracts with Henry Meiggs, a daring, unpredictable and, at times, irresponsible United States contractor, to build railroads over the towering Andes.[3] One specific contract provided for a railroad from Callao, the main sea-port, to Oroya, which was near the rich mineral deposits of central Peru. The cost of railroad construction was too great for the coun-try's antiquated financial system, and in 1876 the nation defaulted on the payment of interest on its foreign debt.

More devastating to national development than any other single event of Peru's history as a republic was the War of the Pacific (1879-1884), in which Chile defeated Bolivia and Peru, and the latter suf-

[2] No treaty of peace had been signed between Peru and Spain at the close of the wars of independence. The mother country adopted an aggressive attitude toward Peru in the mid-sixties which resulted in the Peruvian nation declaring war on Spain in 1866. Hostilities in all sectors during this war with Spain lasted only a few months, yet the treaty of peace in which Spain finally recognized the independence of Peru was not signed until 1879. See Benjamín Vicuña Mackenna for the early period of this conflict. See also: Carlos E. Grez Pérez, Los intentos de unión hispano-americana y la guerra de España en el Pacífico (Santiago, 1928); Gustavo Pons Muzzo, "El conflicto entre el Peru y España, 1864-1866" (thesis, Lima, 1939); Alberto Ulloa Sotomayor, Congresos Americanos de Lima, (2 vols., Lima, 1938); and Carlos Lisson, La república en el Peru y la cuestión peruano-española (Lima, 1865).

[3] Watt Stewart, Henry Meiggs, Yankee Pizarro (Durham, Duke University Press, 1946). For statistics, see: Ernesto Malinowski, Ferrocarril central tra-sandino (Lima, 1869); and Ferrocarriles del Peru (reimpresión, Lima, 1876).

fered occupation and wanton vandalism. A savage civil war broke out in Peru when the die-hards learned that concessions had been made to Chile in the Treaty of Ancón. Early in December of 1885 the two opposing groups fought viciously in the streets of Lima, and bloody engagements between the two Peruvian factions in the interior served further to weaken Peru. The War of the Pacific and the resultant civil wars seriously retarded the general development of the nation for many years.

Nicolás Piérola, founder of the right-wing Democratic Party, was able to form a coalition with part of the *Civilistas* and return to power in 1895.[4] One or the other, Democratic Party or *Civilista* Party, was to prevail over a conservative but steady government for the next thirty-five years. Peruvians took heart again and resumed the work of reconstruction. The year 1895 marked the end of sustained personal rule by military officers; yet, even after 1895 the army continued either to influence or dominate the government in varying degrees. In the period following 1900 it appears at first glance that peace, stability, and industrial growth meant that general progress was being made. This, however, was deceiving, for, as Jorge Basadre has pointed out, the country was ruled by a closed oligarchy.[5] The mestizos and

[4] Peru slowly and laboriously developed a *Civilista* tradition of government which had its first civilian president in the capable Manuel Pardo from 1872 to 1876. Under Pardo the *Civilistas* represented a reaction against the financial mismanagement of Balta's administration and a desire to eliminate military domination of politics. To a great degree, adherents of the *Civilista* Party favored government by the well-born; they would have replaced the military *caudillos* with aristocratic *caudillos*. The War of the Pacific and its tumultuous aftermath brought forth a return of militarism (*el segundo militarismo*), and army figures dominated the presidential scene from 1877 to 1895. Piérola's revolt against Cáceres in 1895 was successful because the *Civilistas* as well as Piérola's democratic party backed the uprising, Piérola attaining popular favor. For general accounts see the following: Jorge Basadre, Clements R. Markham, Víctor Andrés Belaúnde, Francisco García Calderón, José Carlos Mariátegui, Pedro Davalos y Lisson, Nemesio Vargas, and R. J. Owens.

[5] Jorge Basadre, the most notable Peruvian historian of the twentieth century, wrote that it might appear that a great similarity of historical development existed between Peru and Mexico. This, he observed, was only true prior to the wars of independence, for after they became independent nations the two followed different routes. Peru, unlike Mexico, did not attempt government under an emperor. But more significant is the fact that Peru never experienced a prolonged serious struggle for liberalism which paralleled those of Mexico. Nothing in Peru's history is comparable to Mexico's first attempt at reform in 1833, the reforms of 1855-1857, or the twentieth-century revolution. Throughout Peru's

the whites of the coastal region saw some general advancement in living conditions, but the Indians of the mountains and jungles remained submerged in serfdom.

From 1895 to 1919 Peru's major political developments were characterized, in the main, by peaceful and constitutional procedure. During most of that period the *Civilistas* were in control. Eduardo de Romaña (1899-1903) served a quiet term as president and was succeeded by Miguel Candamo (May 1903-May 1904) who died in office. In September 1904, after the temporary presidency of Serapio Calderón, José Pardo assumed the presidency which he held until 1908 when Augusto B. Leguía was elected. Leguía's first administration (1908-1912) resulted in a temporary split of the *Civilista* Party, a split never entirely healed in spite of the return of the *Civilistas* to power from 1915 to 1919. Leguía was able to establish a semi-dictatorship under personal rule, but it collapsed when he tried to have his candidate, Antero Aspillaga, elected to succeed him.[6] Guillermo Billinghurst, grandson of an English officer who had fought with Peru in the War of the Pacific, was president from September 1912 to February 1914. Billinghurst's brusque reform manner and his conciliatory attitude toward Chile were used by his enemies to discredit him, and a revolt supported by a combination of *Civilistas* and militarists was successful. Colonel Oscar Benavides led the successful revolt against Billinghurst on February 4, 1914, and established a provisional *junta* of government with himself at its head. Benavides acted as provisional chief executive until August 1915 when José Pardo (1904-1908 and 1915-1919) was inaugurated as constitutional president for the second time.

José Pardo was the son of Peru's first *Civilista* president, Manuel Pardo (not to be confused with Manuel Prado). His second administration was conservative and fruitful. He fostered general education, strengthened the national economy, and set an example of honesty for the nation. In 1915 the constitution was amended to grant religious liberty to Peruvians. For the first time in its history Peru permitted legal religious toleration. Before he completed his term of office, Pardo introduced scientific sanitary systems and modern roads

---

history the army and the church have enjoyed a great freedom of activity, and a small number of property holders have dominated economically. Jorge Basadre, *Historia de la república del Peru,* I (3rd ed., Lima, 1946).

[6] For a survey of Leguía's relations with the United States (1908-1912) see Chapter 3.

into Peru. Dr. Henry Hanson of the sanitation department of the Panama Canal Zone was instrumental in the survey of Lima which led to the eradication of yellow fever and in the reduction of malaria in Peru's Pacific ports.

Pardo steered Peru through the First World War. During the early years of the war Peru suffered an economic depression, but before the conflict was over the nation enjoyed the prosperity of war prices when its petroleum, copper, sugar, and cotton found a ready market. Under Pardo the country showed itself willing to co-operate with the Allies against the Central Powers. On October 5, 1917, after Germany failed to grant satisfactory reparation for the sinking of a Peruvian ship, the *Lorton,* and in accordance with her ideas on continental co-operation, Peru severed diplomatic relations with Germany. The country did not enter the war against Germany, although considerable sentiment for such a declaration did prevail. After the war, Peru was one of the ten Latin-American countries that became original members of the League of Nations.[7]

Early in 1919, Leguía, who had quarreled with Pardo and Billinghurst in 1913, returned from five years of self-exile in London. In July 1919, he took the presidency by force (after apparently winning the election)[8] and introduced an eleven-year period of personal dictatorship. The internal history of Peru between 1919 and 1930 was one of industrial development, made possible chiefly through the infiltration of foreign capital and accompanied by eleven years of political stability. The period was characterized by a continuance of President Pardo's paving and sanitation operations, by greatly increased borrowing in the United States, and by a regression from republican forms of government.

Political and social progress did not keep pace with physical advancement. President Leguía ruled in a forthright manner. His return to power in July 1919 was followed by a new constitution in January of 1920, which, if it had been conscientiously enforced, would have tended to improve the social, cultural, and general civic patterns of activity of the country. Primary education, labor arbitration, an income tax system, and wide social reforms were promised to the

[7] Eight Latin-American nations declared war, five severed relations, and seven remained neutral. Only Brazil and Cuba took an active part in the war. For further data on Peru's activities in the war see pages 28-31.

[8] See Chapter 3.

masses, but these objectives were never achieved. Because Peru enjoyed a degree of material prosperity in the midst of graft and corruption, many citizens were inclined to disregard the government's indifference to the constitution as long as a progressive program of public works continued.

By convenient modifications of the constitution, Augusto B. Leguía was able to arrange for his re-election in 1920 and 1929. During most of these eleven years, the Peruvian Congress was a sham. This legislative body acted when and in the manner desired by Leguía. Congressmen who chose to oppose the president's plans were often charged by the government with attempted revolt or any other trumped up accusation and were usually imprisoned or exiled. Strong opposition to Leguía came from the *Apristas* and from the old *Civilista* Party; the latter had supported him in his first administration until he attempted in 1912 to have his candidate elected. Leguía controlled the government (1908-1912 and 1919-1930) for almost sixteen years, a period of control longer than that of any other chief executive. His administration might claim another first, if one wishes to call it a first, for he brought Peru under the influence of the United States more than any other president of Peru. By pseudo-constitutional means, Leguía crushed the opposition and maintained himself in the presidency until August 1930, when Sánchez Cerro led a successful revolt.

Sánchez Cerro established himself as president of a military *junta*, but he governed only until February 28, 1931, when uprisings forced him to flee Peru and turn the presidency over to Ricardo Elías. Elías held on but a short time and moved out when *Comandante* Gustavo Jiménez moved in. Under Sánchez Cerro the United States did not attempt actively to influence Peruvian affairs as it had done under Leguía. The official correspondence of the American Embassy reflects the lack of appreciation of the growing popular prestige of *Aprismo*, the movement which provided Sánchez Cerro his greatest opposition.[9]

In the fall of 1931, Sánchez Cerro returned to contest the election with the founder of *Aprismo*, Víctor Raúl Haya de la Torre. There was considerable confusion as to who would have received the most votes in an honest, free election, but there was no doubt that Sánchez Cerro was inaugurated president in December 1931. The new presi-

[9] *Papers Relating to the Foreign Relations of the United States* (Washington), hereafter cited as *US Foreign Relations*.

dent proceeded to try to stamp out the *Aprista* opposition by violent action as he brought in emergency laws of repression.[10] His persecution of *Apristas* caused counteraction and gave the *Apristas* an impetus toward secret organization and active clandestine resistance. His chances of wide public support were doomed from the beginning because of his attempt to eradicate forcibly the *Apristas*, the only popular political movement then rising in Peru. Trujillo, Haya de la Torre's home town, rose in a violent revolt that was accompanied by useless slaughter on both sides. Sánchez Cerro, with his "two eyes for one eye and two teeth for one tooth" methods, put down the rebellion in a merciless manner including the use of airplanes. Scottish-born John R. McKay risked grave danger by hiding Haya de la Torre in Lima.[11] The arrest and imprisonment of Haya de la Torre gave rise to a rupture of diplomatic relations between Peru and Mexico when Peru asked that Mexican Minister Juan Cabral and the legation personnel be withdrawn for alleged "intervention in internal politics." [12] In April 1933, Abelardo Mendoza Leiva (assumed to be an *Aprista*) shot and killed Sánchez Cerro as he was leaving the race track following a military parade-review. Earlier, in March 1932, Melgar Marquez had wounded him in a church at Miraflores.[13] At the time of his assassination, the president-tyrant had provoked a war with Colombia over Leticia. In a more positive approach, he had made attempts at financial reforms as he limited foreigners employed by foreign companies to 20 per cent, and established the Agricultural and Industrial banks of Peru.

On the same day that Sánchez Cerro was killed, Congress selected General Oscar Benavides to take over as temporary executive. Upon completion of the Sánchez Cerro term of office, the Benavides administration presented Jorge Prado, brother of the later President Manuel Prado, as its presidential candidate. Of the four candidates, there is little doubt but that the *Aprista*-supported one, Luis Eguiguren (a former mayor of Lima), was elected. However, the government "failed" to count the votes and, as an alternative, proclaimed Benavides president until the fall of 1939. This postponement of the

[10] See latter part of this chapter for other *Aprista* activities; see also end of Chapter 3.

[11] McKay was later president of the Presbyterian Seminary in Princeton, New Jersey, and a moderator of the Presbyterian Church of America.

[12] Jorge Basadre, *Chile, Peru y Bolivia Independentes*, XXV (Barcelona-Buenos Aires, 1948), p. 652.

[13] *Ibid.*, pp. 655, 652.

election amounted to granting Benavides the right to govern by decree. The *Apra* was still treated as an outlaw party; nevertheless in its clandestine manner it had grown into a powerful force.

Benavides instituted some moderate legislation in the fields of social welfare, health, and social security, but he ruined his chances of a popular government by his persecution of the *Apristas*. Benavides was accused—the accusation was not necessarily just—of permitting the Japanese, Italians, and Germans to gain great influence over the government.[14] This accusation in turn probably worked to increase the influence of the United States in Peru after Benavides stepped down from the presidency and the reaction set in.

In the relatively free elections of 1939, Manuel Prado was chosen to head the government. During this first term, he followed a moderate policy at home by allowing some expression of opposition. Prompt to accept the Good Neighbor Policy, he continued to co-operate closely with the United States during the Second World War. Some temporary economic gain came to Peru when Prado signed treaties with the United States to expedite the sale of cotton, linen, and especially rubber and minerals to the northern giant engaged in war. As will be noted later, friction between Lima and Washington developed over an incident relating to the Peruvian-Ecuadorian boundary dispute and the resultant clashes of 1941.

Haya de la Torre, who had returned to Peru under Prado's administration, openly supported José Luis Bustamante y Rivero for president in the free elections of 1945. With this direct *Aprista* backing, Bustamante won in a landslide. The new president set up a coalition government, with three *Apristas* in the cabinet and considerable *Aprista* influence in key congressional positions during 1946 and 1947. However, the Bustamante government was never an *Aprista* government as some people may have believed.[15] It was a transition period

[14] *Ibid.*, p. 732. See Chapter 7 for additional information; see also same chapter, fn. 5.

[15] Two of Peru's keenest observers of recent political developments stated, when interviewed by this writer (April 1962), that it was not an *Aprista* government, and that neither United States nor Peruvian investors saw fit to support Bustamante. Dr. Jorge Basadre, who has served in several cabinets, and Dr. Luis Echecopar García, the minister of *Hacienda* under Bustamante, have both denied Richard W. Patch's statement, "Apra was in power," in "Testing Time for an Experiment in Freedom," *American Universities Field Staff* (New York, November, 1957), p. 8. Peru's twentieth-century political history has not been written, and it would still be dangerous to write it and try to live in Peru. Some recent

in Peruvian politics with governmental experimentation in democratic reforms. Conservative and reactionary forces opposed the new
liberal coalition which was temporarily in power. Friction between
Bustamante and *Apra* developed and the administration was left
without adequate support from left or right.

Acts of violence (alleged to have been incited by the *Aprista*
Party) provided General Manuel Odría, very anti-*Aprista*, an opportunity and an excuse to seize power in the fall of 1948 when he drove
Bustamante from the country.[16] In the rigged election of 1950 Odría
extended his grip on the executive until 1956. There is no doubt
that militaristic influence in Peruvian politics was strengthened under Odría.[17] At the same time, the United States was an important
factor in building up the strength of Peru's army, navy, and air
force.[18] During most of the time the dictator ruled with an iron
hand backed by the army and a small wealthy minority. He held
Aprista leader Haya de la Torre prisoner in the Colombian Embassy
for five years, while he persecuted or silenced other *Aprista* spokesmen. While the disciplined press usually refrained from criticism,
the army hierarchy, landed aristocracy, and capital-industrial leaders
supported his reactionary political program. Odría welcomed communist assistance and accepted its support when it was to his advantage.[19] Both domestic and foreign interests assisted Odriá, in contrast

---

writings include the following: Fernando Belaúnde Terry, *La conquista del Peru
por los Peruanos* (Lima, 1959); Alfredo Hernández Urbina, *Los partidos y las
crisis del Apra* (Lima, 1956); Enrique Chirinos Soto, *Actores en el drama del
Peru y del mundo* (Lima, 1961); Alfredo Hernández Urbina, *Nueva política
nacional* (Trujillo, Peru, 1962); Carlos Miró Quesada Laos, *Pueblo en crisis*
(Buenos Aires, 1946); Luis Humberto Delgado, *Nuevo Peru* (with more emphasis on social problems than on the political or economic) (Lima, 1945); and
the writings about *Aprismo* of Víctor Raúl Haya de la Torre, Ramiro Prialé,
Manuel Seoane, Luis Alberto Sánchez and Harry Kantor.

[16] President Bustamante sought refuge in Argentina. He has since been appointed a justice of the World Court.

[17] Alfredo Hernández Urbina, *Nueva política nacional* (Trujillo, 1962), pp. 110-
111; Edwin Lieuwen, *Arms and Politics in Latin America* (New York, Frederick
A. Praeger, published for the Council on Foreign Relations, 1960), pp. 81-82.
A slightly more moderate view is taken by Enrique Chirinos Soto, *Actores en
el drama del Peru y del mundo* (Lima, 1961), pp. 55-60.

[18] After Brazil, Peru has received the greatest amount of military aid from the
United States. See Chapter 8.

[19] Robert J. Alexander, *Communism in Latin America* (New Brunswick,
Rutgers University Press, 1957), p. 233. Here the point is made that the communists played a dual role and that one of "the Communist Parties in Peru"

to the experience of Bustamante, who had tried to reduce the power and influence of the army. Nothing of a significant nature was done for the mass of Indian *peones* or for the bulk of the coastal workers in the lowest income brackets. Some school buildings were constructed in this period.

It appears that Washington co-operated closely with Odría and that this co-operation was not appreciated by many young Peruvians. Early in his administration Odría asked for a United States economic mission. This mission filed its report in November 1949. This, the Klein Commission recommendation, may have retarded inflation but it did nothing to solve Peru's basic economic problems. The Odría dictatorship helped business, both national and foreign, but it is not apparent that this stimulant to business aided the majority of Peruvians. In evaluating Peruvian economic activity at that time, one should not overlook the boost provided it by the Korean War. If the economy did react favorably, it might have been expected, for Odría did not have to face either political or economic hardships of the sort which had confronted Bustamante. Especially important, he had the support of United States business interests. This cannot be said for Bustamante during his administration.

Two years after the close of Odría's term, a formal statement drafted by Peru's rising generation reflected their disgust with Odría and with the support which he had gained from United States private investors and the government in Washington.[20] Vice-President Nixon went to Peru at a period when popular political parties, labor unions, and newspapers were experiencing a freedom unknown in Peruvian history. Great numbers of people believed that they deserved a better way of life, but no serious reform program was in operation. In order to understand the background of the anti-Nixon (really, anti-United States) demonstrations one must also consider the tuna fishing problem, anxiety over lead and zinc tariffs, concern with the sugar and cotton markets, a coastal zone controversy, and discontent with United States friendliness toward blatant military dictators. The

gained support under Odría. See also Tad Szulc, *Twilight of the Tyrants* (New York, Henry Holt, 1959), p. 177; Eudocio Ravines, *The Yenan Way* (New York, Charles Scribner's Sons, 1951), p. 314; and the *Aprista* newspaper *La Tribuna*.

[20] The politically powerful—even on a national scale—Federation of University Students of San Marcos, before Nixon's visit to Lima, had made it pointedly clear that they repudiated the United States approval of Odría's coup. See Chapter 11 for further details.

rough reception extended Nixon in May 1958, as well as the implications of this, are discussed in Chapter 11.

Manuel Prado, with last-minute promises to legalize *Apra*, was elected to the presidency in June of 1956, after Odría had surprised the populace by allowing an honest election. Prado's government was generally peaceful and moderate as he determined to allow congressional leaders to try to steer a middle course. This, the second Manuel Prado administration, surmounted many a stormy period before it fell to an army coup on July 18, 1962. Haya de la Torre, who received the largest number of votes in the June election but was still short of the required 35 per cent, was not acceptable to the military and so the Peruvian parliament was denied its constitutional right of deciding the election. The *Junta* forbade Congress to meet, suspended constitutional guarantees, and promised an election at a later date. The general who had led the attack had been trained at American expense in the United States. Peru's military forces, long bolstered by aid from the United States, seemed ready to prevent the broader goals of the Alliance for Progress from being reached. For a time, the United States halted military aid. But, on August 17, the State Department announced its decision to recognize the military *junta* which had promised to hold elections in June 1963.

Competent observers recently reported the following: "Peru . . . is probably on the verge of social and political upheaval based on the extremely low living standards of the great majority and the concentration of ownership and wealth in the hands of a few." [21] Between 1958 and 1963, *Apra* lost some of its popular appeal. A few of the conservative extremists believed that *Aprismo* was too willing to resort to violence. The more radical elements of the *Aprista* Left broke away entirely and called for a political and social revolution that would transform the country's social structure and economic system. This faction of extremists known as *Apra Rebelde* smarted at the marked influence of foreign capital, and *Apra's* softer stand toward "Yankee" investments particularly galled them. *Fidelistas* and communists, or so-called communists, fanned the fires of discontent in the agrarian sierras and in certain mining regions or other areas where United States capital was concentrated. The at least temporary weak-

---

[21] A *Program For the Industrial and Regional Development of Peru* (A Report to the Government of Peru, 1960) (Cambridge, Mass., Arthur D. Little, Inc., 1960), p. 3. It is not that this was such a carefully drawn report, as much as it was made by outsiders and presented to the government of Peru.

ness of *Apra* was displayed in the military-*junta* sponsored elections of June 1963, which were won by Fernando Belaúnde Terry and his *Acción Popular*. Belaúnde insisted that he was not a communist, but it was noted that he accepted communist support. Throughout the first half of 1964, Belaúnde Terry sought a center position on both domestic and foreign issues. Leftists (February 1964) complained sharply when government forces (possibly aided by landowners) killed seventeen peasant men and women, who while armed with slingshots sought to seize and farm nearby land.[22] At the same time, the rightest extreme charged the new President with encouraging incendiary agrarian reforms.

Peru was changing slowly, possibly too slowly. Ownership and wealth were still concentrated in the hands of a small minority. The indigenous problem had never been approached carefully. Living standards were generally low and at the same time a growing percentage of the people were coming to know that there was a better way of life than the one they had. The centers of power were still to be found in the wealthy oligarchy (industrialists and capitalists now in its ranks, along with the great land owners), in the military, and in the Church. Organized labor was still relatively weak. Both the Church and the Army displayed attempts at modernization, albeit belatedly. But would they move rapidly enough to avoid a bloody uprising? Discontent and change jockeyed back and forth as the 1960's unrolled.

THE ECONOMIC OUTLINE

With this scanty political picture of Peru, disconnected in part because of the lack of continuity in historic developments as background, let us turn to the economic scene. Geography has likewise played a major role in holding back the achievement of Peruvian

[22] While addressing a national convention of his party of Popular Action, President Belaúnde charged that "Peru's millionaires" had created a war chest to finance a campaign against the government's program of agrarian reform. *Andean Air Mail and Peruvian Times*, Lima, October 11, 1963, p. 1, hereafter cited as *Peruvian Times*.

The agrarian reform issue has brought out the extremes. Hugo Blanco, who was using violent means to seize the land for peasants, was captured in May 1963. See *El Comercio*, Lima, May 31, 1963. The Sicuani massacre of seventeen peasants took place in early February 1964. See *Hispanic American Report*, XVII (April 1964), pp. 153-154, which cites *Oiga*, Lima, February 6, 13, 1964.

national unity. Three distinct regions—the coast, the *sierra* (lofty Andean mountains), and the *montaña* (interior highlands and jungle)—constitute greatly contrasting areas. Racial, economic, climatic, topographic, and philosophic differences set each of these regions apart from the other two. No single year-round transportation system (except the airlines), no rivers, no valleys link together these three distinct sections. The barren coast, the cold, lofty mountains, and the humid jungle of the interior are, in many respects, isolated from each other even today. At various times it has been said that most of Peru is "too high or too low, too hot or too cold, too wet or too dry." Some observers think a better way to point up the disunity of Peru is to show the contrast between country and town or city. Lima's one million people received approximately half the national income while the other eight million plus averaged less than $50.00 (U.S.) per year in 1960.

In 1948 about 80 per cent of the Peruvian people were dependent upon agriculture in spite of the fact that only 12 per cent of the total area was under cultivation. As late as 1960, somewhere near 62.4 per cent of the total labor force was engaged in agriculture (including animal husbandry and forestry), but that group produced only 23 per cent of the gross national product.[23] In 1957, the Department of Lima, with 6,254 soles per person, had by far the highest per capita income. At the other extreme was Madre de Dios Department with 415 soles per capita.[24] In various departments there are forest Indians who have either no monetary income per capita or almost none. In between these extremes are poor coastal workers and mountain peons who, if they stay alive at all, eke out a miserable existence in a virtual feudal pattern.

The Andes, separating Peru into the three different regions, are

[23] *Basic Data on the Economy of Peru,* World Trade Information Service, Department of Commerce (Washington, 1960), p. 3. Many data are provided in Emilio Romero's *Historia económica del Peru* (Lima, 1939); and *La evolución económica del Peru* (Lima, 1945); J. L. Basombrio, *Estado comparativo de la situación comercial, financiera y económica del país de 1888 a 1938 (En Boletin de la Camara de Comercio de Lima* [Lima, 1938]); Mario F. Bazan, *El proceso económico del Peru* (Buenos Aires, 1954); Rómulo Ferrero, *La historia monetaria del Peru en el presente siglo* (Lima, 1953); Thomas R. Ford, *Man and Land in Peru* (Gainesville, University of Florida Press, 1955); and J. M. Rodríguez Montoya, in the *Economista Peruano* (Lima, 1944).

[24] *Basic Data on the Economy of Peru,* p. 3. One sol was equal to $0.0524 U.S. in 1957.

so steep and rugged that only isolated valleys can be farmed profit-ably.[25] Poor communication and transportation facilities provide lit-tle contact between one valley and another. The ordinary citizen of Europe or the United States has little appreciation of the extreme difficulties of transportation in a country such as Peru. The eastern slopes of the Andes leading to the Amazonian plains (one half of the national territory) are heavily forested and generally isolated from Peru's centers of population. The lower regions are covered with a dense jungle vegetation. Here, hidden away from most of the popu-lation of Peru, is the richest soil, blessed, moreover, by adequate rainfall. The western slopes (where there are slopes, for in many places the Andes extend down almost to the Pacific) constitute an arid coastal belt of near-desert land. Almost no rain falls on this western side, and farming can be carried on only in irrigated sections near the rivers. There are no large rivers on the western slopes of the Andes, and since water is very scarce irrigation is not extensive. Where water can be obtained for irrigation it is used in the produc-tion of cotton, sugar cane, rice, vegetables, and grains. Peru faces various serious problems in her agricultural economy; only a small percentage of the land can be profitably cultivated and the problem of distribution is a tremendous task.

Peru's geographical location on the western coast of South America and the ethnical composition of the people are two more factors which have retarded the economic growth of the nation. Until the opening of the Panama Canal, Peru was, to a large degree, isolated from the main avenues of world trade. European immigration was not as great on the western coast of South America as on the eastern coast. Furthermore, Peru's large Indian population[26] has been pre-

[25] The Central Railway of Peru ascends from sea level at Callao to almost 16,000 feet in 130 miles on the world's highest standard-gauge railway. To the north of the Andes crossing is the mountain Huascarán, 22,180 feet above the sea. Dr. Carlos Monge M., president of the Indigenous Institute of Peru, has made the best studies of acclimatization in the Andes.

[26] The Statesman's Year-Book, 1907 (London, St. Martin's Press, 1907), re-ports that the government of Peru considered the population of Peru to be less than 3,000,000. "According to statistical returns in the census of 1876, no less than 75 per cent of the total population consisted of Indians; 23 per cent was classified under Cholo (mixed Indian and Spanish) and Zumbo (mixed Negro and Spanish); the remaining 2 per cent was of Spanish descent, 18,000 Euro-peans, and 25,000 Asiatics, principally Chinese . . . ," Charles Edmond Akers, A History of South America (rev. ed., London, E. P. Dutton, 1930), p. 572. The Pan-American Yearbook 1945 (New York, Pan-American Associates, 1945),

pared only for subsistence farming, and poorly prepared even for that. Since industrial enterprise is still relatively undeveloped, the nation has remained, even to the present, chiefly a producer of raw materials. While the majority of Peruvians are engaged in the production of cotton, sugar, rice, wheat, fruits, vegetables, grapes, coca, coffee, tobacco, olives, quinine bark, wool, rubber as well as other forest products, it is foreign capital that has taken the lead in developing the mining and petroleum enterprises.

Down to the present time a comparatively few *hacendados* have owned large areas of land and have taken little interest in the Indian laborers attached to the soil. Since the Indians have neither owned the land nor reaped the bulk of the benefits from it, they have little interest in making the soil produce to its maximum capacity. This unfortunate feudal condition, added to the fact that the foreigners reaped the bulk of net profit from mines, oil wells, cotton fields, and the sugar mills, has resulted in a situation whereby the government of Peru either could not or would not develop a financial program dependent upon the resources of the country. In addition to this problem of securing sufficient national revenue, there is the fact that almost all the numerous religious foundations of colonial times were in existence up until 1950, thereby reducing the taxing capacity of the government. Making the burden even greater is the fact that until quite recently wealthy Peruvians were not inclined to invest their money in development enterprises at home. If these few wealthy individuals did invest in Peru, they did so only when an extremely high profit could be anticipated.

In 1926, Charles A. McQueen divided Peruvian financial history into two major periods with a break between them:[27] from the time of independence until the outbreak of the War of the Pacific in 1879;

p. 399, states that in 1940 whites and mixed Indian and whites (mestizo) accounted for 53 per cent of the population while pure-blooded Indians made up 46 per cent. Also see George Kubler, *The Indian Caste of Peru, 1795-1940* (Washington, United States Government for the Smithsonian Institution, 1952); Harold Osborne, *Indians of the Andes: Aymaras and Quechuas* (London, Routledge, 1952); and Moisés Sáenz, *Sobre el indio peruano y su incorporación al medio nacional* (Mexico, D. F., 1933).

[27] Charles A. McQueen, "Peruvian Public Finance," *Trade Promotion Series, Department of Commerce Bureau of Foreign and Domestic Commerce* (Washington, 1926), pp. 3-32. See Peru, *Dirección General de Estadística y Censos, Anuario estadístico del Peru, 1956-1957* (Lima, 1959), and other reports of this *Dirección General* for recent statistics.

and from 1886 to 1926. From 1845 to the outbreak of the War of the Pacific, the economic and financial history of the nation revolved largely around guano. President José Balta borrowed in London and Paris, and part of the money was spent on the "Meiggs" railroad construction. Peru, reluctant to suspend railroad construction, issued paper money beyond its capacity to back it up. The financial situation grew worse and finally collapsed with the War of the Pacific. A third period should be added to McQueen's earlier groupings. With First World War developments stimulating Leguía's interest in both direct and portfolio investments from the United States, the stage was prepared for the third period, that which left the United States in a dominant position in trade as well as finances. The United States, publicly or privately, became the main foreign lender and investor, the principal investor in minerals, the supplier of over half of Peru's imports from 1940 to 1955, as well as the principal buyer of Peruvian exports after 1940.

Peru's fiscal ailments, in part legitimate offspring of the broader economic problems of the land, were aggravated by an inadequate and inefficient system of national taxation. Real direct taxation, according to McQueen, was hardly ever imposed, even in 1926.[28] Vested interests were always reluctant to provide the Peruvian government with adequate financial support. The bulk of tax revenue came from those least able to contribute to the cost of government and from those who received the least benefit. Figures available up to 1925 show that Peru's direct taxes on property, income, or securities contributed a minor portion of the national revenues. Large property owners and the Roman Catholic Church were not predisposed to pay for an active governmental plan of development. Small property holders and the landless masses, living on a mere subsistence level, were in no position to contribute the revenue needed for the development of public works. "In 1840 of a total of about 3,000,000 pesos (national fiscal receipts), the customs contributed 1,600,000 pesos, while the balance came from the poll tax, paid chiefly by the Indians, and various taxes on property and commerce." [29] In 1877, of a total

[28] McQueen, "Peruvian Public Finance," op. cit., p. 46. Very little has been published on Peruvian taxes in the twentieth century, possibly because of the great amount of corruption which is supposed to exist in taxation matters. An earlier account of the system is Fernando Tola, Los impuestos en el Peru (Lima, 1914).

[29] McQueen, "Peruvian Public Finance," op. cit., p. 37.

revenue of 20,110,914 soles,[30] 234,637 soles were exacted in direct taxes while 17,518,069 were collected from customs, guano, and nitrate.[31] The remaining 2,358,208 soles were derived from "various" indirect taxes. For example, all official papers required a stamp (*timbre*), and excise taxes such as the one levied on sugar were collected. The revenue report of 1924 listed the income from government monopolies at 1,855,214 pounds, while the combined rural and urban property taxes amounted to the ridiculously low total of 61,692 pounds.[32]

Government monopolies and indirect taxes on commodities have hindered the development of an equitable fiscal system. During much of Peru's history, national monopolies have been the chief source of governmental income, especially guano and nitrate in the nineteenth century, with salt, tobacco, and matches added to that list in the twentieth century.

Peru's need for foreign capital and technological know-how was comparable to that of any nation with great quantities of undeveloped resources. The introduction of foreign capital into Peru took place gradually. The British position as the largest investor was not challenged until 1926 when United States investments began to approximate those of the British. Dunn estimated that in 1925 Great Britain had $125,000,000 invested in Peru as compared with $100,-000,000 of the United States.[33] Under Augusto B. Leguía the United

---

[30] Until after the middle of the nineteenth century the unit of Peruvian currency was the peso, descendant of the former Spanish silver dollar. For a time the Peruvian sol, of about the same value, took the place of the peso. When the gold standard was adopted in 1897 the sol was stabilized at 24 pence rather than at the 48 pence, or five soles to the pound sterling, which it had rated when silver had been higher. After 1897, the new gold unit was the equivalent of the British sovereign in weight and fineness. The Peruvian pound is written Lp. (*libra peruana*) and is valued at ten soles. Throughout the 1920's the rate of exchange was approximately $4.00 United States money per Peruvian pound. In the main, over the last forty years, Peruvian money has lost in value compared with the dollar.

[31] McQueen, "Peruvian Public Finance," *op. cit.*, p. 39 (see fn. 27 above). For the importance of guano, see Enrique P. Araujo Roman's *La historia del guano en el Peru* (thesis, Lima, 1920).

[32] McQueen, "Peruvian Public Finance," *op. cit.*, pp. 21-22.

[33] Robert W. Dunn, *American Foreign Investments* (New York, The Viking Press, 1926), p. 82. More recent figures are included in Chapter 10 of this volume. Also see J. Fred Rippy, *Globe and Hemisphere, Latin America's Place in the Postwar Foreign Relations of the United States* (Chicago, Henry Regnery Co., 1958), and *British Investments in Latin America, 1822-1949* (Minneapolis,

States took an active hand in supervising fiscal affairs as more private loans were extended to Peru. William Wilson Cumberland, an American financial adviser who had charge of customs collections, served as adviser to the Reserve Bank of Peru, and had influence in all important government financial questions.[34] Private United States capital investments followed the private loans to Peru. But when Peru defaulted on the loans after the outbreak of world economic difficulties and Leguía's fall from power, complications developed between the Peruvian government and the American bondholders. These difficulties were not settled until well after the close of the Second World War.

The stagnated economic condition, which has existed from time to time in this land of considerable natural resources, is reflected in present day figures of the per capita gross national product. We note that in the late 1950's Peru's per capita annual income, with a $108 figure, ranked seventeenth among the twenty Latin-American countries.

Since the Second World War, the Peruvian economy has shown a rate of growth comparable to most of the nations of the world. But with very inadequate transportation and educational facilities, and with a listless domestic economy, a vast amount of natural resources lies almost untouched. Much of this is in eastern Peru (El Oriente). There the great hidden wealth of Peru lies buried in forbidding surroundings, while on the coast where the mass of population lives one finds a dreary spectacle of scarcely a blade of grass that has not been encouraged by the hand of man. An exasperating fact prevails: Peru cannot feed its ten million people, but a land area smaller than Peru feeds nearly twenty times as many. That latter area encompasses Italy, West and East Germany, France, and England. This fact is all the more striking when one notes that Peru is hard put to feed as many people today as did the Inca system of five hundred years ago.

University of Minnesota Press, 1959). For background data, see Louis Clinton Nolan, "The Diplomatic and Commercial Relations of the United States and Peru, 1826-1875," unpublished doctoral thesis, Duke University, 1935.

[34] US Foreign Relations, 1921.

2: WASHINGTON AND LIMA, 1900-1919

It is relevant to note that, on the surface, relations between the United States and Peru have been normal and pleasant for most of the period, 1900-1958. The latter date is that of Vice-President Nixon's rude reception. However, the relationship between the peoples of the two nations has not always been as satisfactory as that between the two governments. Officially—on the exterior, at least—Washington enjoyed the support or acquiescence of Peru on such international affairs as the following: acquisition of the Panama Canal rights; the First World War; position toward the League of Nations; the Second World War; all of the Inter-American Conferences; the Act of Havana (1940); the Rio Pact (1942); and in almost all important matters between the United States and the OAS and the UN. However, in many important issues of international diplomacy and trade the government of Peru has not necessarily had its citizenry behind it. During the administrations of Leguía, Benavides, and Odría—over one half of the period under consideration in this study—there was but little attention given to the wishes of the populace. For that reason, relations should not be judged from a purely official or surface perspective.

The United States was rapidly increasing in wealth and most other forms of power in the early years of the twentieth century. During this period, Washington's official activities through its legation and consulates in Peru were usually economic, involving both individual United States citizens and large corporate enterprises. The range of other activities, in addition to routine diplomatic affairs, included Peru and the gold standard; United States consulate protection of Cuban interests; an extradition treaty; and an investigation of United States consulates.[1] Occasionally noneconomic or nonpolitical

---

[1] *Archives of the United States*, Numerical files (Washington), correspondence between Irving B. Dudley, chargé and later minister of the legation at Lima and the secretary of state in Washington. For Peruvian diplomatic history related to this period see Arturo García Salazar, *Historia diplomática del Peru* (Lima, 1930); and Pedro Ugarteche, *El Peru en la vida internacional americana* (Lima, 1927), as well as other publications by Ugarteche.

matters edged into the pattern, as in the fall of 1900, when the United States legation recommended that the Peruvian government provide for religious freedom.[2]

The investigation of the United States consulates, while less important than other diplomatic matters, nonetheless complicated the assignment of Minister Irving B. Dudley. Charges of financial mismanagement against William B. Dickey, consul in the busy port of Callao, were brought by William G. Herrick, William J. Tryon, and William S. McBride. On July 12, 1901, the Department of State asked the Lima legation to look into matters.[3] No absolute proof of misuse of funds was presented in the official correspondence, but the evidence was damaging to Dickey and he was soon replaced. The Callao consulate provoked further protest by United States citizens when, for a time, a British subject served as consul there. In August 1904, Dudley reported that the Peruvian court had sealed the archives and safe at Chiclayo and had arrested the consul, Theodore Stechmann, on the charge of defrauding creditors. Stechmann himself admitted that he had been imprisoned for debts because he had signed certain obligations for hotel proprietors at Chiclayo.[4]

Activities involving individual United States nationals are typified by the affair of Edward Gottfried. This Polish-born citizen owned extensive agricultural, mining, and commercial operations, and employed one thousand Peruvian families in and around Huamachuco. His problems included what he called "forced loans" and the threat of Peruvian arrest. After two men had been found dead on one of his ranches, Gottfried dropped claims against Peruvian authorities and sought protection of the United States Legation.[5] Fortunately, activities of this sort (including the Landreau claim discussed in Chapter 6) had little continuity or lasting significance in United States policies in Peru.

The interests of the Grace company (as discussed in Chapter 4) and particularly Cerro de Pasco Copper Corporation (later simply Cerro Corporation) were of more significance in United States-Peruvian relations. The Cerro Corporation had gotten its start in 1901 and 1902 when J. P. Morgan the elder, Phoebe Apperson Hearst (mother of William Randolph), D. O. Mills (grandfather

[2] *Diplomatic Register to the Department of State* (Washington, 1900), p. 590.
[3] *Archives of the United States*, October 1, 1901; October 31, 1902.
[4] *Ibid.*, July 26, 1904; August 6, 1904.
[5] *Ibid.*, June 1900.

of Ogden Mills), James Ben Ali Higgins, and several others risked nearly $10,000,000 in the sulphide ores near the two mining centers of Oroya and Cerro de Pasco. The corporation soon found itself in conflict with the Empresa Socavonera del Cerro de Pasco, usually referred to in English as the "Cerro de Pasco Tunnel Company." Matters were complicated by the fact that all the capital stock in the United States concern was owned by United States citizens, whereas Peruvian citizens owned almost all the stock in the Tunnel Company. The United States minister reported in 1908 that the New Jersey mining interests had earlier been ". . . almost in despair [sic] over this matter" of the conflict with the Peruvian company.[6] Furthermore, in 1903-1904, the investment of Grace and the Cerro Corporation in interior Peru depended to a great extent upon the "Haggin" or "Hagan" (apparently Louis T. Haggin) Syndicate. This United States syndicate owned no less than 75 per cent of the rich mines in the inundated zone known as the Rumihallana Tunnel area.[7] The Henry Meiggs contract[8] had been amended in 1877 to provide for railroad extension to the Rumihallana area (the Cerro de Pasco hills nearly 16,000 feet above sea level). A great deal of Minister Dudley's time from 1903 to 1906 and much of the legation's official business of late 1906 and early 1907 were taken up with the clarification and affirmation of Grace and Cerro de Pasco interests. In 1905 the legation became directly involved in securing for these companies equal treatment with the powerful British Peruvian Corporation. On July 16, 1907, the legation urged United States intervention to help Cerro de Pasco.[9]

Matters were settled without serious repercussions, although Peruvian troops did occupy some of Cerro de Pasco Corporation's property in the spring of 1907. It is not clear just what happened to bring about a settlement, but, according to Leslie Combs of the legation at Lima, Secretary of State Elihu Root's "personal expression of interest in the matter" was very important in clearing up the dispute.

[6] *Ibid.*, January 11, 1908. For a general account of the development of mining in Peru, see Carlos Jiménez Correa, *Evolución histórica de la industria minera en el Peru* (Lima, 1924).

[7] *Archives of the United States,* July 16, 1907.

[8] See Chapter 1.

[9] *Archives of the United States,* July 16, 1907. It was not until 1920 that the Legation was raised to the United States Embassy, *Andean Air Mail and Peruvian Times,* Lima, April 15, 1960, III, hereafter cited as *Peruvian Times.*

Late in 1906, W. C. Gulliver, representing the New Jersey Cerro de Pasco interests, had presented the company's case directly and personally to Root and almost immediate action on the part of the Secretary of State followed. On January 11, 1908, correspondence from Leslie Combs to the State Department reported that the settlement ". . . effectually binds, for the present at least, all the local interest now centered in the Tunnel Company, and eliminates for an important period the danger of strike legislation and executive or judicial injustice." [10] During the litigation Cerro de Pasco Copper had capitalized part of its property at $60,000,000, established a bogus investment company, and turned over 5 per cent of the valid stock to the Tunnel Company.

In matters of hemispheric importance from Washington's perspective, Lima usually provided support (such as early recognition of Panama), hoping in turn to have United States assistance. However, close cooperation and significant general exchanges between the two cultures were quite limited up until the First World War. Manuel Ugarte, in *The Destiny of a Continent*, found that few cities had as favorable an atmosphere for his propaganda (an Americanism or Latin-Americanism independent of the United States and even anti-United States in many respects) as did Lima when he visited there in 1913. Before Augusto B. Leguía's first administration (1908-1912), Europe had supplied Peru with the major share of its capital, imports, and foreign technical personnel and intellectual stimulation. Leguía, who had been minister of finance in the cabinet of President Candamo in 1903,[11] admired North American customs and manners

[10] *Archives of the United States*, January 11, 1908.

[11] Augusto B. Leguía, the son of Nicanor Leguía, was born in the Department of Lambayeque on February 19, 1863, and died in prison in Bellavista on February 6, 1932. He was educated in Valparaiso, Chile, having been sent to Chile because he suffered from a bronchial ailment. At the school in Valparaiso Leguía learned the English language. Later he returned to the country of his birth and fought with the Peruvian forces against Chile in the War of the Pacific. He embarked upon a business career early in his life and became the general manager for the New York Life Insurance Company in Peru, Ecuador, and Bolivia. Later he organized and directed La Sud Americana Insurance Company in Peru. On other occasions he was manager for the British Sugar Company, Ltd., and president of the National Bank of Peru. His first active participation in politics came with his selection to the cabinet (minister of finance) in 1903. He remained a cabinet member until his election in 1908. Chapter 3 treats of Leguía's activities in more detail.

more than did other presidents before him. Peru thus shifted her attention from Europe, and during the period 1908 to 1919 came to depend much more upon the United States.

United States relations with Peru now began to assume a more active form in various fields of Peruvian life. A noteworthy example of this participation is public education. In 1905, President José Pardo had attempted reorganization and reform of Peru's ineffective and antiquated educational system by establishing a central directorate of public education for primary, secondary, and higher education. But even four years later, facilities for public education were scanty indeed, consisting of 1,908 school buildings of which 550 belonged to the government and were valued at only $410,199.[12] With the door to reform opened by Pardo, Leguía turned to the United States to recruit some of his officials when he sought to achieve further reorganization.[13] The resulting commission, appointed in 1909, placed United States citizens in the following important positions: inspector of girls' schools in Lima and Callao; adviser to the Peruvian minister of education; director of the Men's Normal School; inspector of the public schools in the Department of Lima; supervisor of commercial courses for Peruvian schools; secretary of a special commission for preparation of a bill to completely reorganize Peru's public school system; and rector of the University of Cuzco.

The commission of 1909 had some competent personnel, headed by educator-consultant Harry Erwin Bard, who was made consultant to the Minister of Education.[14] Others were Joseph A. MacKnight, Joseph B. Lockey, and Albert A. Giesecke. Their interest in Peru was genuine. Bard himself returned as adviser to the minister after the First World War.[15] Giesecke, who married a Peruvian, served for thirteen years as rector of the San Antonio Abad University in Cuzco.

[12] Joseph A. MacKnight, "Education in Peru," *Report of Commissioner of Education for the Year Ended June 30, 1911* (Washington, 1912), pp. 495, 507. Felipe Barreda y Laos has written on this subject from time to time, particularly in the *Revista Universitaria* (Lima, 1919).

[13] MacKnight, "Education in Peru," *op. cit.*, pp. 495, 499, 507. Letter: Dr. Albert A. Giesecke to James C. Carey, written at Lima, October 12, 1947. With the letter was a memorandum prepared by Giesecke with details concerning this first educational "mission" to Peru.

[14] The recommendations of the original group were incorporated into the new education law of 1920 which went into effect during Leguía's second administration.

[15] See Chapter 6.

Later on, in the 1940's, he was employed by the United States Embassy in an advisory capacity.[16] It would appear that a great opportunity for the United States to accomplish much in educational and cultural exchange was thus presented, for the Peruvians were, according to MacKnight, very receptive. "From the President . . . down to the last teacher . . . ," he wrote, "there is the best of good will for our undertaking and a sincere desire to co-operate in the reforms that are to be inaugurated." [17] In spite of the receptive attitude, this first educational commission had a comparatively short life and did little more than prepare the way for the School Law of 1920 and the American Educational Mission of 1920-1921 (see Chapter 6).

The United States was also called upon for help in the work on sanitation. In 1912 the Peruvian government requested personnel from the United States to help improve sanitary conditions in Iquitos, an interior city located at the head of the Amazon River traffic some 2,100 miles from the mouth. The Congress at Lima authorized the Peruvian government to contract a loan of 200,000 pounds to provide Iquitos with a modern sewerage system. The American minister in Peru, H. Clay Howard, wrote optimistically of the work as being "kindred to that of Colonel Gorgas in the Canal Zone." [18]

Secretary of State Philander C. Knox arranged for Peru to secure the services of three United States citizens for the work at Iquitos. Knox consulted the Secretaries of Treasury and War, and in May 1912, Acting Assistant Surgeon George M. Converse of the Public Health and Marine Hospital Service was accepted by President Leguía as sanitary expert. Other United States experts were named for this assignment, but it is evident that little progress of a permanent nature resulted from the diplomatic exchange of 1912 concerning the sanitation program. A report, published in 1925, stated that "there is no sewage or water system, and ditches running down the

[16] *Peruvian Times*, July 17, 1959, pp. 18-19. See also Dorothy Walworth, "Hemisphere Builder, Albert A. Giesecke, A Yankee Teacher in Peru," *The Pan-American Magazine of the Americas*, VIII (October 1947).

[17] MacKnight, "Education in Peru," *op. cit.*, p. 507. Although conditions may have been favorable, MacKnight was overly optimistic. Little information was provided in the *Memorias que el Ministros de Justicia, Culto, Instrucción y Beneficiencia* presented over the years. The annual report of the minister of education was usually included with these *Memorias*.

[18] *Papers Relating to the Foreign Relations of the United States, 1912* (Washington), p. 1280; hereafter cited as *US Foreign Relations*.

center of the streets are used for drainage." [19] The same report does, however, show that Converse reached Iquitos and was engaged in sanitation work there, although there is no indication as to exactly what he accomplished.

In 1912 the governments of Great Britain and the United States carried out a joint investigation of slavery in Peru. Great Britain and the United States were cautious, however, refraining diplomatically from interfering in the internal affairs of the country. The inquiry centered around a region near the Putomayo River rubber-gathering stations. It became evident in 1912 that the American consul in Iquitos had reported cruel slave-like exploitation of the Indians in that section of Peru as early as November 1907.[20] There is no evidence in the correspondence of the *Papers Relating to the Foreign Relations of the United States* to indicate that any action was taken regarding Consul Charles C. Eberhardt's lengthy report until August 1912, when a statement in the London *Times* deplored the "horrible evils" existing in Peru. Secretary of State Knox denied assertions in American journals that "American companies were exploiting the rubber production in the upper Putomayo. . . ." [21] Knox maintained that Eberhardt's investigations uncovered a condition of "virtual

---

[19] William L. Schurz, O. D. Hargis, C. F. Marbut, and C. B. Manifold, "Rubber Production in the Amazon Valley," *Trade Promotion Series, Department of Commerce Bureau of Foreign and Domestic Commerce*, No. 23 (Washington, 1925). For the activity of United States citizens in the discoveries of lost cities see: Hiram Bingham, "The Ruins of Espiritu Pampa, Peru," *American Anthropologist*, XV (1914), 185-199; and Walter Hough, "The Peruvian Expedition of 1912," *American Anthropologist*, XIV (1912), 405. Excellent sources exist in Bingham's writings, as in *Inca Land: Explorations in the Highlands of Peru* (New York, Houghton Mifflin, 1922); and *Lost City of the Incas: The Story of Machu Picchu and Its Builders* (New York, Duell, Sloan and Pearce, 1948).

[20] *US Foreign Relations*, 1913, pp. 1240-1249.

[21] *Ibid.*, p. 1242. Eberhardt's dispatch to Washington (dated December 3, 1907) began as follows: "In view of certain articles which have appeared in different periodicals at home at different times during the past few months (*India Rubber World* of May, September, and October, and *New York Times* of September 6 and 19) regarding the exploitation by an American company, under concession from the Colombian Government, of a large tract of rubber lands in the Upper Putomayo (or Ica) and Yapura (or Caqueta) Rivers district, a territory which is now in dispute between that Government and Peru. . . ." *US Foreign Relations*, as quoted above, has deleted various sections of the Eberhardt report. One of the sections not included stated that Colombians were selling in New York the same land which Peruvians had sold in London. The foreign and local publications had convinced Eberhardt that the Amazon Rubber Trading Company had been formed in New York to exploit the tract in the upper Putumayo (Eberhardt's spelling differs from the usual) district. The full report

slavery" but showed that cruelties "were not the work of American citizens, nor affected American interests." [22]

Investigations revealed that the Peruvian-Amazon Company and certain Peruvians were mainly responsible for the inhumane activities. A Peruvian named Arana had been influential in the formation of the company in London in October 1907. Robertson stated that the American office of the Peruvian-Amazon Company was located at Iquitos.[23] The activities in London and Washington official circles may have had some slight influence in Peru, for in April 1912 President Leguía introduced a program of reform intended to protect the aborigines of the Putumayo region, which was implemented under President Billinghurst.[24]

The United States took a very minor role in the trouble between Billinghurst and Leguía. In September 1912, Billinghurst was inaugurated as president and friction soon developed between ex-president Leguía and the new chief executive. The trouble was caused, to some extent at least, by the fact that Leguía's relatives and followers had considerable influence in, if not control of, Congress. The American minister, H. Clay Howard, ascribed the ensuing violence to Billinghurst's instigation although he did not support his assumption with specific information.[25] When Leguía was attacked in his home, and after he had killed two of the attackers, the United States minister and the secretary of state offered aid and asylum to the ex-president. Leguía, however, was arrested and imprisoned, being later induced to leave the country. In August 1913, the American chargé d'affaires at Panama met Leguía and some of his family and escorted them to a hotel. About the middle of August, the Leguías arrived in the United States en route to Europe. The State Department was especially solicitous in helping Leguía in exile.

---

may be found in *Slavery in Peru, Message From the President of the United States Transmitting Report of the Secretary of State, With Accompanying Papers, Concerning the Alleged Existence of Slavery in Peru*, House Documents, 62nd Cong., 3rd Sess. (Washington, 1913), pp. 111-117.

[22] *US Foreign Relations*, 1913, p. 1242.

[23] *Sir Roger Casement's Report*, Cd. 6266, HMSO (London, 1913).

[24] When the first reports concerning atrocities came from the area, the Peruvian government did nothing. Directors of the company, which was registered in London, denied published accounts of barbarism. Public criticism developed in the Anglo-Saxon area of the world, especially London, and the Foreign Office there sent Sir Roger Casement out to investigate. In the meantime, Peruvian authorities initiated action.

[25] *US Foreign Relations*, 1913, p. 1143.

In a short time, Leguía and his sons went to London where they made their home for the ensuing five years.

Even with Leguía gone, the political situation in Peru did not remain quiet for long and, on February 4, 1914, Colonel Oscar Benavides stepped in to take over as head of a *junta*. Eight days later the Wilson administration reversed its usual policy and instructed Minister Benton McMillin in Lima to recognize the *junta* as a provisional government pending the establishment of a permanent executive.[26] On March 2, 1914, McMillin reported that the Peruvian Congress was opposed to any plan of returning the *Leguísta* faction to power. Diplomatic correspondence in the *Papers Relating to the Foreign Relations of the United States* shows that the officers of the American legation in Lima knew that certain Peruvian politicians had been plotting to restore the *Leguístas* to power.[27] In any event the conspiracy did not take definite form.

Benavides was at the head of the government when the First World War broke out. The national government was sympathetic to the Allies and the United States with the spread of hostilities after 1914.[28] Late that year, it approached the government of the United States and the Governing Board of the Pan-American Union regarding some possible agreement or proclamation whereby joint action of the American republics could be attained which would safeguard the "interests of neutrals in the American Continent" and "free our commerce from the effects of the present European war." [29] The Peruvian government expressed itself in favor of the establishment of neutral shipping lanes in the Western Hemisphere. Because of this interest, and that shown by other American nations, the Pan-American Neutrality Commission was organized to protect the rights of neutral American republics.[30] In 1915, the Peruvian cruisers *Almirante Grau* and *Colonel Bolognesi* convoyed English and Japanese

[26] *Ibid.*, 1914, p. 1063.

[27] *Ibid.*, pp. 1064, 1065.

[28] Thomas A. Bailey, *The Policy of the United States Toward the Neutrals, 1917-1918* (Baltimore, Johns Hopkins University Press, 1942), p. 309. It is likely that the Peruvian citizens were more inclined to be pro-ally and the government of Peru neutral during the early part of the war in Europe. The *Memorias del Ministros de Relaciones Exteriores* and *El Comercio* newspaper for the period reflect more neutralism than anything. For a very general outline of Peru's long-range diplomacy, see Pedro Yrigoyen writing in *El Comercio*, Lima, December 9, 1924.

[29] *US Foreign Relations*, 1914, *Supplement*, pp. 441-446.

[30] *Ibid.*, p. 450.

commercial shipping off the Peruvian coast when German cruisers menaced it.[31] On December 10, 1915, the German Kosmos liner *Luxor* was interned as an auxiliary cruiser when the ship's officers refused to obey orders to leave Callao within twenty-four hours. The event which led to severance of relations with Germany in October 1917 was Germany's failure to grant satisfactory reparation for the sinking of a Peruvian bark, the *Lorton*.[32]

England's relationship with Peru leading up to the First World War had been friendly, and this influenced the favorable tone adopted toward the United States. Influential Peruvian writers contributed to this position. Juan Bautista de Lavalle praised "Yankee" industrial enterprise at work in his nation. In "The City of Copper," which was written for both Spanish and English readers, he praised the work of Cerro de Pasco Copper Corporation as being a magnificent accomplishment of "blessed" and "sublime" qualities.[33] One might think he was on the company's payroll! Something of the same note, but more rational, appeared in the publicity emanating from the Creel Committee. C. N. Griffis, directing this work, said that periodical literature was not so important in Peru. He reported that photographic displays attracted great attention, and that pictures of the industrial might of the United States were a welcome relief from the war-front pictures of the British and the French.[34] Víctor Andrés Belaúnde looked back on the war period as a time when Peru had a sound and strong international position; Alberto Ulloa was of the opinion that Peruvians gave fervent support to Wilson's ideals.[35] Wilson's leadership is recognized in the fact that one of the main avenues of Lima has since carried the name, "*Avenida Wilson*." Some writers no doubt agreed with Ulloa that, for its own good, Peru's

[31] Percy Alvin Martin, *Latin America and the War* (Baltimore, Johns Hopkins University Press, 1925), p. 389. Since Peru's participation in the war was not significant to its national history there is little of a reliable nature in the way of Peruvian sources on this subject. Pedro Ugarteche has done some of the best work in *Revue de l'Amerique Latine* (Paris, 1930), and in various articles in *Revista Peruana de Derecho Internacional* (Lima), especially the years 1953 and 1956.

[32] Martin, *op. cit.*, pp. 395-400.

[33] Juan Bautista de Lavalle, "The City of Copper, Smelter Impressions of the Cerro de Pasco," *Inter-America*, III (December 1919), p. 83.

[34] James R. Mock, "The Creel Committee in Latin America," *The Hispanic American Historical Review*, XXII (May 1942), pp. 273-274.

[35] Juan Bautista de Lavalle, "El Libro de Alberto Ulloa, 'Posición Internacional del Peru,'" *Revista Peruana de Derecho Internacional*, I (Lima, 1941), pp. 175-191.

position was too solidly committed to the United States.[36] In a similar vein was José de la Riva Aguero (see Chapter 7 for a note on his position). And even at the close of the war, the United States and Peru were still little acquainted with each other.

An incident between the United States and Peru during the war —which, although terminated harmoniously, caused some difficulties —was the disposition of ten German ships interned in Peruvian harbors. In negotiations with the United States, Peru insisted that the ships should be utilized under the flag of Peru.[37] Peru ultimately agreed to allow the United States Shipping Board to repair the ships and "charter hire" them at the rate of $8.25 per deadweight ton per month. The Shipping Board was responsible for all expenses.[38] Howland Gardner, representative of the Shipping Board, went to Peru and handled the negotiations of a technical nature relative to the repair and use of the interned ships. At one point in the negotiations prior to the signing of the contract, Peru's hesitancy to act caused Secretary of State Robert Lansing to send, May 29, 1918, the following pointed message:

> In view of the public feeling in the United States, that for the successful prosecution of the war, all ships should be made use of which are controlled by those countries having at heart the desire for the triumph of the cause of the Allies, the Government of the United States feels that it is incumbent upon it to say to the Government of Peru that the above-mentioned hesitation on the part of that Government has produced an unfortunate impression upon the American people.[39]

The contract calling for the use of the interned German ships had been delayed by complications arising when Peru sought guarantees from the United States against possible German claims and retribution.[40] The question was solved on September 6, 1918, when the Peruvian government and the United States Shipping Board signed a contract concerning the repair and use of six steamers and four sailing ships. When it had appeared advisable to do so, the United States agreed to accept responsibility in the event of an international claim.[41]

[36] *Ibid.* See also latter part of this study.
[37] *US Foreign Relations, 1918,* I, *Supplement* 1, p. 675.
[38] *Ibid.,* pp. 666-667.
[39] *Ibid.,* p. 697.
[40] The Spanish minister in Peru, entrusted with German interests there after Peru had broken relations with Berlin, protested Peru's steps in interning ships.
[41] *US Foreign Relations, 1918,* I, *Supplement* 1, pp. 714-718.

After the war, when various Latin-American nations again began to fear the power of the "northern colossus," Peru remained quite friendly to the United States and did not show much apprehension. The Peruvian government, indeed, adopted a cordial attitude in matters of foreign affairs as well as in domestic dealings. Unlike the representatives of several other countries, the representatives of Peru were not responsible during the period following the First World War for raising any issues or questions embarrassing to the United States at the Pan-American conferences, at meetings of the League of Nations, or at other international assemblies.[42] In fact, Pedro Ugarteche (*La política internacional peruana durante la dictadura de Leguía*) viewed his nation's withdrawal from the League in order to serve the interests of the United States as going to the other extreme.

Both national and international developments prompted Peru to look hopefully toward Washington. Peru's view of hemispheric and world affairs was, in those years, conditioned by her problems with Chile. As there was always some hope for United States aid on the Tacna-Arica question, there was also an accompanying tendency for the Minister of Foreign Affairs at Lima to please the Department of State on the Potomac. At the same time, the country was in need of foreign investment capital and technological skills. The United States, seeking to obtain the market which Peru offered and the raw materials needed for American industry, looked with favor upon Leguía's return to the presidency in 1919.

[42] The Dreyfus Case (claims made by the French banking house, Dreyfus and Company) was settled by The Hague without special assistance from Washington. The creditors collected 25,000,000 francs in 1925-1926.

3: LEGUÍA, POLITICS AND THE UNITED STATES

The First World War had made it increasingly clear that Peru offered a favorable climate for closer commercial and financial ties with the North Americans. In its general development of foreign relations in the first nineteen years of the twentieth century, Peru had followed the lead of the United States, and during *el oncenio*, the eleven years of President Augusto B. Leguía's second administration (1919 to 1930), United States policies were seldom indifferent to, or far removed from, internal Peruvian politics. Furthermore, President Leguía was interested in seeing that the already established favorable climate was maintained.

Leguía was an energetic individual possessed of a keen interest in politics and many of the attributes of leadership.[1] In many respects he represented a breaking away from old forms and ideas as

[1] Generally, Peruvians have divided sharply in interpreting the merits or demerits of Leguía. In the very favorable category are such books as that of Manuel A. Capuñay, *Leguía, Vida y obra del constructor del Peru* (Lima, 1951), and José E. Bonilla, *El siglo de Leguía* (Lima, 1928). Denunciatory accounts of note are the following: Jacinto López, *La caída del gobierno constitucional en el Peru* (New York, Carranza and Company, 1927), and Pedro Ugarteche, *La política internacional peruana durante la dictadura de Leguía* (Lima, 1930). Other Peruvian books dealing with Leguía in one degree or another make up a long list, several of which are here mentioned: Víctor Larco Herrera, *Leguía, el martir de la penitenciaria* (Santiago, Chile, 1934); Augusto B. Leguía, *Discoursos y mensajes del Presidente Leguía* (Lima, 1924-1926); Franco Guillermo Forero, *Entre dos dictaduras* (Bogotá, 1935); Víctor Andrés Belaúnde, *La realidad nacional* (Paris, 1931). Under the heading of "Augusto Bernardino Leguía," the Library of Congress in Washington has various pamphlets which are not separately catalogued.

Leguía was an alert, vivacious individual as is pointed out in an article, "Leguía, Lincoln or Mussolini of Latin America?" which appeared in the *Literary Digest*, CVI (September 20, 1930), pp. 32-33. *The Literary Digest* reported that Irvin S. Cobb described Leguía as being "all whipcord and drawn steel" and reminded Cobb of "a dynamo packed inside the case of a wrist-watch." Leguía's weight was 90-100 pounds. See also Lawrence Dennis, "What Overthrew Leguía," *New Republic*, LXIV (September 17, 1930), p. 118.

well as a departure from older institutions. He envisioned a new and greater Peru, but as he stood on the threshold of achievement, his success was limited by dictatorial methods and by corruption in his administration.

After having resided in London for five years, Leguía returned to Peru in the spring of 1919 and immediately entered the Peruvian political arena. His absence from the country during the interval must have restricted his opportunities of regrouping and of building up a strong party following, but it did not prevent his rapid rise to the presidency. This was achieved in spite of the fact that there was little evidence of any well-organized discontent or popular objection to José Pardo's administration.[2] Supporters of Pardo proudly referred to his second term as having been "liberal and constitutional." [3] It did not appear that there were forces at hand in 1919 which were capable of uprooting the well-entrenched *Civilista* (government) Party. Yet, that was just what the surprising Señor Leguía would do. At the outset, it is relevant to observe that he did not lack influential friends in Peruvian business circles, and that he enjoyed the friendship of British and American business leaders.

While returning from London, but before going to Peru to enter the election race, Leguía visited with certain unnamed United States citizens in New York and Washington. There is no complete account available of his conversations with American citizens in those two cities, but it is evident that business interests were of prime importance, for in June 1919, the Peruvian delegate to the Second Pan-American Commercial Conference held in Washington asserted, in part: "When Sr. Leguía was in Washington and New York three months ago, he came in contact with the ablest statesmen and financiers of this country, and the press of the United States has

[2] Pardo was supported by the *Civilistas*, their strength that of the landed proprietors. It has often been asserted that the rapidly increasing business and professional segment of society had insufficient representation and influence among the *Civilistas*. Economic and social changes were slowly exposing the inadequacy of the *Civilista* program, which was representative of political aristocracy and not suitable to an informed populace. Some discontent prevailed because alien labor had been permitted to enter Peru. Yet in spite of the opposition of these groups desiring changes, it is surprising that the *Civilistas* lost control after twenty-five years of domination.

[3] Carlos Concha, "The Reign of Terror in Peru," *Current History*, XVIII (July 1923), p. 699. Critics such as López, *La caída del gobierno constitucional en el Peru*, p. 9 (foreword by Felipe Barreda), believed that Leguía had struck a terrible blow at constitutional government and left Peru in ruins.

given publicity to his ideas and plans for closer commercial and political relations, and for encouraging the investment of North American capital in the exploitation and development of the incalculable and inexhaustible wealth contained in the Peruvian territory. . . ."[4] More concrete evidence that Leguía had talked with important United States financiers was brought out later, in hearings before a subcommittee of the Committee on Banking and Currency of the United States Senate. This inquiry into stock-exchange practices disclosed a memorandum written December 3, 1925, by Claude W. Calvin, representative of the National City Bank in Peru for the preceding eleven years. Speaking of Leguía, Calvin wrote:

> On his way to Peru from England, Leguía stopped in New York in the spring of 1919 and called on President Vanderlip, of our institution. He stated that he desired to consolidate the various government agencies and monopolies operating in Peru, eliminate all unnecessary overhead and put the entire government machine upon an economic and efficient basis. To do this would require the refunding of various loans secured by such monopolies. Mr. Vanderlip indicated some interest in the matter and promised to send a man to Peru to investigate after Mr. Leguía had been inducted into office.
> When I arrived in Lima in October, 1919, to install the branch of the National City Bank, President Leguía thought I was the man sent by our institution pursuant to his conversation with Mr. Vanderlip, and was much disappointed to learn that my visit had no such significance. . . . It was his idea to make us the approved bankers of his government, which would take care of all his financing and advise and assist him in his program of improving and building up the country, which advice and assistance would be at all times most welcome.[5]

There is no evidence to conclude that the prospective president of Peru and the head of the National City Bank entertained other than honorable intentions. When it is noted, however, that the conversations took place *before* the elections were held in Peru, it is evident that some presumptuous planning was done with a man who had not yet returned from a five-year absence. This made it

[4] José Corbacho, "Peruvian Trade and Internal Conditions," *Pan-American Commerce, Report of the Second Pan-American Commercial Conference* (Washington, 1919), p. 203.

[5] *Stock Exchange Practices: Hearings before a Subcommittee of the Committee on Banking and Currency, United States Senate,* 72nd Cong., 2nd Sess., S. Res. 84 and S. Res. 239, Part VI (Washington, 1933), p. 2104.

apparent that the New York bankers had a direct interest in the politics of this South American country.

Other United States businessmen also felt that they benefited by Leguía's return to the presidency. Representatives of the Electric Boat Company recognized a link with Leguía and dated it back to his first administration (1908-1912).[6] Henry R. Carse (later the company president) wrote, prior to the 1919 elections, that "Captain Buenano states that President Leguía will be returned to the Presidency in three or four months, and it is he who is asking for the data on submarines, as the sentiment throughout the whole country is to secure land and naval armaments to protect themselves from Chile." [7] In 1924, Lawrence W. Spear, vice-president of the company, wrote that a Peruvian named Aubry, an employee of their concern in 1923, had been "intimately connected with the restoration of President Leguía to power in Peru." [8] We are not told what part, if any, Aubry played in Leguía's restoration, but it is clear that the Electric Boat Company looked upon Leguía as especially favorable to their business activities.

It is difficult to determine the exact returns of the 1919 election or to justify Leguía's use of force to assume power. Many informed persons feel that Leguía *did* receive a majority of votes cast, and it seems probable that this was the case.[9] If Leguía feared (justifiably or unjustifiably) that the ballots would not be honestly counted, he may have felt obliged to take office by means of a military *coup d'état*. Still there is no sound evidence that Pardo intended to rob Leguía of the fruits of victory if Leguía deserved them. On the other hand, there is no logical explanation for the coup except that Leguía (1) feared a dishonest election, (2) doubted that he had obtained a majority, or (3) wanted to employ a coup to strengthen his position regardless of the election. It has been suggested that Leguía executed the coup so that when he charged the Pardo ad-

[6] *Munitions Industry: Hearings before the Special Committee Investigating the Munitions Industry, United States Senate,* 73rd Cong., pursuant to S. Res. 206, Part I (Washington, 1934), p. 377.

[7] *Ibid.,* pp. 85-86.

[8] *Ibid.,* p. 377.

[9] Jorge Basadre, Víctor Andrés Belaúnde, Charles Edmond Akers, Dana Gardner Munro, and J. Fred Rippy are only a few of those who believe Leguía won the election. Akers affirmed that "he [Leguía] was officially announced to have received 160,000 votes out of a total of 200,000 cast." Charles Edmond Akers, *A History of South America* (London, E. P. Dutton, 1930), pp. 597-598.

ministration with fraudulent elections he could find an excuse for
changing the Constitution and holding new congressional elections.
The old Constitution of Peru (art. 57) provided that elections to
Congress should be held every two years, at which time a third of
the members would stand election. The Congress that existed in
1919 at the time of Leguía's election was made up of many former
senators and deputies, among whom Leguía had various foes. "It
was much easier for him to have new elections for Congress and
have all his partisans as deputies and senators." [10] He could hardly
have expected to gain public favor by the coup. In any event, it
initiated an eleven-year period of absolute dictatorship masquerading
as constitutional rule.

The overthrow of the legal government came on July 4, 1919,
although Pardo's tenure was to expire on August 18. Antero Aspillaga, however, the candidate enjoying Pardo's support, had disputed
the election, and his claim was to have been pleaded before the
Peruvian Congress on July 28. Rather than wait for further developments, Leguía seized the Government Palace in a military move
directed by Colonel Geraldo Álvarez and General A. A. Cáceres,[11]
with some of the regular army and the police force joining in the
coup. Leguía entered his new post as provisional president amid an
air of festivity; the Fourth of July was at once proclaimed a national
holiday.[12]

The principal United States consular official in Peru, William W.
Handley, cabled Washington a series of messages which demonstrated his interest in the revolt. Correspondence in the *Papers Relating to the Foreign Relations of the United States* gives a broad
outline of what happened. On May 20, 1919, the United States
consul general at Callao, Handley, reported that Augusto B. Leguía
appeared to have been elected president. On July 4 Handley cabled
the news of the revolt, elaborating on the ease with which the coup
was carried out. According to the consul general, President Pardo

---

[10] Personal letter: Luis Echecopar García (cabinet member in the José Luis
Bustamante y Rivero administration) to James C. Carey, dated Lima, May 17,
1948. Jacinto López (see fn. 15 of this chapter) is in general agreement with this
interpretation.

[11] *New York Times*, July 5, 1919, p. 11. In September, 1919, Álvarez was appointed minister of war and navy.

[12] *Ibid.*

was imprisoned and Leguía was "installed . . . president of Peru." [13] The army was reported to be patrolling Lima, and Handley expected no trouble.[14] Also on July 4, the American minister, Benton Mc-Millin, wired similar information, but his report included more specific details showing that there was violence and loss of life involved in the coup.

The Government Palace was seized at 3:00 A.M., and in less than twelve hours Consul General Handley had made a visit to Leguía in the Government Palace, his telegram to the assistant secretary of state in Washington confirming the visit having been filed at 3:00 P.M. on July 4. The consul general of the Netherlands informed the American Legation that the American consul general had made the call on Leguía.[15] Minister McMillin relayed the information to Frank L. Polk, the Acting Secretary of State. Polk immediately wired Handley and asked why he had had an interview with Leguía. Handley replied that his presence at the presidential quarters was purely accidental since he had merely accompanied Leguía's legal adviser on a mission. According to Handley, he also had been "on very friendly terms with Leguía" since the latter's return from Europe.[16] Polk then instructed Handley to ascertain from McMillin the attitude of the United States toward the events in Peru and to be "governed accordingly." [17]

It is difficult to measure the pro-Leguía influence of this apparently official visit (even if Handley intended no such implication), especially since rumors encouraged greater speculation. We have the following report from Minister McMillin which shows how rapidly propagandists were able to take advantage of what some of them

[13] *Papers Relating to the Foreign Relations of the United States, 1919*, II (Washington), p. 720, hereafter cited as *US Foreign Relations*.

[14] *Ibid.*, p. 720.

[15] *Ibid.*, p. 724. For an anti-Leguía account see López, *La caída del gobierno constitucional en el Peru*, or Belaúnde, *La realidad nacional*, p. 253. Belaúnde, a later president of the United Nations, launched the following bitter attack: "En realidad, la obra, el espíritu de Leguía era la destrucción de la independencia. . . . No la celebramos con las macabras fiestas del 21 y del 24, coronadas por la mutilación territorial, la venta de Arica y la esclavitud ante el imperialismo Yanqui."

[16] *Archives of the United States*, Numerical files (Washington, July 8, 1919), Handley to the secretary of state.

[17] *US Foreign Relations, 1919*, II, p. 728.

viewed as a formal visit: "*La Prensa* July 5th reported that the Nuncio, American Minister and the British Chargé d'affaires called on Leguía. The British Chargé d'affaires and I [McMillin] did not go and [by] private notification *La Prensa* made correction on own responsibility." [18] Of the three mentioned in *La Prensa* only the Nuncio had paid his respects at the Government Palace; he had gone for personal reasons.[19] It is pertinent to note also that regardless of the wisdom of Consul General Handley's call on Leguía, his visit could not commit the United States formally. While Handley[20] was not the United States diplomatic representative in Peru, his action may well have provided Leguía with valuable support or prestige.

Once in power as provisional president, Leguía moved rapidly to consolidate his position. The Peruvian Supreme Court was to have ruled on the legality of the election, but Leguía ordered the court to suspend this work, and the judiciary duly announced its suspension.[21] Minister McMillin reported on July 9 that Leguía promised to release Pardo from prison and allow him to leave the country providing Pardo would sign a renunciation of the presidency.[22] Upon Pardo's definite refusal to renounce his position, Leguía consented to Pardo's departure from the country without the resignation.

The general diplomatic response of the world to Leguía's *coup d'état* was one of calm deliberation. Many countries turned to Washington in expectation of some indication of approval or disapproval. An American Legation report informed Washington on July 9 that the newly-appointed minister of foreign affairs had received only three replies to his letter announcing the change in government and the incoming cabinet: China alone recognized the new government; the Argentine minister answered that he had referred the communication to his government; and the Uruguayan chargé d'affaires

---

[18] *Ibid.*, p. 724.

[19] The Nuncio's visit was not of great significance. Leguía had often extended favors to the Church and in return received the support of the clergy. According to *Time*, XXIII (April 9, 1934), every Leguía heir had at least once in his life served forty days in his hereditary position as a Colonel of the Papal Guard in Rome. This honorary office held by the Leguía family dated centuries back.

[20] Handley had held the position of consul general at Callao-Lima since his appointment on November 24, 1913. Handley died at his post (Callao-Lima) on September 27, 1919, at forty-eight years of age. *Register of The Department of State, 1918* (Washington, 1922), pp. 117, 128. See page 97, Chapter 6, for unpleasantness later experienced by Mrs. Handley.

[21] *US Foreign Relations, 1919*, II, p. 723.

[22] *Ibid.*, p. 725.

simply acknowledged receipt.[23] A meeting of the diplomatic corps, July 8, revealed that various nations, including Brazil and Uruguay, would take action in accordance with the wishes of the United States.

Diplomatic correspondence has disclosed that Washington attempted to ascertain, first, if Leguía had had enough popular support to win the election, and second, if the majority of Peruvians continued to back him after he had executed the *coup d'état*. Both of these questions proved complicated and could not be answered with a simple yes or no. On August 9, McMillin cabled that Leguía had a strong popular following, but the American minister did not know whether this would have been "sufficient to elect." [24]

The second question—was the will of the majority expressed in support of Leguía's coup?—received an answer from Minister Mc-Millin, but this answer was not printed in the *Papers Relating to the Foreign Relations of the United States*.[25] On August 9, 1919, McMillin reported that he believed a majority of people "have acquiesced in (the) overthrow of Pardo but not in calling new congressional elections." [26] The Peruvians did not, according to Mc-Millin, see the need of new congressional elections. It seemed inconsistent that Leguía should feel that the elective procedure could be "regular as to the President of the Republic and irregular as to the Senators and Deputies when all were conducted at the same time and place and by same officers." [27]

Leguía faced turbulent conditions for several months after taking over the presidency.[28] William Walker Smith, United States chargé in Peru, on October 4 informed Washington that he believed Leguía would be able to maintain the presidency if the army remained loyal

---

[23] *Ibid.*, p. 732.

[24] *Ibid.*, p. 732. *Aprista* literature does not demonstrate a strong denunciation of Leguía's coup. However, Haya de la Torre did maintain that many people in July 1919 looked toward modernization to be achieved through a new national emphasis, that civic spirit was high, and the people were desirous of working for the national interest as never before under the *Civilistas*. He believed that Leguía dissipated this well of energy and scattered the idealism in a way which brought about widespread dissolution. See *El proceso—Haya de la Torre* (*Documentos para la historia del ajusticiamiento de un pueblo*) (Guayaquil, 1933), pp. xxx, xxxi, xxxii.

[25] *US Foreign Relations, 1919*, II, p. 733.

[26] *Ibid.*

[27] *Ibid.*

[28] *Ibid.*, pp. 736-737.

to him.[29] As Washington attempted to determine the basis for Leguía's position, the British government showed its willingness to accord either full or *de facto* recognition of the government in Lima.[30] The United States Department of State studied the problem of recognition carefully, and on August 25, eight weeks after the coup, Washington decided to recognize Leguía as head of the *de facto* government of Peru.[31] England, France, Belgium, Bolivia, and Ecuador soon followed the example set by Washington.

If leaders in Washington had followed President Wilson's earlier policy of nonrecognition of governments that assumed power by force, it is doubtful that Leguía would have been recognized by Wilson's government. The *New York Times* of July 6 in a speculative tone asked if the United States would sever relations with Peru as it had with Costa Rica, where Washington had looked with disfavor upon the Tinoco government.[32] Although Leguía's case merited greater consideration, the *New York Times* had pointed out a timely analogy.[33]

Leguía's friendly attitude toward the United States was widely known. Minister McMillin reported, September 5, 1919, that Leguía was credited with being friendly to all foreigners in Peru and hopeful of participation by United States economic interests in the development of Peru.[34] Americans in Peru followed up the revolt by making "strong representations to have the Washington Government retain Benton McMillin not as Minister at Lima, but as Ambassador." [35]

[29] *Ibid.*, p. 738. Numerous developments proved that Leguía did not have and could not obtain co-operation from all segments of Peruvian society. His Democratic Reform Party was able to maintain itself in office until August 1930, but only by treating political opponents harshly. Yet opposition continued and on July 3, 1921, bombs destroyed the northwest wing of the Government Palace. Arrests were made on suspicion, as was often the case when the offenders were not definitely known. For one account of persecution under Leguía, see F. Cossío del Pomar, *Haya de la Torre el indoamericano* (Mexico, D. F., 1939), pp. 72-77.

[30] *US Foreign Relations, 1919*, II, p. 729.

[31] *Ibid.*, p. 734.

[32] *New York Times*, July 6, 1919, p. 11.

[33] In January 1917, Federico A. Tinoco executed a *coup d'état* and overthrew Alfredo Gonzales Flores, the president of Costa Rica. The United States refused to recognize the Tinoco regime and in May 1919 Tinoco was ousted by the Flores supporters. Refusal by the United States to recognize Tinoco was a factor in bringing about his downfall.

[34] *US Foreign Relations, 1919*, II, p. 735.

[35] "Among the Nations," *Current History* (April-September, 1919), p. 247.

A Peruvian writer, Víctor Andrés Belaúnde, suggested another explanation for the action taken by Washington toward the new government in Lima. Belaúnde believed Wilson's recognition of Leguía constituted a departure from his policy of nonrecognition of revolutionary governments. He suggested that Wilson in this case discarded the usual procedure because he did not wish to deprive Peru of "the continuity of her international representation" while the League of Nations was holding its initial session, and "when the hopes of the Peruvian people were focused on the solution through the League of the great problem of the Tacna Arica nationality." [36]

Recognition of a *de jure* government in Lima came early in 1920. Chargé Smith reported the promulgation of the new Constitution on January 18, and suggested that recognition of a *de jure* government be granted.[37] The United States diplomatic agency in Lima was soon afterward raised from a legation to an embassy with the appointment of William E. Gonzales as ambassador.[38]

Let us now turn to those internal Peruvian developments of a political nature which drew the attention of the United States government. As Leguía tightened his hold, he found the United States to be openly friendly to him in many Peruvian domestic matters. Although the United States government did not approve of all of Leguía's domestic policies, the American ambassadors in Peru between 1920 and 1930 (William E. Gonzales, Miles Poindexter, Alexander Pollack Moore, and Fred Morris Dearing) were in general very laudatory of Leguía and his administration.

In September 1919 Leguía announced that there had been a plot to assassinate him and therefore initiated a campaign against all opposition to his new government. Leguía and the more radical elements of his party secured the passage of a confiscation bill on December 26, 1919. This drastic piece of legislation was retroactive and provided for the confiscation of the property of all who had conspired against the government since July 4, 1919, or who might in the future do so.[39] Prior to promulgation of the law, Leguía requested an opinion on it from Chargé Smith. Smith pointed out

[36] Víctor Andrés Belaúnde, "Latin America and the United States" (lectures of the Harris Foundation, edited by Quincy Wright) in *Interpretations of American Foreign Policy* (Chicago, University of Chicago Press, 1930), p. 123.

[37] *US Foreign Relations, 1920*, III, p. 359.

[38] Gonzales had formerly been United States ambassador to Cuba. He was to remain at his Lima post for less than a year.

[39] *US Foreign Relations, 1920*, III, pp. 360-361.

that the bill might affect commercial interests, including those of American citizens, since transactions with conspirators could be declared null and void.[40] On December 31, President Leguía informed Smith that the cabinet had decided to eliminate the retroactive features of the bill.[41] When Leguía asked the State Department for an opinion, Washington expressed its disapproval of the remainder of the bill. On January 3, 1920, Secretary of State Lansing instructed Smith to find another opportunity to discuss it and to intimate to Leguía that the United States considered its passage a "grave error of judgment."[42] Leguía also stated that if Lansing found objection to such a law, it would not be put into effect. American Ambassador Gonzales took up the matter, and on June 17, 1920, suggested to Washington that it would be wise to soft-pedal the matter since American interests were not involved.

This entire affair demonstrates one of the paramount political enigmas of Latin-American politics which faced Leguía throughout his presidency: how to maintain a large degree of stability without employing tyrannical methods. Clarence H. Haring, writing as late as 1931, recognized the scope and complexity of Leguía's political problems when he attributed the statement "Dictatorship is more popular than anarchy" to the Peruvian president.[43] It does seem that Leguía decided in favor of ruthlessness and oppression in dealing with political opponents. His administration was marked constantly by deportations of political dissidents and possible challengers for governmental offices.

Some unofficial voices, especially those of Latin Americans, decried the Leguía government as being dictatorial and harmful to the best interest of Peru. On May 20, 1923, the *New York Times* published a letter written by a Peruvian exile, Emilio Delboy, which placed responsibility upon the Peruvian government for the unex-

[40] Part of the press, many commercial houses, and especially the banks voiced discontent with the confiscation bill. It was thought that the legislation would tend to restrict the free flow of business activity.

[41] *US Foreign Relations*, 1920, III, p. 362.

[42] *Ibid.* The resolution had already passed in Congress but lacked the president's promulgation. It is not clear just why Washington official opinion was so definitely opposed to this domestic legislation. Although the bill was weak in several respects, it was not aimed at foreigners. An early study of the rights of foreigners in Peru was that of Félix Cipriano Coronel Zegarra, *La condición jurídica de los extranjeros en el Peru* (Santiago, 1872).

[43] Clarence H. Haring, "Revolution in South America," *Foreign Affairs, an American Quarterly Review*, IX (January 1931), p. 287.

pected death of Dr. Augusto Durand, April 2, 1923, while being transported aboard a Peruvian ship as a prisoner. The government denied the charge and stated that the immediate cause of death was an abdominal rupture caused by an old wound.[44] Nevertheless, many recalled that Durand had been owner of the newspaper *La Prensa*, which, while retaining its name, was soon transformed into an official organ of the administration.[45]

Professor Carlos Concha was the author of another strong denunciation of Leguía's suppressions, expropriations, and deportations.[46] Concha charged that Leguía had squandered public funds. He also took the former ambassador, William E. Gonzales, to task for a defense he had made of the internal financial policy followed by Leguía. Víctor Andrés Belaúnde, exiled professor of San Marcos (later a president of the United Nations General Assembly), indicted Leguía's administration for the severe blow which it struck at the constitutional advancement Peru had made in the years between 1895 and 1919. "Those who have greeted the rise of . . . Leguía in Peru as the latest step toward democracy and constitutionalism," he protested, have not realized that those countries which apparently have enjoyed for decades a constitutional regime under middle-class and bureaucratic control "are in reality going back to a dictatorship" perhaps worse in certain respects than the earlier personal regimes.[47]

One writer, using the pseudonym Guillermo Pérez, described by the editor of *Current History* magazine as "a well-known, experienced and respected Latin-American statesman and diplomat of high standing throughout South America, the United States, and Europe," launched a bitter attack upon Gómez of Venezuela, Leguía of Peru, and Saavedra of Bolivia.[48] In an article entitled "Three South American Despots," he pictured the three dictators as being the worst kind of tyrants.[49] Appealing to the American public and the State Department, he insisted that "to profit by the misfortune of the South American peoples, to exploit them by means of shame-

[44] *Current History*, XVIII (April-September 1923), 525.
[45] Concha, "The Reign of Terror in Peru," *op. cit.*, p. 670.
[46] *Current History*, XVIII (April-September 1923), pp. 669-672.
[47] Belaúnde, "Latin America and the United States," *op. cit.*, p. 111. See also, Belaúnde's *La realidad nacional*, p. 253.
[48] *Current History*, XXX (September 1929), p. 1143.
[49] *Ibid.*, XVIII (April-September 1923), p. 91. *Current History* aroused considerable United States interest in dictatorial governments of Latin America.

ful contracts, is neither just nor human." [50] He asked if it would
not be proper for the secretary of state in Washington to "warn
the bankers and businessmen of the United States of the risk that
they were running in concluding contracts with dictatorial Governments which in no way represented the will of the peoples in whose
name contracts were entered into containing most burdensome conditions."

These statements form a sharp contrast with the views presented
by representatives of the United States government, and were almost
lost sight of in the praise which flowed from much of the North
American press. Defenders of the status quo in Venezuela, Peru, and
Bolivia were quick to answer Guillermo Pérez. The *Wall Street
Journal*, speaking of the requests to declare null and void the contracts between the dictators and American interests, argued that the
suggestion made by Pérez could scarcely be taken seriously.[51] The
next issue of *Current History* carried an article by a United States
citizen, Grand Pierre, which credited the three dictators with being
benevolent despots.[52]

Press statements which had their origin in official sources in Washington were most laudatory of Leguía and United States-Peruvian
relations. William E. Gonzales, first American ambassador to Lima,
was one of several American diplomats who praised Leguía's administration. Soon after leaving his post at Lima, Gonzales prepared
a statement defending Leguía against those who criticized his dictatorial methods. In an article entitled "A Vindication of President
Leguía of Peru," appearing in the same issue of *Current History*
as Pierre's article, Gonzales said: "Knowing Augusto B. Leguía,
President of Peru, to be most cordial to Americans, to be forward-
looking, progressive in spirit and effort and to be striving for the
advancement of his country, it is surprising to find him classed by
Guillermo Pérez in the April number of the *Current History Magazine* as one of 'Three American Despots.' " [53] Gonzales enumerated

[50] *Ibid.*, p. 74. *Aprista* writings also presented a concern for the spread of
"Yankee imperialism." See fn. 57 of this chapter and later references; also Víctor
Raúl Haya de la Torre, *El antimperialismo y el Apra* (Santiago, 1936), pp. 99-
100, and *El proceso—Haya de la Torre* (Guayaquil, 1933), p. 16.

[51] *Current History*, XVIII (April-September, 1923), p. 189.

[52] *Ibid.*, pp. 191-195.

[53] William E. Gonzales, "A Vindication of President Leguía of Peru," *Current
History*, XVIII (May 1923), p. 195.

the achievements of the Peruvian president and, at the same time, attempted to prove that it was necessary for Leguía to exile some of his opponents in order that he might maintain a degree of political stability.[54]

On another occasion Gonzales suggested that the United States press carefully sift the news dispatches from Peru in order to determine which reports should be printed. He noted that news attacking Leguía might have a depressing effect upon the negotiations with Chile over Tacna and Arica.[55] Another State Department figure of note, Ambassador Alexander Pollack Moore (widower of Lillian Russell and ambassador to Spain before going to Peru), also lauded and eulogized Leguía. Moore was reported to have said that "Leguía has the courage of Caesar, the power of Napoleon and the diplomacy of Richelieu," and that Leguía would go down in history as one of the world's greatest men. As might be expected, this statement caused considerable comment.[56] *Apristas*, Haya de la Torre and Luis Alberto Sánchez, were disturbed since they believed that the ambassador's words encouraged exile or deportation of political opponents. These two believed it important to oppose both the local oligarchies and the foreign corporation-giants at the same time. Pedro Ugarteche was appalled when he learned that Ambassador Moore tried to obtain the Nobel Peace Prize for Leguía.

Using whatever means necessary, including spoliation of the Constitution, Leguía arranged for his re-election in 1924 and 1929. Leguía and his Democratic Reform Party met stiff resistance from parties representing two different segments of Peruvian society: the *Civilistas*, supported by rightist landed proprietors and part of the upper middle-class middle-roaders; and the *Apristas* (*Alianza Popular Revo-*

[54] One can claim that Leguía, in employing dictatorial measures, only followed the route taken by numerous past presidents of Peru. It can be pointed out that powers of the presidential office in Peru are quite extensive, as Graham H. Stuart has done in *The Governmental System of Peru* (Washington, published by the Carnegie Institution of Washington, 1925), p. 41. This, of course, does not prove that it was necessary for Leguía to use suppressive methods in order to maintain political stability in Peru.

[55] *New York Times*, June 10, 1923, II, p. 4.

[56] Ernest Galarza, "Debts, Dictatorship and Revolution in Bolivia and Peru," *Foreign Policy Reports*, VII, No. 5 (May 13, 1931), p. 117. See also, Luis Alberto Sánchez, *Haya de la Torre y el Apra* (Santiago, 1954), pp. 148-149, and Ugarteche, *La política internacional peruana durante la dictadura de Leguía*, pp. 30-31.

lucionaria Americana) who were backed by noncommunist and anti-communist leftist groups, representing the Indians, laborers, and a large section of the university student body. The leaders of these two opposition parties were exiled and imprisoned if they showed any inclination to criticize the administration.

Apra had had the longest record of persistent agitation for social reform in Peru. In addition, the movement gained considerable influence in at least six other nations south of the Rio Grande. Víctor Raúl Haya de la Torre, the leader, picked up where Manuel Gonzalez Prada had left off. Haya de la Torre was exiled from Peru in 1923 and while living in Mexico the following year founded the *Aprista* organization. With its co-operative efforts of laborers and intellectuals, its blend of Marxist economics and democratic philosophy, its free night-universities, and its direct attacks on the feudal patterns of Peru, it was destined to gain great popular support. At times, in the early years, it was more of a social movement or a popular crusade than a political party. The program at the beginning was centered around the following five points: (1) action against "Yankee" imperialism (the word "Yankee" was later dropped); (2) political unity of Latin America; (3) the nationalization of lands and industry; (4) the internationalization of the Panama Canal; and (5) solidarity with all oppressed peoples and classes of the world.[57] On the other hand, ultraconservatives and reactionaries under Leguía, Sánchez Cerro, and Benavides made spurious charges that *Apristas* were nothing more than communists.

Eudocio Ravines, Peruvian communist in the 1920's and a bitter critic of Haya de la Torre, shows that *Apra* and communism never had any real mutual goals or common ideological grounds beyond

[57] The *Apristas* have been socialistic—and even Marxist in certain economic approaches—but they have disagreed (especially since 1936 or 1937) on most matters and even violently opposed the communists. The following *Aprista* publications provide important insights into this complex movement: Haya de la Torre, *Por la emancipación de la américa latina* (Buenos Aires, 1927); *Ideario y acción Aprista* (Buenos Aires, 1930); *Teoría y táctica del aprismo* (Lima, 1931); *A donde va indoamerica?* (Santiago, 1936); *El antimperialismo y el Apra* (Santiago, 1936); *Treinta años de Aprismo* (Mexico, D. F., 1956); also F. Cossío del Pomar, *Haya de la Torre el indoamericano* (Mexico, D. F., 1939); Luis Alberto Sánchez, *Haya de la Torre y el Apra* (Santiago, 1955); and Harry Kantor, *The Ideology and Program of the Peruvian Aprista Movement* (Berkeley, University of California Press, 1953). Kantor's work is not an "*Aprista* publication" in the sense that he is an active participant, but it is sympathetic to much of the *Aprista* point of view.

some starting points.[58] In Peru they may have suffered in common but that was about the extent of their common experience. Earlier, Haya had accepted some Marxist economic arguments as meritorious, but it is generally believed that by 1928 the *Apristas* had separated completely from the communists—if there had ever been anything to separate. José Carlos Mariátegui (1895-1930) was the ideological leader of Peruvian communism until his death. Luis Alberto Sánchez writing in *Haya de la Torre o el político* refers to one of Haya de la Torre's letters dated 1928, which stated that he (Haya) always sympathized with Mariátegui but that they were never in the same struggle; "Pero, Mariátegui nunca ha estado en la lucha misma." *La Tribuna*, the *Apra* newspaper, makes clear how much enmity existed between communism and *Apra* before the end of 1945.[59]

[58] Eudocio Ravines, *The Yenan Way* (New York, Charles Scribner's Sons, 1951). This work must be used with caution to avoid confusion over implications and insinuations. The excessive use and careless handling of quotations is evident; for example, the person identified merely as Herrera, p. 97, who is reported to have said that in *Apra* "you have all the big landholders in the mountains, the most reactionary and primitive gentlemen in the country."

For the *Aprista* leader's statement as to when communism and *Aprismo* took different routes, see Haya de la Torre, *El antimperialismo y el Apra*, pp. 118, 183-185, 190, 210. Enrique Chirinos Soto, *Actores en el drama del Peru y del mundo* (Lima, 1961), p. 123, wrote that Haya de la Torre always kept his distance from communism and later fought it openly and without reserve. For the later years this is true; however, the early relationship between communism and *Aprismo* is not so clear. Precursor Manuel Gonzalez Prada seems to have stood apart, but the association of Haya de la Torre with José Carlos Mariátegui leaves some unanswered questions. Harry Kantor (see fn. 57 above) reported that international communism has continually fought the *Apristas*. This is correct, but how much of an ideological debt does *Aprismo* owe Mariátegui? See Eugenio Chang-Rodriguez, *La literatura política de Gonzalez Prada, Mariátegui y Haya de la Torre* (Mexico, D. F., 1957). For the position at the close of the Second World War see Chapter 7 of the present work and *La Tribuna*, *Apra* party newspaper, for the years 1945 and 1946. Robert J. Alexander, *Communism in Latin America* (New Brunswick, Rutgers University Press, 1957), maintains that *Apristas* and communists early followed separate roads (see pages 221, 225, 226, and 229). Alexander also views *Apra* as having been the chief "stumbling block to the advancement of Communism" (pages 220 and 232). For background on *Aprismo*, this writer has also depended upon personal interviews with Haya de la Torre, Luis Alberto Sánchez, and Julian Petrovich. These interviews were in or near Lima on June 14, 1945, and again on October 16, 1945, at party headquarters. Luis Alberto Sánchez was not present at the second interview, but on another occasion (probably September 1945) he and this writer had dinner together.

[59] Luis Alberto Sánchez, *Haya de la Torre o el político* (Santiago, 1936), p. 83.

United States officials in Peru during Leguía's administration made little effort to distinguish between leftists and extreme leftists or between *Apristas* and communists. In December 1928, United States authorities at the Panama Canal Zone refused Haya de la Torre permission to disembark at Balboa or to board a ship for Mexico. These officials offered no explanation for detaining the *Aprista* leader or for placing him on a German ship which carried him to Bremen, Germany.[60] The only interpretation given Haya, unofficially tendered him by the Canal Zone doctor at Colon, was: "I think you are a too powerful speaker." [61] In 1928 the *Apristas* were the recognized opponents of Leguía. At that same time the United States government looked upon them as hostile to the United States because of their vocal discontent with the growing influence of Washington over Peru's internal affairs and the large shadow cast by the "Yankee dollar." Not until the Second World War would there be a real rapprochement between the government in Washington and this, the strongest and most popular of all of Peru's political parties for the first sixty years of the twentieth century.

Leguía may have had confidence that American dollars would help build Peru, but many of his compatriots did not agree. During the *oncenio*, when open domestic criticism of the regime was not permitted, publications from exile (such as *La Republica*) registered an early protest. Later, complaints from both home and abroad poured forth to decry Peru's political and economic subservience to Washington and New York. While most saw the need for foreign capital, they protested, however, that too high a price was being paid for it. The list of well-known Peruvian writers who expressed dissatisfaction with the influx of "Yankee" money included the following: Felipe Barreda y Laos, Víctor Andrés Belaúnde, Luis Humberto Delgado, José Carlos Mariátegui, Pedro Ugarteche, Genaro Arbaiza, and at one time or another, all of the principal *Aprista* editorialists and literary figures, as well as many others not mentioned here.

Leguía apparently hoped for the growth of an atmosphere which would be friendly to the United States. By the end of the *oncenio* the result was something far different, for influential Peruvians such as Víctor Andrés Belaúnde, Haya de la Torre, Luis Alberto Sánchez, Manuel Seoane, Felipe Barreda y Laos, Alberto Ulloa and many

[60] Haya de la Torre, *A donde va indoamerica?*, pp. 65-66.
[61] *Ibid.*, p. 67.

others became more and more critical of the spread of "Yankee" influence. Ugarteche protested because the major positions of finance, public education, political administration in many instances, and additional areas of public responsibility were given over to the North Americans. Other foreigners were granted privileged posts also, but it was a United States physician and a United States dentist who administered personally to the president of Peru.[62] Then, as if in derision, it is mentioned that he had a Chilean jockey for his racing stable. The nature of this "anti-Yankeeism" is clarified in later chapters, but it was principally Leguía's subservience to the forces of Wall Street or the Potomac which caused resentment. Those Peruvians who were happy with the status quo were willing to overlook the slaps at the nation because the might of "Uncle Sam" made them feel all the more secure. Newspapers such as El Comercio, along with powerful hacendados, identified Aprismo with communism and appeared to be fearful of any serious social reform program.[63]

From the right came some voices of protest against Leguía, as well as bitter criticism of his allegiance to the United States. One of the most distinguished was Víctor Andrés Belaúnde. Pro-Catholic in tradition, this intellectual protested Leguía's subjection to Washington in economic and political matters. Belaúnde lamented that Peru was the only Latin-American nation to voice approval of the Marine occupation of Nicaragua.[64] In this respect, the Apristas were going even further in order to help Sandino. Pedro Ugarteche decried the fact that at the Havana meeting in 1928 his country did not stand up to be counted in the ranks of those who opposed intervention. It was Ugarteche's opinion that there was no need for Peru's subjugation, and that such subjugation merely hurt Peru. His criticism of the United States singled out the Republican Party, although not as directly as did that of Belaúnde. "Frente al problema social universal, hay tres posturas: la individualista o conservadora,

[62] Ugarteche, La política internacional peruana durante la dictadura de Leguía, pp. 23, 40-42.

[63] El Comercio, Lima, January 1932. See also Sánchez, Haya de la Torre o el político, pp. 204-205; and Kantor, The Ideology and Program of the Peruvian Aprista Movement, fn. 82, who reports that after the Apristas had developed a successful agricultural co-operative with the yanacones (type of sharecropper), the rich landowners decided it was communism and destroyed it.

[64] Belaúnde, La realidad nacional, pp. 242-244. For Aprista backing of General Sandino in Nicaragua, see A donde va indoamerica? (fn. 59), p. 7.

la reformista y la revolucionaria. La primera, desacreditada con justicia, es la de la majoría del partido republicano en los Estados Unidos, expresión suprema del capitalismo moderno." [65] Another powerful voice of discontent was raised in exile when Felipe Barreda y Laos, by means of the periodical, *La Republica*, criticized Leguía and his dependence upon the United States. Although Leguía silenced the domestic press and the university, he was never able to gain wide acceptance of his objectives in Peru. It is quite possible that after 1931, the pendulum of anti-Leguía feeling swung to the extreme and even some of his constructive achievements were ignored or interpreted in a negative manner. Leguía had slighted the nation, and, since nationalism is not limited to either the right or the left, he was looked down upon from all sides. The generations which had grown up under the exaggerated onus of defeat by Chile wanted to raise their heads without seeing "Uncle Sam" loom always before them.

To a significant degree, then, Leguía was to find himself more and more committed to the United States. And if officially the United States was not committed to Leguía, at least it was willing to overlook most of his shortcomings. He was able to retain power as long as he had the backing of official Washington and the financial support of private United States interests. Later we will note that he would fall from the presidency as soon as the credit strings to New York were cut.

[65] Belaúnde, *La realidad nacional*, p. 312.

4: THE INCREASE OF DIRECT INVESTMENTS

As a result of the conditions outlined in the preceding chapter, it became evident that United States capital would flow into Peru in the 1920's. Peru's need for foreign capital and technological know-how was comparable to that of any nation with great quantities of undeveloped resources and a great potential in the extractive industries. The statement of Leguía read before the Second Pan-American Commercial Conference emphasized his desire to have closer contacts with United States business interests.[1] Prior to the First World War, England had been first and Germany second in the amount of goods sold to Peru. Under Leguía this changed, and between 1925 and 1930 United States investments in Peru would loom larger than those of the British or German. In addition, the Peruvian government borrowed heavily from private United States investors. National governmental expenditures increased from 54,500,000 soles annually in 1918 to 200,000,000 soles in 1929. Víctor Andrés Belaúnde, claiming that expenditures had been excessive under Leguía, pointed out that Peru reduced its cost of government in 1932 when Sánchez Cerro was president.[2] Historian Jorge Basadre has pointed out that much of the public works program was of a constructive nature, but it was costly. A summary of the loan situation appears in the following chapter.

That the United States Department of Commerce encouraged large-scale rather than small-scale investments in Peru is shown by the following statement from the report of the Acting Commercial Attaché of the United States, Daniel Waters, at Lima, August 23, 1921: "Peru as a market should be carefully cultivated, even though

[1] General Session, *Pan-American Commerce—Report of the Second Pan-American Commercial Conference* (Washington, 1919), p. 85.

[2] Víctor Andrés Belaúnde, *La crisis presente, 1914-1939* (Lima, 1940), pp. 120-129. Felipe Barreda, in a foreword, claimed that Leguía's internal improvements which were built for show could not hide the ruin of Peru; see Jacinto López, *La caída del gobierno constitucional en el Peru* (New York, Carranza and Company, 1927), p. 9.

sales at the present time are restricted. The field for North American investments is extensive. . . . Peru is primarily a country for large capital, and there is no place there for the small investor." [3]

Diplomatic efforts were made by the United States to encourage general investments and, on various occasions, the government acted on behalf of specific companies. L. Y. Spear of the Electric Boat Company told the committee conducting Senate hearings that the United States government had aided his firm most directly:

> The Chairman: Mr. Spear, speaking generally now, how far could the Electric Boat Company have gotten as respects business in South America without such aid as came from the State Department, the Navy Department, and your activities with money which you do not pretend to know definitely how it was spent—how far could you have gotten without resort to those influences?
>
> Mr. Spear: I think they were helpful, but I do not think they were the deciding factor. [4]

Governmental aid to private business was by no means an exclusively "Yankee" characteristic; other nations bid for South American and Peruvian business in similar fashion. [5] It is pertinent to note, however, that, although the Electric Boat Company solicited submarine business in numerous South American countries, it succeeded only in Peru. [6] It was in Peru that the Electric Boat Company received its greatest assistance from the United States Departments of State and Navy. [7]

Other instances demonstrate how diplomatic assistance was extended to United States private business concerns. In June 1921,

[3] *Commerce Reports, Bureau of Foreign and Domestic Commerce*, III, Nos. 152-153 (Washington, 1921), p. 943.

[4] *Munitions Industry: Hearings before the Special Committee Investigating the Munitions Industry, United States Senate*, 73rd Cong., pursuant to S. Res. 206, Part I (Washington, 1934), pp. 127-128; hereafter cited as *Munitions Industry: Senate Hearings*.

[5] Albert E. Carter, *The Battle of South America* (New York, Bobbs-Merrill Company, 1941), pp. 217-218, 224.

[6] *Munitions Industry: Senate Hearings*, Part I (1934), p. 152. During the disturbances in Peru in 1933, the Electric Boat Company asked the State Department to assist the company by providing it with information about one of its Peruvian employees. The company also tried unsuccessfully to obtain the assistance of Washington in the collection of debts owed it by the Peruvian government.

[7] *Ibid.*, pp. 150, 151. For the part played by the American Naval Mission to Peru in the sale of American goods to the Peruvian government see Chapter 6.

United States Ambassador William E. Gonzales accompanied C. W. Calvin, head of the Peruvian branch of the National City Bank of New York, on a visit to President Leguía. The purpose of the visit was to attempt to influence Leguía in favor of the American concern. Apparently a British bank had almost completed negotiations for a loan, when Gonzales tried, unsuccessfully, to change the President's views on the matter.[8]

In March 1921, the Peruvian government was preparing to close a contract with the British-owned Marconi Company to take over, develop, and operate the Peruvian wireless service. Ambassador Gonzales informed Secretary of State Hughes that he hoped that All American Cables wanted the business. Immediately—March 31—Hughes cabled Gonzales that "you are instructed to state to the President in a further audience that this government trusts the Peruvian Government will at least delay the closing of the rumored contract with the Marconi Company until an opportunity is given to American companies which may be interested to make propositions to the government of Peru."[9] Throughout this month-long diplomatic interchange, it was apparent that the State Department in Washington wanted All American Cables to bid for the business; but the company could not, according to Leguía's interpretation of its capacity and ability, undertake such operation.

Air transportation services provide another example of official policy aiding private enterprise. German interests offered the competition here. On January 19, 1928, Secretary of State Kellogg informed Ambassador Miles Poindexter in Lima that since American aeronautical interests planned to develop aviation along the west coast of South America, it was important that "the Government of Peru grant no exclusive concessions to foreign aeronautical interests to operate in Peru, and it is highly desirable that the Government

[8] *Papers Relating to the Foreign Relations of the United States, 1921*, II (Washington), pp. 663-665, hereafter cited as *US Foreign Relations*. C. W. Calvin had become worried when Leguía prepared to give the Anglo-South American Bank (a British bank) business which the New York bank desired. The business concerned was the handling of $800,000 accumulated interest on gold which the government of Peru had in deposit in the National City Bank of New York. In July 1921, Leguía ordered the conversion into sterling of a $12,000,000 gold reserve deposit in New York. The Bank of England made a better offer than did the National City Bank, and thus again the transactions were turned over to British bankers.

[9] *US Foreign Relations*, 1921, II, p. 667.

of Peru grant no concessions at all to foreign interests for air transport in Peru until American companies . . . have had the opportunity to develop their projects. . . ." [10] Kellogg was acting in support of the Keystone company and Huff-Daland Dusters, who in
turn were connected with Hayden Stone (financial) and Pan American Airways (later associated with W. R. Grace in this project).
German and isolated American private interests opposed the Keystone company's advance into Peru.[11] Diplomatic dispatches to
Washington reported, "We owe a debt of genuine gratitude to
President Leguía for his staunch stand in favor of American aviation
interests here." [12]

Washington officials, with the aid of Harold B. Grow (formerly
of the American Naval Mission to Peru) and the propaganda about
a proposed flight to Peru by Charles A. Lindbergh, were successful
in maintaining Leguía's interest in favor of Pan American-Grace
Airways.[13] Leguía would not permit the Peruvian government to par-
ticipate in a conference which Faucett of Peru, Scadta of Colombia,
the Bolivian Lloyd Aerial, and the Chilean military air service were
planning to hold in Lima. Grow, a United States citizen, was Peru's
Director General of Aviation.

There were fewer than a dozen important American concerns
operating in Peru in the 1920's. The largest ones were the Cerro de
Pasco Copper Corporation engaged in mining and related operations;
W. R. Grace and Company, the principal American trading and
manufacturing concern; International Petroleum Company (Standard Oil of New Jersey), the largest petroleum producer and distrib-
utor in Peru; Pan American-Grace Airways, the largest international
air transportation concern; All America Cables, with cable and radio-
telegraph concessions (especially after 1929); Frederick Snare Corporation, with an interest in the Callao dock and port works it had
constructed; the National City Bank of New York, operating a

[10] US Foreign Relations, 1928, I, p. 800.
[11] US Foreign Relations, 1929, I, p. 601.
[12] Ibid.
[13] US Foreign Relations, 1929, I, pp. 573, 576, 587. Protests that Leguía was
turning Peru into a colony were made by various persons. Here are two: Víctor
Andrés Belaúnde, La realidad nacional (Paris, 1931), p. 253; and Pedro
Ugarteche, La política internacional peruana durante la dictadura de Leguía
(Lima, 1930), pp. 34, 39, 40. These two writers were exiles from Leguía's Peru.
For a general account of the Naval Mission activities see Chapter 6.

branch office in Lima; and Wessel Duval and Company, an early United States trading firm with a long record of involvement in general merchandising in Peru. Cerro de Pasco, Grace and Company, and International Petroleum long maintained their economic empires in Peru.

Five other concerns had invested only small amounts of capital in Peruvian enterprises but had entered into contracts of importance with the Peruvian central government or with regional or local agencies of Peruvian government. These were three investment-banking houses dealing in foreign securities: the J. and W. Seligman and Company; the Guaranty Trust Company of New York; the National City Company; a construction concern called the Foundation Company; and the Electric Boat Company, producers of naval armaments.

Lesser American mining interests were represented by the following firms: the Vanadium Corporation of America, owner of 2,372 acres of vanadium mines, concerning which Max Winkler reported, "The ore deposits are among the richest and most productive vanadium deposits in the world";[14] the Inca Mining Company, which operated one of the largest gold-mining concerns in Peru; the American Smelting and Refining Company, owners of the capital stock of the Northern Peru Mining and Smelting Company. These three concerns are not to be compared in size to the mammoth Cerro de Pasco Corporation prior to 1950. Cerro de Pasco's investments in Peru for 1925 were conservatively estimated at $50,000,000.[15] The market value of these holdings would have been much more than the book value. By 1926 the mines had reached a production of more than 100,000,000 pounds of copper annually, with the record output for the corporation up until the Second World War being attained in 1929.

W. R. Grace and Company had a long history in Peru, dating

[14] Max Winkler, *Investments of United States Capital in Latin America* (Boston, World Peace Foundation Pamphlets, 1928), p. 149.

[15] *Stock Exchange Practices: Hearings before a Subcommittee of the Committee on Banking and Currency, United States Senate*, 72nd Cong., 2nd Sess., S. Res. 84 and S. Res. 239, Part VI (Washington, 1933), p. 2105, hereafter cited as *Stock Exchange Practices: Senate Hearings*.

Ugarteche, *La política internacional*, p. 42, singled out Cerro de Pasco Copper Corporation and W. R. Grace along with other companies to say that all of them exploited Peru's great riches through concessions given them by "the dictatorship" of Leguía.

back to 1850 when young W. R. Grace went to Callao and started a small business.[16] By the time of Leguía's tenure in office, in addition to its shipping interests the company and its subsidiaries owned cotton and woolen mills, sugar plantations and mills, light and power properties and terminal facilities for shipping. Meanwhile, the Grace Steamship Company, controlled by W. R. Grace and Company, developed a virtual monopoly on passenger and freight traffic between the United States and Peru.[17] In 1929 the steamship company owned thirteen freight and passenger vessels of an aggregate dead weight tonnage of 105,565, all engaged in South American trade.[18] From 1928 to 1934 the company collected $9,500,000 annually from the United States government for carrying mail which at the regular United States poundage rate would have been worth $1,200,000.[19] This type of subsidy has not been uncommon in our history. The Cartavio Sugar Company, a subsidiary of W. R. Grace, operated the second largest sugar mill in Peru.[20] By 1935 Cartavio was producing 60,000 tons of sugar a year, making many gallons of rum, and em-

[16] "Casa Grace," *Fortune*, XII (December 1935), p. 158. A more detailed account may be found in Eugene W. Burgess and Frederick H. Harbison, *Casa Grace in Peru* (Second Case Study in an NPA Series on United States Business Performance Abroad) (Washington, National Planning Association, 1954). In 1850 William Russell Grace went to Callao with his father who headed a colony of 200 Irishmen. The colony expected to farm a large estate between Lima and Callao, but malaria took such a heavy toll that this project was abandoned. W. R. Grace started to work as a ship's chandler. Soon he entered the guano trade and by 1860 had made enough money to branch out; for a time the company was the sole United States agent in Peru for guano. Grace sold supplies to ships and developed a shipping and trading business. The business continued to grow until it had spread over much of the west coast of South America and into New York. In 1935 W. R. Grace and Company (Casa Grace) controlled forty-three companies, most of which it owned outright. The *Fortune* article reported: "Since W. R. Grace and Company is a closed corporation, the gentlemen of 7 Hanover Square will reveal no earnings figure. . . . If Grace had cut managerial bonuses to the bone (they averaged $821,000 a year from 1916 to 1933) it could have translated its $2,000,000 gross profits into net profits of $1,500,000 a year. . . ."

[17] "South America II: Peru," *Fortune*, XVII (January 1938), p. 126.

[18] *Moody's Manual* (1929), p. 2156.

[19] "Casa Grace," *Fortune*, XII, p. 97.

[20] W. E. Dunn, "Peru a Commercial and Industrial Handbook," *Trade Promotion Series, Department of Commerce Bureau of Foreign and Domestic Commerce* (Washington, 1925), p. 24. The Grace 17,000-acre sugar hacienda at Paramonga has a large paper mill and produces numerous other by-products. See *Peru*, Pan-American Union (Washington, D.C., 1957; reprint 1960), p. 24.

ploying 3,000 men on 9,000 acres of cane.[21] Grace entered the Peruvian textile industry in 1912, after rapid expansion in the 1920's had developed three mills which produced 2,500,000 yards of cotton goods per month, five-eighths of the entire output of Peru.[22] With much W. R. Grace cargo filling the holds of W. R. Grace ships, it is evident that that firm exercised broad influence over the export and import trading of Peru as well as over domestic industry.

International Petroleum Company, an $85,000,000 concern in 1938, had been incorporated under the laws of Canada in 1920. It was controlled by Imperial Oil of Canada which in turn was a majority-owned subsidiary of Standard Oil of New Jersey.[23] In 1926, International Petroleum controlled 70 per cent of the Peruvian oil output. By that same year British companies, gradually losing out to North American interests, controlled only 27 per cent of the Peruvian oil business, and Italian concerns 3 per cent.[24] It was estimated that International Petroleum Company exported about 90 per cent of Peru's outgoing petroleum in the mid-twenties.[25] The refinery at Talara owned by International Petroleum was not only the largest in Peru but the largest on the west coast of South America as well, with a potential capacity in 1925 of 10,000 barrels a day. The North Americans built up model towns at Talara and at Negritos, the center of field activity.[26] The International Petroleum Company was granted a concession by the Peruvian government to import Mexican oil free of duty in order to make products not ob-

---

[21] "Casa Grace," *Fortune*, XII, p. 96. See also Chapter 10.

[22] "Casa Grace," *Fortune*, XII, p. 96.

[23] Winkler, *Investments of United States Capital in Latin America*, pp. 144-145. Companies holding concessions under the Peruvian law of January 2, 1922, were to be legally domiciled in Peru. Often this resulted in a superficial incorporation in Peru of foreign concerns, with the home corporation existing outside. Advantages, especially in taxation, were gained by the foreign interests.

[24] Robert W. Dunn, *American Foreign Investments* (New York, Viking Press, 1926), p. 183. In 1922 the International Petroleum Company purchased the properties of the London and Pacific Petroleum Company and its subsidiary, the Lagunitas Oil Company.

[25] *Ibid.*, p. 83.

[26] *American Petroleum Interests in Foreign Countries: Hearings before a Special Committee Investigating Petroleum Resources, United States Senate*, 79th Cong., 1st Sess., S. Res. 36 (Washington, 1945), p. 352; hereafter cited as *American Petroleum Interests in Foreign Countries: Senate Hearings*.

tainable from Peruvian oil.[27] This company's Peruvian investments rose in value from $45,000,000 in 1919 to $68,500,000 (only book value—not market value) in 1929 and its production increased five-fold between 1919 and 1929.[28] An account of the more recent activity of I.P.C. is included in Chapter 10, "The Mighty Dollar at Work."

A variety of utility operations and public service or quasi-public service enterprises came under control of the dollar in the 1920's. International Telephone and Telegraph, which had bought out All America Cables in 1927,[29] extended its influence in Peru by acquiring ownership of the Lima and Callao telephone service (*Compañia Peruana de Teléfonos Limitada*) on January 3, 1930. The Frederick Snare Corporation constructed dock and port works at Callao valued at about $1,000,000. By arrangement with the Peruvian government in 1929 the profits on the port works were to be turned over to the corporation until it was paid in full. Meanwhile the government was to pay 8 per cent interest on the amount owed for construction of the port works.[30]

The armaments field provided another lucrative arena. The Electric Boat Company of New York and New Jersey sold four submarines to the Leguía government, two in 1924 and two in 1926, the aggregate price being $5,785,987. According to an official of the company, sums amounting to $15,000 were paid out in Peruvian circles for special commissions and to eliminate "some sore feeling of some political friends . . . that are trying to introduce Bethlehem into our small Peruvian market."[31] In January 1929, the company agreed to pay President Leguía's grafting son, Juan, a commission of $40,000 on a prospective order for two submarines, and the Electric Boat Company "expressed its willingness to pay $145,000 in commissions altogether" in negotiating this matter.[32] This 1929 sale was,

[27] Dunn, "Peru a Commercial and Industrial Handbook," *op. cit.*, p. 202.

[28] Cleona Lewis, *America's Stake in International Investments* (Washington, Brookings Institution, 1938), p. 588. See also, *American Petroleum Interests in Foreign Countries: Senate Hearings* (1945), p. 354.

[29] *Poor's 1931 Public Utilities* (New York, 1931), p. 2138.

[30] *Sale of Foreign Bonds or Securities in the United States: Hearings before the Committee on Finance, United States Senate*, 72nd Cong., 1st Sess., S. Res. 19, Part III (Washington, 1932), pp. 1711-1712; hereafter cited as *Sale of Foreign Bonds or Securities: Senate Hearings*.

[31] *Munitions Industry: Senate Hearings*, Part III (1936), p. 84.

[32] *Ibid.*

however, never completed. L. Y. Spear of the company was of the opinion that graft was the essential feature and the "real foundation" of all South American business.[33] Thus it was a very fine line, if any at all, which existed between a commission and a bribe. The submarine builders were not successful in making full collections on their sales, and in 1931 they asked the United States Department of State to assist them in making collection.[34]

The Foundation Company contracted in October 1920 with the Peruvian government on the basis of cost plus 19 per cent.[35] This New York firm arranged for the expenditure of $10,000,000 to $15,-000,000 over a three-year period on water, sanitation, and other public works. The total assets of the Foundation Company, as listed in 1922, amounted to $4,530,440.[36] Some roads were built and various sanitation projects came to completion.

There was little United States banking activity in Peru before October 1919, when C. W. Calvin of the National City Bank of New York went to Lima to install a branch office. Since 1920 the institution has carried on regular banking business in Peru. The National City Company was the investment affiliate of the National City Bank, the latter owning all the stock of the former. Most of the business of the National City Company in Peru revolved around buying Peruvian securities and selling them to the general public in the United States. The company was actively engaged in the sale of the ill-fated 1927 and 1928 Peruvian bonds which will be discussed in the following chapter.

Smaller United States business interests began to enter the field, too, especially in the manufacturing of by-products and the importing of industrial products. In a diversified exchange, much of it dependent upon sound business practices, trade between Peru and the United States continued to increase. There was interest in the development of Peruvian rubber but it did not prove to be successful in the 1920's.

There is reason to believe that, in the main, Peru benefited by this influx of United States capital, but it is not an easy matter to evaluate in specific terms. By 1929, American businesses nearly monopolized certain fields of development such as copper mining, vana-

[33] Ibid.
[34] Munitions Industry: Senate Hearings (see fn. 6 of this chapter), p. 87.
[35] Munitions Industry: Senate Hearings, Part I (1934), pp. 354-355.
[36] Moody's Manual (1922), p. 656.

dium mining, oil production, communications, and foreign financing. The growth of American capital in Peru was accompanied by an increase of Peruvian exports, but the increase in exports did not bring a commensurate benefit to the Peruvian economy. An official report of the United States Department of Commerce maintained that the profits from mining interests, to a great extent, went abroad.[37] J. H. Durrell, vice-president and overseas manager of the National City Bank, put it in the following way (July 1927): "Its principal sources of wealth, the mines and oil wells, are nearly all foreign-owned, and excepting for wages and taxes, no part of the value of their production remains in the country. . . . As a whole, I have no great faith in any material betterment of Peru's economic condition in the near future." [38] It would not be difficult to show that United States interests benefited by the operations in Peru, but it is another thing to try to demonstrate that Peruvians—that is, other than those few who were closely aligned with foreign capital—gained appreciably. Another explanation of Peru's situation was forthcoming in a report dated January 12, 1928, and later read before the Senate investigation of stock exchange practices: "The present low value of Peruvian money is due primarily to the fact that the balance of international payments is unfavorable to Peru, although the commercial scales show a favorable balance, and this is apparent at a glance when one considers that metals, minerals, and oils bring into the country only a part of the real value as shown by the customhouse statistics, for the reason that the production of these articles is largely in the hands of foreign companies which sell exchange only sufficient to cover their operating costs, and many other articles leave a part of their value abroad." [39] Into this general picture we must fit the fact that about 83.4 per cent of Peru's total exports were accounted for in sugar, cotton, copper, and petroleum. Then note that most of these exports were owned by non-Peruvians, especially United States citizens.

The real need which existed for outside capital did not insure its willing acceptance when the "Yankee" investors rushed in. The

[37] *Commerce Reports, Bureau of Foreign and Domestic Commerce*, II, Nos. 14-26 (Washington, 1930), p. 6.

[38] *Stock Exchange Practices: Senate Hearings* (1933), p. 2071.

[39] *Ibid.*, p. 2078: Report of Ralph Dalton, vice-president of the Foundation Company, forwarded to Victor Schoepperle, vice-president of the National City Company.

better-known Peruvian writers of the period, other than some Leguía apologists such as Pedro Dávalos, Manuel A. Capuñay, and José E. Bonilla, were inclined to decry the subjugated condition of the sol (*enfeudado*, as Belaúnde put it) which the influx of dollars brought. In writing of Latin America's economic problems, Peruvian Luis Humberto Delgado said, "Laws are determined by the great companies which conceal the capitalists." [40] Privileged domestic groups joined with outside capital and divided the profits, he wrote. Delgado lamented that the major share of the benefits were drained off to the banks in New York in one way or another. Of course, Peruvians often invested or deposited their profits in the northern centers just as did foreigners. Delgado, although not seeking to shift responsibility to foreigners, believed that foreign financing would in the long run be debilitating unless it helped build real markets and, at the same time, halted the entrenchment of vested interests. *Apristas* such as Manuel Seoane, Haya de la Torre, and Luis Alberto Sánchez compared Peru to a colony or semi-colony in its economic and political relationship to the United States.[41] Alberto Ulloa aimed his argument at "United States imperialism" because it worked in opposition to Peru in international matters. So, although in a real sense United States investments helped Leguía just as Leguía helped them, by the same token some critics of Leguía may have been inclined to oppose such investments simply because the dictator and the dollar were associated. There were other reasons why the dollar might have been viewed with cynicism, but when it was affiliated with tyranny it was almost inevitable that it would be unwelcome.

Foreign capital contributed financial backing for Leguía and made it possible for him to pay his army promptly and to spend lavishly on public works. The loans floated by New York banking houses provided the Peruvian president with the funds he needed to maintain his hold on the presidency.[42] Although H. E. Henneman, vice-

---

[40] Luis Humberto Delgado, *Nuevo Peru?* (Lima, 1945), p. 89. This is a compilation of earlier writings which includes the essay, "La Tierra," first published in Berlin in 1933.

[41] See Luis Alberto Sánchez, *Haya de la Torre o el político* (Santiago, 1936); *Haya de la Torre y el Apra* (Santiago, 1954); Belaúnde, *La realidad nacional, op. cit.*; Manuel Seoane, *La garra yanqui* (Buenos Aires, 1930); Alberto Ulloa, *Posición internacional del Peru* (Lima, 1941); and *Revisita Peruana de Derecho Internacional*, V (1945), pp. 292-293.

[42] *Sale of Foreign Bonds or Securities: Senate Hearings*, Part III (1932), p. 1603.

president of the National City Company, was not convinced of this, he admitted that a number of prominent Peruvians thought that Leguía "did not dare reduce his public-works expenditures for fear of the effect upon his political fortunes and throwing any large number of men out of work."[43] Henneman believed that the Peruvian president's security rested more upon the loyal, well-paid army behind him.

In summary, it is fair to say that Leguía needed United States capital—at least foreign capital—and that United States capital found a friend in Leguía. J. H. Durrell opined that Peru's financial standing was affected by Leguía's poor health and the fact that he needed an operation. This officer of the National City Bank reported (July 1927) that many believed "a revolution or worse" would result if the dictator-president should die or retire.[44] Well-informed senators in Washington believed that loans had made it possible for Leguía to maintain himself in office.

When the inflow of capital stopped with the 1929 crash, Leguía's downfall was not long in coming. The suspension of incoming capital was probably a factor in bringing about his fall, although in an indirect way. Also important was the decrease in Peruvian export values as the 1920's came to a close. The incoming Sánchez Cerro regime was not as generous to foreign investors, although in the long run it was not as adverse to them as some had expected it would be. In October 1930, shortly after taking over, Sánchez Cerro canceled the contract between Peru and the Foundation Company and ordered liquidation of accounts.[45] Leguía had, of course, left many concessions in operation between Peru and United States interests. Senator Hiram W. Johnson of California, who conducted the Senate investigations of the sale of foreign bonds, discerned a relationship between the loans made to various countries that defaulted, such as Peru, and the granting of concessions to companies wishing to do business in the countries which received the loans.[46] Johnson believed that the

[43] Stock Exchange Practices: Senate Hearings (1933), p. 2113.

[44] Ibid., p. 2071.

[45] New York Times, October 21, 1930, p. 11.

[46] Sale of Foreign Bonds or Securities: Senate Hearings, Part IV (1932), p. 2106. A search of the following two Peruvian documentary sources revealed a most incomplete statement regarding the concessions granted to foreigners: El Peruano (1919-1931), which was the Peruvian governmental official record that corresponded to the United States Federal Register, carried part of the concessions and contracts concerning Yankee firms; and Memorias, Ministerio de Hacienda

loans aided the concessionaires in gaining favors, but he did not have concrete evidence at hand. R. P. Lamont, Secretary of Commerce, was of little help to Johnson when he reported that "the activities of the American companies you specified in many instances are entities not reported on. . . ." [47]

The influence of private business interests upon official policy of the United States was clearly demonstrated by events relating to Leguía's overthrow and imprisonment.[48] Washington declined to use the full weight of its good offices on Leguía's behalf when it appeared that such action would prove harmful to American interests operating in Peru. The American chargé d'affaires in Lima, Ferdinand L. Mayer, on August 25 asked Peru for special protection for the National City Bank. Mayer also contended that "immediate preparatory steps should be taken at Panama looking toward despatch of naval force here for protection of American lives and interests." [49] This was not necessary, and gradually the resentment came to an end. But before this happened other interesting developments took place.

After Leguía had fallen and Sánchez Cerro had taken over, the American chargé d'affaires indicated that he was taking Harold Kingsmill, manager of the Cerro de Pasco Corporation, with him on his first visit to the new chief executive.[50] Kingsmill also suggested to Mayer the advisability of having "war vessels" brought to Peru. Secretary of State Henry Stimson and Chargé Mayer both believed it desirable to exert "friendly good offices" on behalf of the ousted President Leguía whose life was endangered in late August 1930. Shortly after these opinions were exchanged as to what communication should be made to Sánchez Cerro's *junta*, Mayer wired Stimson this message: "Feeling throughout the country is so strongly con-

---

y *Comercio* (1919-1930), which were the annual reports of the minister of finance presented to the Peruvian Congress. These general reports contained very little specific information related to United States investments in Peru.

[47] *Sale of Foreign Bonds or Securities: Senate Hearings*, Part IV (1932), p. 2097.

[48] *US Foreign Relations*, 1930, III, pp. 732-737.

[49] *Ibid.*, p. 724. Admiral Pye of the United States Naval Mission was in agreement in this respect.

[50] *Ibid.*, p. 729. Mayer's telegram shows that his main reason for going to see Sánchez Cerro at that time was to introduce Kingsmill, who wanted to discuss the Cerro de Pasco difficulties.

demnatory of the Leguía regime and all its works (please see my 170, August 29, 10 P.M.) that, to be effective and at the same time not to result unfortunately for our interests here, any efforts on our part respecting the President's personal safety must be couched in terms immediately responsive to the present psychology." So, in respect for the "Yankee dollar," the communication to Sánchez Cerro made no specific mention of the United States hope that Leguía and his family would be saved from bloodshed.

The ousting of Leguía encompassed a real threat to American investments, although it was only temporary. Sánchez Cerro had built up popular favor in various ways, one of which was the intimation that he would check American economic exploitation in Peru. Before it was all over, he adopted an approach not very different from Leguía's. Sánchez Cerro did create a tribunal to bring charges of improper use of funds against Leguía, while at the same time the Leguía relations to various American firms were called into question.[51] A wave of anti-foreignism, as well as anti-Americanism, caused the State Department and American business interests considerable anxiety during August and September 1930. Several thousand port workers from Callao called upon Sánchez Cerro on the evening of August 29, and the following speech was attributed to one of them: "Free us, sir, from Yankee imperialism. Peruvians do not hate foreigners who came to work with us and to help us, but we do hate those who come to exploit us."[52] At least four United States citizens were imprisoned during the confusion in Peru at that time.

The American business suffering the greatest amount of property damage was the Cerro de Pasco Corporation.[53] The United States Embassy sought the protection of the Peruvian government for this business. The company's manager reported to Ambassador Fred Morris Dearing that the laborers were "rioting, pillaging houses and

[51] Henry Grattan Doyle, "Charges Against Ex-President Leguía," Current History, XXXIII (November 1930), p. 281.

[52] New York Times, August 30, 1930, p. 2. The criticism of Víctor Andrés Belaúnde and Pedro Ugarteche, although phrased in terms of "Yankee imperialism," is not made on a narrow economic (short-range) basis. Rather they protested that Leguía lacked confidence in Peruvians and that he turned the management of his government over to foreigners, even when there was no reason to do so. See Belaúnde, La realidad nacional, p. 253; and Ugarteche, La política internacional peruana durante la dictadura de Leguía, pp. 22, 39-42.

[53] New York Times, September 10, 1930, p. 5.

dynamiting." [54] One foreigner had been injured and the rest fled the mining region, but not before two United States citizens lost their lives.

During the time when the problem of recognizing or not recognizing the Sánchez Cerro government was being studied, as well as during the period of the 1930 revolt, it was evident that United States policy was determined to a significant extent by the views of American businessmen operating in Peru.[55] Six of the most influential companies and the Naval Mission to Peru were canvassed on the matter of recognition. As their responses were favorable, the provisional government of Sánchez Cerro was recognized by Washington on September 18, 1930.

The 1920's, then, were years when the dollar assumed a commanding position in Peru. At the same time, known or unknown, "Uncle Sam's" responsibilities there had increased rapidly. It is manifest that loans made by private United States concerns were important in the flow of both portfolio and direct investments.[56] Because of this, and because of the default and discontent with the loans, it is necessary that we examine the details of these financial operations.

[54] *Ibid.* As late as 1942 the foreign residents' homes near the mines were still under the "protection" of an armed Peruvian soldier who stood guard at the entrance to the area.

[55] *US Foreign Relations,* 1930, III, pp. 752-753.

[56] Some Peruvians jokingly compared Leguía's procedure of borrowing and spending to the cablegram from Monte Carlo: "System working fine; send more money."

5: LOANS IN THE 1920's

Between 1890 and 1919 Peru had ordinarily operated within its national budget (in many years there were minor deficits), but after Leguía attained power the government depended on deficit financing with foreign investors supplying the capital. Most of the loans were floated by New York bankers as Peru altered its entire fiscal system. The lending bankers derived the necessary capital for the loans from the sale of bonds to private American investors. In most cases these foreign securities were listed on the New York Stock Exchange in glorified and misleading terms.

Within Peru, publicity concerning foreign financing was subdued. As a result, it is not likely that the man in the street understood public policies. Official Peru, newspapers (such as *Tiempo*) under the influence of the government, and captive presses had little to say about the loans, and what they did print was guardedly favorable. Most of the opposition was forced underground or pushed outside the nation. The non-*Aprista* critics of Leguía writing in exile were more critical of the dictator's New York financing than were the *Aprista* writers. The former group identified Peru's economic subjugation with loss of national sovereignty. The loans were bitter medicine, in their view, because they helped Leguía stay in power while at the same time they inflicted damage to the national pride. Haya de la Torre held that *Apra* was not opposed to bringing in foreign capital unless that capital was predatory with respect to raw materials or engaged in excessive exploitation of cheap labor.[1] Haya

[1] F. Cossío del Pomar, *Haya de la Torre el indoamericano* (Mexico, D.F., 1939), pp. 225-226; and Haya de la Torre, *Construyendo el Aprismo* (Buenos Aires, 1933), pp. 123-124. From the first mentioned, under "Sobre El Capital Extranjero," we read: "El capital extranjero es necesario al Peru, mientras exista el capitalismo como sistema económico imperante y mientras nuestro país se halle en las condiciones elementales de desarrollo en que se encuentra. Lo que el Aprismo considera ruinoso para el Peru es que en nombre de nuestra sociedad de capitales extranjeros, el pais se convierta en un esclavo de ellos, y en vez de servirse del capital extranjero para su progreso, no sea sino su servidor. . . . Condicionar, limitar, sistematizar el ingreso de capitales extranjeros a nuestros países no es ahuyentarlos, como algunos creen ingenuamente" (pp. 225-226).

de la Torre, Seoane, Luis E. Heysen, and others feared that United
States capital under Leguía was supporting the feudal minority which
already dominated Peru. Within the Peruvian records there is little
accurate information available which deals with finances under
Leguía; however, the sources in the United States are quite revealing.

During this period five generalizations apply to South American
loans on the whole and to the Peruvian loans in particular: (1)
officials of the United States Departments of State and Commerce
encouraged lending, and the State Department (knowingly or un-
knowingly) helped the bankers build up unwarranted confidence
in South American securities; (2) investment bankers of New York
made a profit on unsound loans and were able to do this even while
the American investor suffered heavy losses; (3) the bankers with-
held a portion of the capital which they obtained by means of bond
flotations, and for this reason the borrowing nations did not receive
the full amount of credit which the loan contract specified as the
principal figure; (4) Wall Street bankers were guilty of unethical
practices in dealing in South American securities; (5) Peru's poor
debt record and general fiscal situation did not merit the heavy
credit which New York bankers extended it.

Officially, the United States encouraged loans because loans were
not only supposed to lead to the development of business but were
often directly equated with American foreign policy. Those who
voiced the government view included Grosvenor M. Jones, Chief of
the Finance and Investment Division of the Bureau of Foreign and
Domestic Commerce, and Oliver C. Townsend, commercial attaché
at Lima from December 1926 to December 1929. In the middle
1920's Jones stated: "Investment abroad is no longer quite the risky
thing it was a decade or so ago. . . . We are a long way from a
permanent foreign policy, but every hundred million dollars invested
by Americans in foreign securities brings us that much nearer to a
fixed attitude on foreign affairs." [2] Townsend testified that the
United States Department of Commerce had informed him that
"optimistic reports were what were needed." [3] In support of this
statement he produced a personal letter, written directly to him,

[2] "Foreign Conditions," *The Industrial Digest*, IV (December 1925), p. 65.

[3] *Sale of Foreign Bonds or Securities in the United States: Hearings before the
Committee on Finance, United States Senate*, 72nd Cong., 1st Sess., S. Res. 19,
Part III (Washington, 1932), pp. 1613-1614, hereafter cited as *Sale of Foreign
Bonds or Securities: Senate Hearings*.

from Thomas R. Taylor, Assistant Director of the Bureau of Foreign and Domestic Commerce, in which Taylor suggested that Townsend should make his own reports optimistic wherever possible.

United States government officials, however, had no authoritative check on investment banks offering the foreign securities for sale. The State Department "had no objection" to particular issues, according to Senate hearings on the sale of foreign bonds in 1932, and this attitude became a factor in inducing people to purchase bonds. Bond brokers regarded the State Department's lack of objection as an indication of its approval, although the Departments of State and Commerce were actually unaware of details of the bond loans. All of this led to unfortunate results for citizens of the northern republic, for within a few years bonds that had been sold to United States investors dropped to an average of less than 10 per cent of their par value.[4]

J. and W. Seligman and Company and the National City Company (affiliate of the National City Bank of New York) were the most active in placing loans. Even when the foreign securities, which they had sold, depreciated 80 per cent in value or proved to be nearly worthless, these investment houses netted a substantial profit by reselling most of the bonds before Peru defaulted.[5] The failure of the Peruvian government to maintain service payments became a serious matter to those American purchasers who were of limited financial means; small banks around the United States or small moderate investors carried most of the loss.

There were four principal reasons why the borrowing nation never received the full amount of credit stipulated in the loan contracts.[6] First, the loans to Peru were often sold to the United States investor at 91 or 92 per cent, par being 100. Second, the bankers computed the interest on the par value of the bonds and not on the selling price. Third, the investment bankers collected an initial commission for their services in the arrangements; the commissions must have been substantial since profits on loan transactions ran as high as 8 and 10 per cent. Fourth, the bonds often sold at a higher price than that originally agreed upon between the bankers and the borrowers.

[4] *Sale of Foreign Bonds or Securities: Senate Hearings*, Part II (1932), pp. 323-327.

[5] *Sale of Foreign Bonds or Securities: Senate Hearings*, Part III (1932), p. 1718.

[6] *Ibid.*, p. 1373.

Then, if there was no definite price specification in the contract, the marginal difference was retained by the Wall Street firms. Deductions were also made for cables, printing, stock exchange listings, legal counsel, Peruvian legal stamps, engraving expenses, compensation of the trustee, and collection agency fees.

Other stipulations guarded the banker's interests even further. For instance, in the loan contract for the $15,000,000 issue of 1927 arranged by J. and W. Seligman and the National City Company these points were included: the bonds were to draw 7 per cent interest annually, payable semi-annually; the J. and W. Seligman and Company, as fiscal agent, was to receive from the Republic one-fourth of 1 per cent of all amounts paid to the fiscal agents for the sinking fund "or for the payment of the principal and premium of the bonds at maturity"; and the Republic was also to reimburse the fiscal agents for all expenses "incurred in connection with the service of the bonds." [7] In addition, Peru was to bear all expenses connected with the administration of the sinking fund.[8] It is apparent that Peru received considerably less than $15,000,000 of this 1927 flotation, although bonds totaling $15,000,000 were marketed in the United States.

The New York bankers may have been well protected, but the same cannot be said for the American citizens who purchased the bonds. Whatever the cause, the Peruvian loans were characterized by a general atmosphere of poor, and at times unethical, financing. In the case of certain early loans to Leguía there was some competition among the various investment firms attempting to secure the business. However, during the 1920's a tendency toward monopoly in the marketing of these securities developed. At one time Leguía protested because he felt that there was no actual competition for the Peruvian loans and because he was unhappy with the bankers' activities.[9] Another problem arose because the banking houses failed to ascertain whether or not the proceeds of the loans were applied "toward the purposes specified in the loan contracts . . . whether revenues pledged for the service of loans were collected. . . ." [10] In fairness to the bankers it should be noted that the

[7] Ibid., p. 1369. The provisions listed here were taken almost verbatim from a copy of the contract.

[8] Ibid., p. 1385.

[9] New York Times, February 16, 1924, p. 22.

[10] Stock Exchange Practices: Hearings before a Subcommittee of the Committee on Banking and Currency, United States Senate, 72nd Cong., 2nd Sess., S. Res.

process of supervising the expenditures of foreign loans was a difficult matter, probably more complex than they had anticipated.

The sponsors of the foreign loans were guilty of numerous abuses, which in Peru's case included payments of bribes, a disregard of Peru's poor credit history, the extension of loans beyond Peru's ability to pay, misrepresentations to the American public in the published material, and a general negligence in investing funds obtained from private investors. Townsend, the commercial attaché in Lima from 1926 to 1929, pointed out that graft was customarily used by the banking promoters in the "undignified scramble" to obtain the loan business.[11] Indeed, the Peruvian issues of 1927 and 1928 (see page 74) constitute one of the seamy chapters in the history of American investment banking. Such activity prompted a committee on banking and currency of the United States Senate, investigating stock-exchange practices, to launch a scathing attack on the methods employed in the flotation of foreign loans in general.

One of the most serious mistakes made by the sponsors of Peruvian bonds was that large loans were extended in spite of the fact that Peru's credit rating and debt record did not warrant even moderate borrowing. The Senate committee concluded that the financiers had disregarded all business precedents and all warnings. "The financial history of the Republic of Peru," the committee reported, "which had been under examination by the bankers for years prior to the offering (1927-1928 issues), was of such a nature that even a casual regard for the interests of the American investor would have led the bankers to shun this financing." [12] Various exiled Peruvians (as in *Current History*, April-September 1923) tried to warn investors of the fact that Leguía's negotiations did not have the support of the people. Correspondence in the files of the National City Company also disclosed numerous warnings advising against the extension of further loans to Peru, and yet that company joined with J. and W. Seligman to take the lead in the sale of Peruvian bonds.[13] Between 1925 and 1927 the National City Company received several encouraging reports from its agents in Peru; but in general the regu-

---

84 and S. Res. 239, Part VI (Washington, 1933), p. 126; hereafter cited as *Stock Exchange Practices: Senate Hearings*.

[11] *Sale of Foreign Bonds or Securities: Senate Hearings*, Part III (1932), p. 1612.

[12] *Stock Exchange Practices: Senate Hearings* (1933), p. 126.

[13] *Ibid.*, pp. 130-131.

lar statements in 1927 (prior to the large bond issues) maintained that little improvement in Peru's economic condition could be expected in the near future. Of course, a security-buying craze had hit the United States and warning signs were everywhere being disregarded. A general trade depression prevailed in Peru throughout 1925 and 1926, while at the same time, Peru's sugar and cotton brought low prices. Victor Schoepperle, vice-president of the National City Company, admitted that he did not know of a country, for which his company had undertaken to sell bonds, with as bad a debt record as that of Peru.[14] On the next page is a resumé-outline of the loans made from United States private sources during the Leguía *oncenio*.

The Foundation Company and the Guaranty Trust Company of New York conducted joint negotiations with Peru in the early twenties. Three important results were: (1) a public works contract for the Foundation Company; (2) the first foreign loan of Leguía's second administration as arranged by the Guaranty Trust Company; and (3) the appointment of an American, William Wilson Cumberland, as administrator of Peruvian customs. Correspondence of the United States ambassador to Peru, William E. Gonzales, shows that Leguía believed he did not have the confidence of his people behind him in making this contract.[15] Gonzales informed Washington that Leguía wanted the administrator of customs to take over his duties before the loan was made, so that it would appear that the appointment of Cumberland and the loan were unrelated. "This will obviate wounding sensibilities of those who, whether for political reasons or otherwise, may be sensitive about sovereignty," declared the ambassador. Diplomatic correspondence demonstrates how the United States Department of State used its influence to help prepare the way for loans from the private banks of New York.

Cumberland's authority over Peruvian finances was extensive. He could revise the system of collecting customs or the rate of imports and exports duties. He was also to be consulted in advance of admin-

[14] *Stock Exchange Practices: Senate Hearings* (1933), p. 2103.

[15] *Papers Relating to the Foreign Relations of the United States*, 1921, II (Washington), p. 655. Gonzales sent this dispatch to Washington June 7, 1921. Pedro Ugarteche, *La política internacional peruana durante la dictadura de Leguía* (Lima, 1930), p. 40, protested that although a representative of the New York bankers controlled public finances of Peru, the finances were badly mismanaged; and that under the provisions of the Cumberland mission, both the customs collection and Peruvian finances were badly handled, pp. 40-41.

PRINCIPAL PERUVIAN LOANS FLOATED BY UNITED STATES BANKERS (1921-1928)

Usual Name Applied to Loan	Date of Loan Contract	Rate of Interest	Principal Banking Interests Affiliated with Loan	Amount
Loan confirming Cumberland's Contract	1921	*	Guaranty Trust Co. of New York	$200,000
Petroleum Loan of 1922	1922	8%	Guaranty Trust Co. of New York	$2,500,000
Sanitation Loan of 1924	1924	8%	Guaranty Trust Co. of New York and others	$7,000,000
Petroleum Loan of 1925	1925	7.5%	Guaranty Trust Co. of New York and others	$7,500,000
Sanitation Loan of 1926	1926	8%	Guaranty Trust Co. of New York and others	$2,000,000
Gold Bond Loan of 1926	1926	7.5%	Guaranty Trust Co. of New York and others	$16,000,000
Province of Callao	1927	7.5%	Alvin H. Frank & Co., J. & W. Seligman & Co., and others	$1,500,000
Tobacco Loan	1927	7%	J. & W. Seligman & Co., National City Co., and others	$15,000,000
Peruvian National Loan (First Series)	1927	6%	J. & W. Seligman & Co., National City Co., and others	$50,000,000
Peruvian National Loan (Second Series)	1928	6%	J. & W. Seligman & Co., National City Co., and others	$25,000,000—U. S. £2,000,000—Gr. Brit.
City of Lima	1928	6.5%	R. H. Rollins and Sons	$3,000,000

* Ernest Galarza reports this loan and cites the *Ministerio de Hacienda, Memoria, 1922*, pp. 6-9. Max Winkler and Edwin Walter Kemmerer do not mention this loan; Galarza failed to list the rate of interest charged by the Guaranty Trust Company of New York.

istrative action or recommendations in regard to all financial policies of the Republic of Peru, and he was to become a director of any government financial fiscal agency which the Republic might establish. The Peruvian government accepted the financial obligations for the operation of the position. Cumberland's salary, paid by Peru, was $16,000 a year plus all reasonable and necessary traveling expenses of Cumberland and his immediate family from Washington to Peru and return. The Guaranty Trust Company loan of 1921 confirmed Cumberland's appointment as chief of the customs service, and at the same time made his office the protector for the first loans. Later, there was trouble between the Peruvian government and the Guaranty Trust Company. The State Department answered Leguía's complaint by saying that the Guaranty Company had not been guilty of unusual or unfair practices, and since it was a private institution the United States government had "no control over its legitimate operations." [16] The Guaranty Trust Company floated six loans, its final one being the "Gold Bond Loan of 1926," which called for 7.5 per cent interest with various tax revenues pledged as security.

The Electric Boat Company had been one of the first United States concerns interested in a loan to Peru when, in 1920, it tried to sell four submarines to the Leguía government. Leguía's first plan to borrow $18,000,000 in New York for the launching of a naval expansion program was unsuccessful. When, in 1926, the company did sell its second pair of submarines to Peru, Becker and Company of Chicago purchased the notes and resold them throughout the United States.[17]

The largest and most controversial loans during Leguía's second administration came in 1927 and 1928, when J. and W. Seligman and Company and the National City Company issued securities totaling $100,000,000 ($90,000,000 in United States and $10,000,000 in Europe).[18] Bonds totaling $100,000,000 were sold under arrangement of three contracts, the third one being divided into two series:[19] on March 15, 1925, the $15,000,000 "Tobacco Loan" bonds were arranged to be sold to the American public; then on December 19, 1927, a $50,000,000 "Peruvian National" loan contract was signed; and on October 1, 1928, the New York bankers agreed to market $25,000,000 in the United States and $10,000,000 in Europe.[20]

The tobacco loan of March 1927 called for 7 per cent interest, and the bankers paid Peru 90 per cent of par for it. About one

[16] *New York Times*, April 16, 1924, p. 15; see also *Stock Exchange Practices: Senate Hearings* (1933), p. 2104.

[17] *Munitions Industry: Hearings before the Special Committee Investigating the Munitions Industry, United States Senate*, 73rd Cong., pursuant to S. Res. 206, Part I (Washington, 1934), p. 111.

[18] In 1927, J. and W. Seligman and Company was also associated with Alvin H. Frank & Co., and Hunter, Dulin, & Co., in a $1,500,000 loan to the Province of Callao. This $1,500,000 is not included in the $100,000,000 figure.

[19] See pages 74-76.

[20] *Sale of Foreign Bonds or Securities: Senate Hearings*, Part III (1932), pp. 1741-1744.

quarter of the proceeds of the loan was allocated to develop the tobacco industry (tobacco manufacturing plant, equipment for the plant, and service on the loan). The proceeds of the already existing tobacco tax were supposed to furnish security for the loan.[21]

The first issue, $50,000,000, of the Peruvian national loan, as well as the second of $35,000,000 ($25,000,000 in United States and $10,-000,000 in Europe), was made on the basis of 6 per cent interest. This in reality was not a cheaper rate, since the bankers paid Peru only 86 per cent of par for them and sold the bonds to the American public for 91.5.[22] According to the contract, the Peruvian government was to apply the proceeds of these loans to irrigation and sanitation projects, highway and railroad construction, and for the redemption of older bonds (the 1924 and 1926 issues).[23] The Senate's investigating committee in Washington charged the National City Company with omitting notice of Peru's unfavorable debt record in the prospectus published to accompany these bonds.[24] In 1933 Hugh B. Baker, president of the National City Company, admitted that the bond buyers would not have purchased the bonds at 91.5 per cent of par if they had been given a true picture of Peru's fiscal situation.[25]

Promoters and grafters collected at least $567,000 in commissions for their dealings in the flotation of the three 1927-1928 loans. Juan Leguía, the president's son, obtained $416,000 for helping the Wall Street firms get the loan contracts, in spite of the fact that all he seems to have done was to "permit" the loans to go through.[26] The president's son was known for "spoiling business" around Lima if he did not get a part of the profits.[27] Frederick J. Lisman, investment

[21] *Ibid.*, p. 1741.

[22] *Stock Exchange Practices: Senate Hearings* (1933), p. 128. Additional data are found in the *Annual Reports* of the Foreign Bondholders Protective Council, Inc. (see fn. 50, this chapter).

[23] *Sale of Foreign Bonds or Securities: Senate Hearings*, Part III (1932), pp. 1759, 1760. Lawrence Dennis testified that the 6 per cent bond flotation scheme was a "ruinous operation that needlessly increased the net debt about $10,000,-000," for 5 per cent and 5.5 per cent bonds were refunded with 6 per cent bonds.

[24] *Stock Exchange Practices: Senate Hearings* (1933), p. 129.

[25] *Ibid.*

[26] *Sale of Foreign Bonds or Securities: Senate Hearings*, Part III (1932), pp. 1288-1289. Ferdinand Pecora referred to the commission as, ". . . bribe, a gift, a gratuity, whatever it was.

[27] *Stock Exchange Practices: Senate Hearings* (1933), p. 220. In February 1927 Townsend wrote that Juan Leguía is "always willing to serve as blind tiger to

banker, believed that Juan Leguía "blackmailed us (the bankers) into paying him." Lisman thought that President Leguía did not receive any of the "commission money." [28] Henry C. Breck of J. and W. Seligman testified that his company had never paid so high a commission to promoters of foreign loans as it did in the case of these three Peruvian transactions.[29]

Samuel Abbot Maginnis, formerly the American minister to Bolivia, was one of the promoters involved in the $100,000,000 Peruvian transactions of 1927-1928. Maginnis, a representative of J. and W. Seligman and Company in 1927, went to Peru early in that year and negotiated the details of the so-called tobacco loan.[30] He received $40,000 for his efforts in securing the business for J. and W. Seligman and Company.[31] The company also paid other United States citizens commissions for bringing the 1927-1928 loan business to them, T. V. Salt receiving $10,000 and Harold Bolster collecting $67,373.[32]

Oliver C. Townsend described a banquet which Maginnis gave for fifty some guests at the Hotel Bolívar in Lima in February 1927 as being "entertainment by promoters seeking favors of one sort or another from the Government." [33] Among the group in attendance were American Ambassador to Peru Miles Poindexter, former Peruvian Ambassador to the United States Federico A. Pezet, and Juan Leguía. Maginnis persistently urged Pezet to welcome the Americans to Peru in the name of the Peruvian government, and finally Pezet reluctantly did so; but "the American Ambassador steadfastly declined to rise from his seat." [34]

Throughout the marketing of the 1927-1928 bonds, the bankers did not disclose the fact that the Peruvian president's son was receiv-

---

ambitious negotiators who know the ropes—and he's doing a good business these days." Oliver Townsend, U.S. commercial attaché in Lima from December 1926 to December 1929, quoted in the *Washington Star*, January 12, 1932.

[28] *Sale of Foreign Bonds or Securities: Senate Hearings*, Part III (1932), p. 1770.

[29] *Ibid.* Lawrence Dennis was also of the opinion that President Leguía did not receive any of the "commission money." Dennis, "What Overthrew Leguía," p. 118 (see fn. 1 of Chapter 3).

[30] *Sale of Foreign Bonds or Securities: Senate Hearings*, Part III (1932), p. 1297.

[31] *Ibid.*, p. 1288.

[32] *Ibid.*, pp. 1284, 1289.

[33] *Ibid.*, pp. 1611-1613.

[34] *Washington Star*, January 12, 1932.

ing almost a half-million dollars for merely agreeing not to interfere with the transaction. J. and W. Seligman and National City Company were aware of the arrangement to pay Juan Leguía one half of 1 per cent of the loan before the $50,000,000 issue was floated,[35] although Victor Schoepperle, vice-president of the latter, testified that he did not know of the proposed payment at the time the arrangements were made. At the Senate hearings, the bankers admitted that publication of the commission-bribe to Juan Leguía would not have added to the buyer's desire to purchase the bonds.[36] Peruvian Genaro Arbaiza, in an article appearing in *Current History* in 1938, graphically described Leguía's position when he wrote that "Leguía sat at the dollar feast table . . . enraptured by the golden saxophones of American financial jazz." These commissions were the basis for one point of the attack which Leguía's successor, Sánchez Cerro, and other Peruvians directed against the administration. In 1930, Sánchez Cerro established the Tribunal of National Accounting to weigh charges against Leguía and his son Juan, and the prosecution was so vigorous that the American diplomatic corps at one time feared for the lives of the two men. Juan fled the country and his father died in prison.

The Peruvian Congress sought to determine if Peruvians, other than Juan Leguía, had received money, and the government of Peru became keenly interested in the United States Senate hearings which looked into the background of the loans. In January 1932 the Peruvian Congress asked its government to request further investigations by the United States Senate as to which individuals had received commissions at the time the loans were made. The Peruvian ambassador in Washington requested that any investigation be as ". . . thorough as possible so that the responsibility of all those who participated in the said transactions affecting Peru's vital interests may be closely defined." [37] The ambassador also wished to have a copy of the evidence taken in the hearings.

Associated with the loans is the thorny question of what they meant in the way of aid to United States concerns. Did the Leguía loans result in new concessions, the extension of earlier agreements,

[35] *Stock Exchange Practices: Senate Hearings* (1933), pp. 220-221. See also *Sale of Foreign Bonds or Securities: Senate Hearings,* Part III (1932), p. 1295.

[36] *Stock Exchange Practices: Senate Hearings* (1933), p. 221.

[37] *Sale of Foreign Bonds or Securities: Senate Hearings,* Part IV (1932), pp. 1930-1931. A letter from Ambassador Manuel Freyre y Santander to Secretary of State Henry L. Stimson was brought to the attention of the committee.

or merely in giving one or both of these impressions? Senator Hiram Johnson, as noted in the preceding chapter, believed there was a connection between the loans and concessions, but he did not provide proof. Víctor Andrés Belaúnde, writing in 1931, accused Leguía of selling the nation's resources to the highest bidder in New York.[38] Luis Alberto Sánchez, Haya de la Torre, Pedro Ugarteche, Manuel Seoane, and Luis Humberto Delgado were a few Peruvians who supported Belaúnde's criticism. Here follows a statement (1933) of Delgado's which does not single out Peru but refers to Latin-American nations as such: "We must free the governments from the economic oppression which is imposed upon them by the foreign money lenders." He continued by alluding to voracious governments who used the methods of capitalists which could limit or destroy their markets. One would think "they have the joint objective" of "mutilating or pruning the plant which serves as the shelter of society." A miserly system is the result, he said, for they give to the people with one hand and take it away with the other. They collect more than they provide, and "they do it with deceit," Delgado opined.[39] Up until the present (1964) there is no indication that the loans-concessions enigma has been unraveled. In *La realidad nacional* (1931), Belaúnde protested the oil concession arrangements made by Leguía.[40] Some of these problems appear to be very much with us even after the passing of a full generation.

In looking back upon the "lending spree" of the 1920's one can document the opinion that investment bankers, as well as officials of the State Department, made some honest mistakes. These errors in judgment paralleled similar faults in financing which went on within the United States. It also appears that the Senate committee investigating the chief causes of default on the loans which began in 1931 made broad generalizations, some of which were not based on the results of objective study. It is clear, however, that many of the foreign loans went into default because the lending bankers had been guided by very narrow pecuniary considerations rather than by sound financial principles.[41]

[38] Víctor Andrés Belaúnde, *La realidad nacional* (Paris, 1931), p. 247.

[39] Luis Humberto Delgado, *Nuevo Perú?* (Lima, 1945), p. 100. Included in "El Equilibrio," first published in Berlin, 1933.

[40] Belaúnde, *La realidad nacional*, p. 247.

[41] John T. Madden, Marcus Nadler, and Harry C. Sauvain, *America's Experience As a Creditor Nation* (New York, Prentice-Hall, 1937), p. 231, show that the loans to Peru were not entirely set apart.

To anyone familiar with the Peruvian loans the default, discontent, and repayment problems which resulted should not have come as a surprise. Leguía was ousted in August 1930, and Peru began to default on its debt approximately six months later. Before the end of 1931, Peruvian bonds had dropped to an average of less than 10 per cent of their par value. Peru was the second South American nation—Bolivia, with a somewhat similar background, was the first—to default on bonds held by private American investors. The $50,-000,000 Peruvian national loan of 1927, originally sold at 91.5 per cent of par, was reported in November 1931 to be selling at 5.25 per cent. This was less than the figure originally set for interest alone.

Peru's announcement of March 1, 1931, that she could no longer keep up payments on her external debt was not a repudiation of those contractual obligations; it was an admission of inability to meet the payments. The Republic claimed that continued payment of the service on the loan would "jeopardize the economic life of the country." [42] On June 23, 1931, the Peruvian budget commission announced that a critical financial condition existed, and that revenues for the year were not expected to reach $32,000,000 (90,000,000 soles).[43] As of January 1932, it would have taken 34.3 per cent of the annual national revenue to maintain foreign debt services. Debt services came to $8,639,000, while the estimated national revenue was $25,200,000 for 1932.[44]

The causes of Peruvian default lie within a complex pattern of both national and international characteristics. Winkler and Maxwell listed the following reasons for general default on loans around the world: exorbitant or unjust terms, unwise investment, fall of commodity prices, maldistribution of gold, and tariffs or other restrictions.[45] The weaknesses of Peru's financial and commercial system made that nation susceptible to severe losses when the economy

[42] Max Winkler, *Foreign Bonds An Autopsy* (Philadelphia, Stevens and Brown, 1933), p. 258. Winkler's comprehensive study constitutes a fundamental background of information for this chapter.

[43] *New York Times*, June 24, 1931, 48. See Max Winkler and Stewart S. Maxwell, "Recent Defaults of Government Loans," *Foreign Policy Reports*, VII, No. 22 (January 6, 1932), pp. 402-423. On January 1, 1932, Peru was in arrears on interest payments to the amount of $3,955,525—so fast did the interest alone accrue.

[44] Winkler and Maxwell, "Recent Defaults of Government Loans," *ibid.*, p. 398.

[45] *Ibid.*, pp. 395, 408.

of the United States and the world at large collapsed after 1929. Peru's minister of finance in 1947, Luis Echecopar García, stated Peru defaulted on the loans because of: (1) their unpopularity; (2) the collapse in prices of Peruvian exports, produced, in part, by the loss of American market for certain commodities; (3) the general economic depression which followed; (4) the unsound way in which such loans were invested, since they did not produce incomes (in Peruvian or foreign currencies) to pay for their interest or amortization.[46]

According to Grosvenor M. Jones, "the default of Peru really was a sequel to the overthrow of the government of Leguía, and of the political disorder that followed thereon, as well as of the collapse in the prices of the principal commodities which Peru exports." [47] Added to this list is the opinion of Senator Johnson of the investigating committee that the "hush payment" of $416,000 to Juan Leguía had been one of the reasons for default. Carter Glass, who had three years previously cautioned policy makers, denounced the State Department for having a ". . . clerk passing on the loans who didn't know any more about them than my cat." [48] Involved in the entire matter was a problem seldom mentioned, at least not in Washington circles during the twenties. Did the United States government have any direct responsibility for loans to Peru? If so—what responsibility? What was private interest and what was public interest?

In many respects the beginning of default marked the end of an era in Peru as well as in the United States, but the problems, created earlier, were to linger on. In 1933, National City Bank and J. and W. Seligman and Company settled out of court on three lawsuits involving Peruvian bonds. In Peru, foreign exchange matters created pressing fiscal problems which were complicated by the fact that that nation did not maintain the service on the foreign debt. The Foreign Bondholders Protective Council [49] tried from 1934 to 1948 to induce the Peruvian government to embark upon an active program of servicing the dollar bond debt of Peru. For over twenty

[46] Personal letter (dated March 12, 1948 at Lima): Luis Echecopar García to James C. Carey.

[47] *Sale of Foreign Bonds or Securities: Senate Hearings*, Part II (1932), p. 726.

[48] *New York Times*, January 7, 1932, p. 1.

[49] The Corporation of Foreign Bondholders Act, approved by President Franklin D. Roosevelt on May 27, 1933, as a part of the Securities Act of 1933, was enacted in order to protect the interests of the holders of foreign securities in default.

years, Peru was reluctant to restore the service on the debt. In 1934 the Council cabled the Peruvian minister of finance the following message: "The feeling is growing among the American holders of Peruvian dollar bonds that now the difficulties between Peru and Colombia have been adjusted, the Government of Peru should consider the early renewal of service upon the Peruvian bonds." [50] But as late as the beginning of 1946 Peru was still in total default.

Unfortunately, for both the government of Peru and the American bondholders, the dollar bond loans did not engender good feeling, and out of them came some ill will which lingered on for thirty years. Early in 1946, *Aprista* newspapers mentioned the fact that a former under-secretary of state had visited Peru as a representative of the bondholders.[51] If Washington could not decide just what was official or unofficial in this international financing, Lima could hardly be expected to untangle the problem. Bondholders in the United States continued until 1952 to press for some sort of a mutually satisfactory settlement. (For further information see Chapter 7 on the Second World War.) In 1953 repayment on a very limited scale was started, financed to some extent out of aid funds coming south from Washington. The music had stopped about 1928, but the dance had gone on grotesquely for another twenty-five years or more.

[50] *Annual Report, Foreign Bondholders Protective Council* (Washington, 1934), p. 98. For further difficulties caused by the bonds, see prior to page 98.

[51] *La Tribuna*, Lima, January 4, 1946, p. 5. *Aprista* leaders, Haya de la Torre and Manuel Seoane, had long advocated paying off the foreign debt if a suitable settlement could be reached.

6: "YANKEE" ASSISTANCE AND INTERCESSION: MISSIONS, BOUNDARIES, AND CLAIMS

The years between the two world wars mark a kind of "middle period" in United States-Peruvian relations. This was a time when the "Yankee" power from the north was being heavily relied upon to assist in matters of both internal and international importance, not always with fully satisfactory results as far as Peru herself was concerned. Of greatest significance to Peruvian national dignity were the boundary disputes with neighboring Chile, Colombia and Ecuador. Years of wrangling and complex negotiations among the four nations had arrived nowhere. The Lima foreign office continued to look toward Washington for support in these controversies, mainly on the basis of a real hope that Peruvian diplomats held, both before and after the First World War, that the United States would assist their nation in various international matters. With this hope, Peru withdrew from the League of Nations—according to Pedro Ugarteche, in order to serve the interests of the United States.[1] This explanation is an oversimplified one. However, there seems little doubt but that Leguía's acceptance of United States action in international affairs offended the national pride of many Peruvians. The settlement agreements eventually reached with Washington's help in regard to Colombia and Chile were disappointing to Peru, but results seemed better in the later controversy with Ecuador.

Before discussing the boundary disputes in more detail, it should be pointed out, however, that in affairs of lesser import, such as

[1] Alberto Ulloa, *Posición internacional del Perú* (Lima, 1941), pp. 378-379; and Pedro Ugarteche, *La política internacional peruana durante la dictadura de Leguía* (Lima, 1930), pp. 15-21. Ugarteche bitterly criticized Leguía for his servile attitude toward Washington in the boundary questions as well as in economic matters. See also Víctor Andrés Belaúnde, *La realidad nacional* (Paris, 1931), p. 253. Arturo García Salazar, *Historia diplomática del Perú*, Vol. I (Lima, 1930), is more kindly in his treatment of Leguía's negotiations over the Chilean boundary questions (pp. 293-296, for example).

educational and naval missions, or certain financial claims, the northern nation was more co-operative.

THE EDUCATION MISSION

President Leguía was particularly active in his attempt to place important educational offices in the hands of North Americans. In 1920 Harry Erwin Bard, who had headed Leguía's 1909 commission (see Chapter 2), was requested to secure thirty United States educators for "positions of responsibility and of unusual opportunity for creative service." This 1920 scheme took up where the 1909 program had left off, and part of its aim was to introduce vocational studies into the secondary schools and institutions of higher education. Bard, who became the Director General of Instruction, while retaining the post of adviser to the Ministry of Education, informed applicants for this program that it was not necessary to know how to speak or write Spanish so long as their academic training involved "a sufficient grounding in other Latin languages. . . ." [2] Twenty-four American educators were engaged. Some of the recruits were appointed to national posts, described as being similar in importance to college deans, while three others were given regional positions comparable to those held by commissioners of education or superintendents of public instruction within the United States.[3] One member of this educational mission, much impressed by his belief that Peru had become the first Latin-American nation to turn over "its entire system of public education to an American mission on the ground," [4] held that the project was a "third great experiment in modern education."

But not everything proceeded as well as these optimistic comments would indicate. As might have been expected, conservative Peruvians and venerable old San Marcos University supporters raised objections to the "Yankee-directed" educational reforms. The spirit of nationalism would naturally impel Peruvians to resent the influx of American educators into important positions, but the United

[2] "Notes," *The Hispanic American Historical Review*. Under news items entitled "Notes" is this article which quotes Bard, III (1920), p. 593.

[3] *Ibid.*

[4] William E. Dunn, "Peru's Progressive Educational Program," *The Hispanic American Historical Review*, IV (1921), p. 511.

States citizens working in Peru did not seem sufficiently conscious of this important obstacle to their mission's success. As a result, several of the proposals for secondary and university programs never got beyond the paper-planning stage. Moreover, at least three members of the mission soon resigned and returned to the United States, making it clear that there was friction within the mission itself as well.

Various petty matters constantly interfered with the hoped-for progress. Some ill will developed over the fact that Peru paid for an order for desks, but never received them.[5] The educators charged that the Peruvian government did not fully comply with various points of the initial agreement. The general deterioration of the situation was reflected in an anonymous article by a member of the mission that appeared in February 1923. Although ostensibly not written in the "spirit of complaint or criticism," it did reflect the pessimism of a discouraged and disillusioned individual. The author of this bitter article concluded that it was not advisable to send a group of American educators to Peru or any other Latin-American country without the "direct intervention of our own government." [6]

The concrete achievements of the American educational mission, as a body of educators, were not significant. The lack of accomplishment is especially underlined when compared with the criticism engendered. The constructive work of one member of the mission who stayed on in Peru, Albert Geisecke, has been mentioned in Chapter 2.

THE NAVAL MISSION

The Naval Mission sent to Peru in 1920 became the first of its kind to be authorized by the United States under the act of June 5 of that year. In October 1919, during the civil disorder of the early years of the oncenio, Leguía expressed hope that the United States would send a naval mission "as soon as possible," and that one high naval officer would be provided for reorganization of the Peruvian Navy. Peru needed power to offset the growing Chilean Navy because the Tacna-Arica boundary problem was as yet un-

[5] "Reorganizing Peru's Schools," an anonymous article, School and Society, XVII (January-June 1923), pp. 117-118.
[6] Ibid., p. 115.

settled. At the same time, American Marine police were sought for the purpose of maintaining order in Callao.[7] The request for a naval commission received prompt action in Washington, but the matter of police for Callao is not clear, because that request was not openly treated in the *Foreign Relations* publications of the Department of State.

While Washington diplomats and naval officers worked out details of the arrangement, there were various other forces at work on its behalf. For instance, Stephen G. Porter of the House Committee on Foreign Affairs favored it and referred to it as "a measure that the State Department is very much in favor of for reasons I would not care to state."[8] The Navy considered the move to be one which would increase the "efficiency of the naval strength of the countries of the Western Hemisphere," and which should also promote friendly feelings between the United States and other American republics. Senator James Beauchamp Clark, citing the Secretary of the Navy, stated that one purpose of the Mission was to sell armaments and induce South Americans to install United States equipment.[9]

An American firm, the Electric Boat Company, was also eager to see the Naval Mission established. The company's interest in the sale of armaments to Peru dated back to before the First World War, to Leguía's first administration. Luis Aubry, the Electric Boat Company's representative in Peru in 1923, was Peru's naval attaché to Washington in 1920, and had been credited with being "intimately connected with the restoration of President Leguía to power" in 1919.[10] In 1920 and 1923, while still in the employ of the Peruvian government, Aubry had received $4,170 from the company for "certain services." The record makes it clear that the Naval Mission was a great asset to the Electric Boat Company in its Lima sales, al-

[7] *Papers Relating to the Foreign Relations of the United States, 1920*, III (Washington), p. 367, hereafter cited as *US Foreign Relations*.

[8] *Congressional Record*, 66th Cong., 2nd Sess., May 25 to June 5, 1920, LIX, Part 8 (Washington), p. 8580. For official Peruvian statements concerning the establishment of the Mission see: *Memoria que el Ministro de Marina y Aviacion Contralmirante don Augusto Loayza presenta al Congreso Nacional· 1928-1929* (Lima, 1929).

[9] *Munitions Industry: Hearings before the Special Committee Investigating the Munitions Industry, United States Senate*, 73rd Cong., pursuant to S. Res. 206, Part I (Washington, 1934), p. 109.

[10] *Ibid.*, p. 377.

though this is not to say that the Mission had aid to the company as one of its objectives. On at least one occasion, when the Mission recommended destroyers rather than submarines, Electric Boat was unhappy since it made only the underwater craft.

Any consideration of the significance of the Naval Mission should pay heed to the boundary dispute question. In 1928, when the United States Department of State was attempting to settle the Tacna-Arica problem, the Electric Boat Company looked unfavorably upon the restoration of friendly relations between Peru and Chile since peace would lessen the chances of company sales.[11] Most Peruvians probably distrusted or envied Chile's naval strength and, therefore, looked with favor upon any support from Washington in strengthening its own force. On the other hand, there were some who opposed the whole plan of naval armaments. Dora Mayer de Zulen, a Peruvian writer living in Callao, was one who protested because she believed that the Mission was not acting in the interests of Peruvian peace. Her views were printed in *The Nation* in January 1924.[12] The editor of *The Nation* also criticized the Naval Mission on the basis of an article in a Lima newspaper. The heart of these objections seems to have been the fact that the head of the Mission had issued some "war-breeding" statements which were not conducive to a peaceful Tacna-Arica settlement.

Annual reports of the *Ministro de Marina* (later *Ministro de Marina y Aviación*) lack significant details regarding the activities of the Mission. In addition to assisting in the purchase of equipment and the supervision of construction work, the American Naval Mission aided in the administration of cadet-training at the national Naval School in La Punta near Callao. By 1930, the Peruvian Navy consisted of two cruisers, four submarines, an auxiliary cruiser transformed into a submarine tender, one destroyer, a sailing ship, and three gun boats on the Amazon River. Adequate information is not available for definite statements, but in the main it appears that the

---

[11] *Ibid.*, p. 340.

[12] "War Mongers," *The Nation*, CXVIII (January 23, 1924), p. 79. The editor of *The Nation* stated that his source of information was an article in *El Comercio*. Even allowing for an overemphasis and reaction of one political party to another as in the *Senate Hearings* regarding munitions' sales, these sources are of considerable value in throwing light on the complexities of the Mission. Of course, such material should be treated with care in order that the high feeling of a particular era does not clutter or befuddle the record for the future.

Mission was well received in Peru up until the time that Leguía fell from power. As the dictator was being ousted, the Mission faced a predicament.

Many of the high-ranking officers of the Peruvian Navy were pro-Leguía, but this loyalty did not prevent them from obeying the order of Sánchez Cerro and the *junta* when they were ordered to bring Leguía back to Callao as a prisoner of the new government. By returning to Callao, the officers of the Cruiser *Grau*, to which Leguía had fled, forfeited all chance of aiding Leguía in his attempt to escape from Peru. Also the Naval School cadets joined the 1930 revolt and fought with other rebellious students against the small segment of troops which continued to support the dictator. The American Naval Mission was implicated to some degree, since Captain William O. Spears, the American naval officer in command of the Mission, was aboard the *Grau* from time to time during the revolt. The United States diplomatic and naval officers in Lima, during Sánchez Cerro's revolt, misjudged the attitude of the Peruvian Navy and the cadets of the Naval School when they opined that Peruvian sailors would stand behind Leguía.[13] Chargé Ferdinand L. Mayer had asked Washington for advice as to what part the Naval Mission and its American officers should play in case the revolt matured. Nothing in the published *Papers Relating to the Foreign Relations of the United States* reported the answer to Mayer's question. This information has remained confidential.[14]

As a result of Sánchez Cerro's successful revolt, Harold B. Grow, a reserve officer of the United States Navy who had served under Leguía as chief of the air forces, was imprisoned at Arequipa.[15] He faced severe punishment and a Peruvian court-martial. At Leguía's order and against the orders of the head of the Mission, Grow had flown to Arequipa in an armed bombing plane intending to distribute propaganda to demoralize the rebellious Sánchez Cerro faction. After being captured, Grow admitted carrying one twenty-five-pound bomb, but denied any intention to use it other than to attract attention of the rebels. Chargé Mayer was informed by a re-

[13] *US Foreign Relations, 1930*, III, p. 720.

[14] Leguía and his son, Juan, were arrested and placed in Peru's bastille for political prisoners, the island fortress of San Lorenzo. The elder Leguía was later placed in the Naval Hospital in Bellavista where he died on February 6, 1932. For a softening of attitude of the *Apristas* toward Leguía, see *La Tribuna*, Lima, December 18, 1945, p. 4.

[15] Grow had gone to Peru as a member of the Naval Mission.

liable source that Grow's plane had been equipped with machine guns and bombs for the trip. *Time* magazine suggested that there was always a strong argument, in reserve, to be used in Grow's defense—Sánchez Cerro would need the official recognition of the United States.[16] A special Peruvian court tried Grow and, after intercession on the part of the United States embassy, found him not guilty of taking sides in the civil conflict.

On August 27, Mayer reported that he had conferred with British and Chilean colleagues on the possibility of having British, United States, and Chilean warships come to Callao. "The concurrence of Chile in any such action would also make for Pan-American unity," he explained.[17] Mayer did not seem to realize that the approach of a Chilean warship could have set Peru and Chile at odds and stirred the Peruvians to fierce national hatred of both Chile and the United States. Even the conservative newspaper, *El Comercio* (November 16, 1930), protested against any suggestion that Washington might send a warship to Peruvian waters at that time. A cursory reading of contemporary history (the Tacna-Arica problem had been settled only the preceding year) would have pointed out the foolishness of Mayer's notion. Sometime prior to August 27, both the Chilean and American embassies had been placed under the guard of large cavalry patrols. All in all, the Naval Mission, which functioned from September 1920 to March 1933, came out of the revolt and the ousting of Leguía better than would have been the case if the ideas of Chargé Mayer had been fully implemented.

Under Sánchez Cerro the three Mission members remaining in Peru were "relieved of all administrative duties" and relegated to a position where they could carry out "strictly educational efforts." In March 1933 it was reported that the Mission had terminated because of "financial and international reasons." [18]

If one can judge from the scanty information published, it seems that two threats, one to Continental security and the other to the market advantages of United States goods, were the principal factors

[16] *Time*, XVI (September 8, 1930), p. 23.

[17] *US Foreign Relations, 1930*, III, pp. 724-728.

[18] *New York Times*, March 24, 1933, p. 7. The mission agreement, however, was soon renewed. On July 31, 1940, an agreement was made with Peru which provided for the addition of a Naval Aviation Mission: see *US Foreign Relations, 1940*, V, p. 1146. See also *Revista Peruana de Derecho Internacional*, VII (Lima, 1947), p. 123, for confirmation of a 1946 agreement establishing the United States Air Mission to Peru.

influencing the actions of the United States Naval Mission to Peru. Maintenance of hemispheric defenses and protection of United States economic enterprise were motives behind the United States appointment of the Mission in 1920 and the operation of the Mission after it was in the field. But the long-range results and ramifications cannot be seen in clear perspective. Chile, Ecuador, and probably other neighboring nations were not pleased with the United States for supplying part of the wherewithal for Peru to strengthen her navy. In the years that followed, Washington made additional military agreements with Peru as part of an over-all Latin-American pattern. United States aviation and army missions were established in Lima prior to Western Hemisphere participation in the Second World War.

BOUNDARIES

The United States devoted considerable effort to effecting peaceful settlements of the Peruvian boundary disputes with Chile, Colombia, and Ecuador. United States involvement deserves more attention than space allows here, two reasons precluding further development at this time. Although the Tacna-Arica dispute with Chile was an important factor in Peruvian-United States relations, it has already been so carefully investigated by others that only a brief summary is included. The second reason for limited treatment is the fact that the problem runs back into the nineteenth century, which is not under consideration in this study.

The Tacna-Arica question occupied more space in the *Papers Relating to the Foreign Relations of the United States* than did any one specific topic concerning Peru from 1908 to 1940. This thorny problem centered around 9,250 square miles of land which was disputed by Chile and Peru. Peru's interest in the fate of the region was based largely on sentimentality,[19] although a minor economic matter was also at stake. The complications which attached themselves to the main question of what to do with the territory kept the

[19] Graham H. Stuart, *The Tacna-Arica Dispute* (Boston, World Peace Foundation Pamphlets, 1927), p. 8. William Jefferson Dennis, Iowa City, and Edwin M. Borchard, Washington, D.C., also from north of the border, studied this problem. Víctor Andrés Belaúnde, Víctor Manuel Maurtua, Arturo G. Salazar, Carlos A. Tellez, and Pedro Ugarteche are only a few of the Peruvians who have studied and written on the Tacna-Arica dispute. Documents alone would constitute a voluminous collection at Lima, Santiago, or Washington.

issue alive from 1883 to 1929. Here we will discuss only the developments which had a direct bearing upon United States policy in Peru.

At the close of the War of the Pacific in which Chile defeated her two neighbors, Chile took possession of Bolivian Atacama and the Peruvian province of Tarapaca. By the Treaty of Ancón, drawn up in 1883 and ratified in 1884, Chile would be allowed to occupy Tacna and Arica for a ten-year period, after which a plebiscite was to be held. Internal political conditions in Peru and Chile, national pride, hatred engendered by war, purchases of armaments from the United States and England, and numerous other factors contributed to the complicated situation which prevented a settlement until 1929.[20] In this interim, the two nations could not agree on the conditions of the plebiscite and the administration of the area. A process of Chileanization took place before any plan was adopted, and 1894 passed with no progress made toward a settlement. In 1898 it appeared that the Queen of Spain would be allowed to submit plans for a plebiscite. This attempt at settlement, the Billinghurst-Latorre protocol, was not approved by the Chilean government and consequently resulted in failure and a continued stalemate. Leguía's message to Congress in 1909 stated that Chile had "disregarded" the treaty of Ancón since 1894 while Peru had tried to "carry it out." This provoked a refutation from Agustín Edwards, Chilean minister of foreign affairs. In 1909-1910 another attempt to reach accord over details of the plebiscite failed. On March 21, 1910, Peru broke off diplomatic relations when its southern neighbor adopted an uncompromising attitude.[21] When Peru withdrew its diplomatic representa-

---

[20] The Electric Boat Company of New York and Groton, Connecticut, helped Chile arm and then induced Peru to order two submarines in 1924 and two more in 1926. When Chile requested two submarines in 1927, the Electric Boat Company agreed to turn the business over to Vickers in England provided the American concern collected its 5 per cent royalty. William T. Stone, *The Munitions Industry—Analysis of United States Senate Investigation*, Geneva Special Studies (New York, published by arrangement with the Foreign Policy Association, 1934), pp. 5, 10.

During the War of the Pacific, American diplomacy engendered a "feeling of antagonism against the United States in both Chile and Peru." Blaine "had blunderingly tried to befriend" Peru, and he failed with that nation as well as with Chile for his policy was "inconsistent and changeable." Herbert Millington, *American Diplomacy and the War of the Pacific* (New York, Columbia University Press, 1948), p. 142. With that as a background, Tacna-Arica was necessarily difficult.

[21] US Foreign Relations, 1910, p. 196.

tives from Santiago, it requested the United States government to protect the Peruvian citizens living in Chile.[22] The entire question remained deadlocked, and little effort was made to settle it until after the First World War. In the meantime, Chile continued the Chileanization process in the disputed area.

After 1919 the United States took a more active part in the negotiations relating to the problem. In 1922 Chile and Peru accepted President Harding's offer of mediation, and a conference at Washington resulted in the signing of a protocol of arbitration on July 20 of that year. The American president was chosen as arbitrator; but he died before a decision was rendered, and Calvin Coolidge inherited the responsibility.

President Coolidge handed down his award on March 4, 1925, in a document of 17,000 words (a large number for a man with a reputation for brevity). His decision was grounded on three points: (1) the plebiscite, which had been provided for more than forty years before, was to be held; (2) according to a plan of supervision, persons born in Tacna and Arica, as well as those with an established residence, were to be allowed to register and vote; (3) the boundary questions, Tarata and Chilcaya, were to be determined by the report of a special commission "consisting of three persons, one to be nominated by Chile, another . . . by Peru, and the third to be designated by the arbitrator." [23] The plebiscite was not to be delayed in awaiting the decision of the boundary commission.

The award of President Coolidge was favorable to the Chilean viewpoint and caused "great rejoicing" because Chile had desired the plebiscite. The decision was considered a "national calamity" in Lima.[24] Peru had maintained that the plebiscite should not be held, since the conditions of the Treaty of Ancón were no longer applica-

[22] Possibly, Peru depended too much for its own good upon the chance that help over Tacna-Arica might come from Washington. As Herbert Millington has concluded, it appears that James G. Blaine had tried to befriend Peru during the course of the war. Although Peruvian writers did not at first present their case with as much finesse as did their Chilean rivals, the Lima arguments were well prepared by the 1920's. It may be that the delay on the part of Peru was more the result of the destruction and postwar confusion than it was a waiting for aid from the United States.

[23] *US Foreign Relations*, 1925, I, p. 346. According to Salazar, *Historia diplomática del Peru*, p. 295, Peru was willing to accept the United States invitation, January 18, 1922, to the Washington meeting which was scheduled for July 20 of that year.

[24] Stuart, *Tacna-Arica Dispute*, pp. 55-57. See also regular diplomatic dispatches.

ble in 1925.[25] The Peruvian protest centered around the interpreta-tion of the words, *"expirado este plazo,"* from the Treaty of Ancón, dealing with the period of time during which the vote should be taken. Peru argued that it should be understood as "at the expiration of that time" and not as some time after the ten years had elapsed. The reaction was so violent, in fact, that Peruvian soldiers were called out in Lima to disperse a crowd which tore the United States coat of arms from over the embassy doorway. Ugarteche thought that the events of this period demonstrated that the "Yankee" diplomacy was incapable of comprehending the international prob-lems of South America.[26] He, along with a good many other Peru-vians, believed that the participation taken by Washington was not beneficial to Lima. Víctor Andrés Belaúnde, writing in the heat of the 1931 partisanship, claimed that his country put itself at the mercy of the United States with the "Question of the Pacific."

Plans for the plebiscite were drawn up, but the final settlement was impeded by the lack of any system of voting. General John J. Pershing resigned as chairman of the plebiscite commission with a statement that he needed "dental treatment," [27] General William Lassiter, Governor of the Panama Canal Zone, replacing him. In June 1926 Lassiter reported that a plebiscite was impossible and that Chilean police in Tacna and Arica had encouraged, rather than prevented, outrages on peaceful Peruvians. Toward the close of that year Secretary of State Kellogg advocated that Tacna-Arica be ceded or sold to a third country (Bolivia was suggested in Kellogg's memo-randum), or that part of it be made into a neutralized area.[28] Kel-logg's proposal was unacceptable to Peru. The Secretary of State soon made progress, however, by helping to establish direct diplo-matic relations between the disputants. Then in May 1929 President Hoover, complying with the request of both countries, offered a

[25] William Jefferson Dennis, *Tacna and Arica* (New Haven, Yale University Press, 1931), and others have concluded that Coolidge was guided in this de-cision more by doctrinaire legalism than by practical considerations.

[26] Ugarteche, *La política internacional peruana durante la dictadura de Leguía*, pp. 17, 80, 84, 89. See also Belaúnde, *La realidad nacional*, p. 222; Ulloa, *Posición internacional del Peru*, p. 379, and Stuart, *Tacna-Arica Dispute*, p. 56.

[27] Stuart, *Tacna-Arica Dispute*, pp. 55-57.

[28] *US Foreign Relations, 1926*, I, pp. 505-509. The memorandum suggested that the promontory known as the "Morro of Arica" (which held a sentimental attrac-tion for most Peruvians) be internationalized and that the City of Arica be made forever a free port.

plan of settlement. The details of the plan had earlier been accepted
orally by both South American nations. With the formal approval
of Chile and Peru, this complicated "Question of the Pacific" (the
Alsace-Lorraine of South America) came to a close. President Leguía
was insistent that the proposal appear to originate in Washington.
This, he felt, would offer less of an opening for attacks from his
political opponents.

The final settlement was a compromise agreement. The disputed
area was divided, with Tacna going to Peru and Arica to Chile. Chile
consented to pay Peru $6,000,000 and to construct for Peruvian use
a port with a wharf and customhouse in the harbor of Arica as well
as a station in Arica for the Tacna-Arica railroad. In this way Peru
was provided with port and transportation facilities in the area incorporated into Chile.

In looking back, it is evident that from the Treaty of Ancón until
the final settlement almost a half-century later, the internal political
conditions of Peru were affected by this vexatious situation of Tacna
and Arica. It is not surprising that various Peruvian presidents were
caught in its web of complications. During Leguía's first administration (1908-1912) it was apparent to the American minister in Lima
that the Peruvian president used the Tacna-Arica problem to play
upon the patriotic sentiment of the people. Minister Leslie Combs
reported, November 17, 1909, that President Leguía ". . . confirmed
the opinion I have expressed in former dispatches that political use
is being made of the controversy by his administration to bid for
popularity, or at least to distract the people from thought of revolution." [29] Peru was sensitive and demonstrated it by insisting that no
settlement be made which would "wound any fibre of its nationality." Kellogg's memorandum[30] in 1926, proposing cession, sale, and
internationalization, created a sharp political crisis.[31] Again in April
1929, when Chile and Peru agreed on terms of settlement, President
Leguía told the American ambassador that he expected President
Hoover to "offer the compromise as coming from him and both
countries will accept it." [32] This would not run as great a risk of
alienating Peruvian public opinion as would an offer from either the

[29] US Foreign Relations, 1913, p. 1176.
[30] US Foreign Relations, 1926, I, p. 528.
[31] US Foreign Relations, 1926, I, pp. 517-518.
[32] US Foreign Relations, 1913, p. 1176.

president of Chile or the president of Peru. It was understood that the two nations would agree to accept the terms even before Hoover presented them in a formal proposition.

To a degree, this dispute with Chile conditioned Peru's activity in the League of Nations. The Peruvian people were disappointed when the League could not or would not do justice to the "Question of the Pacific," and their government turned elsewhere for prospective aid.[33] Peru's relations with Washington had been cordial, and as hope for a satisfactory League settlement of Tacna and Arica died, Peruvian hope for United States support grew. Chile's favorable position as a member of the Council was also a cause of Peru's indifference to the international meetings in Geneva.[34] From 1921 to 1928 it was obvious that Peru cared little about maintaining League membership. Thereafter, following settlement of the Tacna-Arica matter in 1929, the government at Lima took a much more active part in League proceedings.

Various major financial matters involving American concerns and the Peruvian government also hinged upon the Tacna-Arica enigma. A memorandum of 1925, which C. W. Calvin prepared for the vice-president of the National City Company, showed that Peru's chances of obtaining loans in the United States were linked to the outcome of the quarrel. Leguía's influence and popularity in Peru were also closely tied up with the solution. "If the Tacna-Arica territory is assigned to Peru as a result of Leguía's diplomacy and management," wrote Calvin, "his hold on the Peruvian public will, in my opinion, be so firmly entrenched that he will serve out his present term of office less hampered than in the past and will be able to shape matters up so as to bring about a continuance of his policies." [35] In

[33] Warren H. Kelchner, *Latin American Relations With the League of Nations* (Boston, World Peace Foundation, 1930), p. 104.

[34] In 1922, Chilean Agustín Edwards was elected president of the League Assembly. Peruvian hope for aid from the United States appears to have gone up and down—up prior to 1910, down for a time, and up again after 1921. By 1929, those who knew what had happened could not be pleased with Washington. Belaúnde wrote of the territorial mutilation and the sale of Arica along with the "slavery" before "Yankee imperialism," *La realidad nacional*, p. 253. This last, from a man who would later be a friend of the United States.

[35] *Stock Exchange Practices: Hearings before a Subcommittee of the Committee on Banking and Currency, United States Senate*, 72nd Cong., 2nd Sess., S. Res. 84 and S. Res. 239, Part VI (Washington, 1933), p. 2105.

other words, the winning of those two provinces, in themselves unimportant economically, meant increased political and economic stability in Peru. Calvin suggested that the National City Company
withhold its plan for financing the Peruvian government until the
question of Peru's southern boundary was cleared up. The attempts
of the Electric Boat Company to prevent a settlement of the issue
demonstrated its narrow attitude toward the State Department's
effort to preserve peace between the two disputants.[36]

It is clear that various aspects of Peruvian-United States inter-
course were dependent, in one way or another, upon the "Question
of the Pacific." Leguía's control over the government, Peru's political
stability, Peru's general commercial and financial operations, as well
as Peruvian friendship for the United States, hinged on the outcome
of that troublesome problem.

The Leticia boundary dispute between Colombia and Peru was
one which arose from colonial confusion over the exact boundary
line separating the vice-royalties of New Granada and Peru. Colombia was, however, unable to do little but protest when Brazil and
Peru signed a treaty in 1851 by which the two nations agreed that
the boundary line between them would be a "straight line from
Tabatinga to the Yapura opposite to the confluence of the Apa-
poris." [37] On various occasions between 1900 and 1912 Peruvian
and Colombian settlers and military detachments clashed along the
Caqueta River. Peruvian rubber collectors operated (but not without gunfire) in the disputed area. By 1912 Peru's claims to the region appeared to be well supported and her treaty with Brazil (1851)
encouraged Peruvians in the belief that they would not have to re-
linquish territory south of the Putumayo River.

A new phase of the hundred-year-old Colombia-Peruvian struggle
over the Leticia area began soon after Leguía started his second
administration. Washington, desirous of improving relations with
Colombia after the First World War, supported Bogotá in the
Colombian-Peruvian negotiations which led to the signing of the

[36] L. Y. Spear, vice-president of Electric Boat Company, wrote on August 6,
1928, to Commander C. W. Craven of Vickers the following: "It is too bad the
pernicious activities of our State Department have put a brake on armament
orders from Peru by forcing resumption of formal diplomatic relations with
Chile." William T. Stone, *The Munitions Industry, Analysis of United States
Senate Investigation*, p. 10, is the source here.

[37] Gordon Ireland, *Boundaries, Possessions and Conflicts in South America*
(Cambridge, Mass., Harvard University Press, 1938), p. 188.

Salomón-Lozano treaty in March 1922.[38] The treaty gave Colombia possession of a narrow corridor of dense jungle land extending south from the Putumayo River to the Amazon.[39] The Peruvian government consistently postponed ratification of the Salomón-Lozano treaty so that its execution was not realized until 1930.

Leguía, who had favored (or made it appear that he did) the Salomón-Lozano treaty of 1922,[40] found the following various reasons or excuses for not submitting the treaty to the Peruvian Congress for ratification: the approaching presidential elections in 1924, the danger that the opposition forces would defeat it unless it appeared before Congress at the opportune time, the tension in Peru aroused by the Tacna-Arica question, and Brazil's memorandum to Peru attacking the treaty as being injurious to Brazilian interests in the disputed region. Alberto Ulloa claimed that Peru was coerced into agreeing to the treaty, since Leguía was dependent upon Washington for aid and upon private United States brokers for loans.[41]

The United States Department of State was in agreement that there was little value in pushing the matter prior to the 1924 elections, but repeatedly (1924-1927) urged Peru to take action so that the matter could be terminated. The United States government made at least eight oral or written statements to the Peruvian president and minister of foreign affairs indicating a desire for direct action by the Peruvian government.[42] Brazil's avowal that the Salomón-Lozano treaty was an infringement of her rights brought about more

[38] Arthur P. Whitaker, *The United States and South America, The Northern Republics* (Cambridge, Mass., Harvard University Press, The American Foreign Policy Library, 1948), p. 178.

[39] John C. de Wilde, "South American Conflicts, The Chaco and Leticia," *Foreign Policy Reports*, IX, No. 6 (May 24, 1933), p. 66.

[40] *US Foreign Relations*, 1924, I, p. 298. Peruvian Foreign Minister Salomón told American Ambassador Poindexter that he had never approved of the treaty and had signed it because Leguía favored it. One of Peru's most influential diplomats and a student of international law, Alberto Ulloa, made it clear that Peru resented the dominant role played by the United States in continental matters. Ulloa held that, when Leguía tried to get United States help on Tacna-Arica, Washington was interested only in political solutions which strengthened the United States influence in the continent and around the world. He also criticized the Leticia role of Washington: Ulloa, *Posición internacional del Perú*, pp. 378, 379, 381-384.

[41] Whitaker, *The United States and South America, The Northern Republics*, p. 178.

[42] *US Foreign Relations*, 1923, I, p. 352; 1924, I, p. 299; 1925, I, pp. 443, 448, 454, 460, 468; 1926, I, p. 535.

direct participation by the United States. Secretary of State Hughes, at Colombia's request, took the matter up with Brazil and sent "his opinion to Peru" in December 1924 by Leo S. Rowe, Director of the Pan-American Union.[43]

Secretary Hughes, desirous of an agreement before he left office, secured the signing by Brazil, Colombia, and Peru of a *procès-verbal* which contained three provisions: (1) the withdrawal, by the government of Brazil, of its observations regarding the 1922 boundary treaty between Colombia and Peru;[44] (2) the agreement of Colombia and Peru to ratify this boundary treaty; and (3) the signing of a convention between Brazil and Colombia by which the boundary between those countries would be agreed to on the Apaporis-Tabatinga line, Brazil agreeing in perpetuity in favor of Colombian freedom of navigation on the Amazon and other rivers common to both countries.[45] The *procès-verbal* was signed on March 4, 1925, in the office of the secretary of state at Washington, by Charles E. Hughes; Peruvian Ambassador Hernan Velarde; Colombian Minister Enrique Olaya; and Brazilian Chargé Samuel de Souza Leso Gracie.

Secretary of State Frank B. Kellogg took up the matter at this point, but he too could not move rapidly toward a settlement, since Leguía was hesitant to ask congressional ratification of the Salomón-Lozano treaty. The United States government urged Peruvian ratification and the Colombian government intimated the probable severance of relations if the settlement were not ratified, but Leguía still hesitated to insist upon congressional approval. In October 1925, Colombia approved the treaty, but it was not until December 1927 that Peru acted favorably upon it.[46] Ratifications were exchanged March 19, 1928, and the mixed commission to demarcate the boundary terminated its work at Iquitos in March 1930.[47]

The treaty was unpopular in Peru. At first, Peruvians did not even hear the details of the Salomón-Lozano treaty. But after pressure from Washington brought about its ratification by a Peruvian Congress subservient to Leguía, there was no way of preventing educated Peruvians from learning these details. Ireland concluded that "nego-

[43] Ireland, *Boundaries, Possessions and Conflicts in South America*, p. 198.
[44] In November 1924, Brazil had presented Peru with a memorandum which declared the Salomón-Lozano treaty to be injurious to Brazilian interests in the region; Ireland, *Boundaries, Possessions and Conflicts in South America*, p. 198.
[45] *US Foreign Relations, 1925*, I, pp. 461-462.
[46] *US Foreign Relations, 1927*, I, p. 343.
[47] Ireland, *Boundaries, Possessions and Conflicts in South America*, p. 198.

tiations and execution of this treaty played a considerable part in the downfall of the Peruvian president Leguía. . . ." [48] The fact that Peruvians were soon ready to fight to regain possession of the Leticia corridor is proof that they did not sanction the Salomón-Lozano treaty. Hostilities occurred when an aggressive frontier band of Peruvians seized the Colombian Amazon port of Leticia. United States Ambassador Dearing carelessly reported from Lima that a band of *Apristas* from Loreto, Peru, had broken the peace of 1922 on September 1, 1932, and had taken Leticia. There was no more reason to identify this as an *Aprista* attack than there was for President Sánchez Cerro to claim it was caused by communists, as he later did. [49] When Washington expressed a desire that there be no further bloodshed, the Peruvian chief executive suggested that the State Department refrain from mixing in a solely domestic matter. Sánchez Cerro shifted his position from one of alleged ignorance of the attack to one of sending reinforcements to the Amazon headwaters for purposes of trying to reopen the 1922 settlement. When it became evident that Peru did not intend merely to withdraw from Leticia and return to a position of accord with the Salomón-Lozano treaty, the Colombian government described itself as "very gratified" at the attitude taken in Washington. [50]

By early 1933, relations between Washington and Lima were placed under even greater stress, as a result of developments occurring in Lima at the precise time the United States was preparing to assume charge of Colombia's Peruvian interests. Bogotá-Lima relations were broken. Colombians were leaving Peru, and other foreign diplomats feared for their safety. Among those departing was Mrs. Teresa Handley, a former Colombian who was also the United States-born widow of an earlier United States consul general. Consul Handley had displayed an unusual interest in Leguía's coup of 1919. [51] Ambassador Fred Morris Dearing (February 19, 1933) made an urgent request that Secretary of State Stimson "consider most seriously" sending a war vessel to Callao. The jittery Dearing thought that one "vessel and equipment should be adequate for dealing with

[48] *Ibid.*, pp. 198-199.
[49] *US Foreign Relations,* 1932, V, pp. 270-273. See *US Foreign Relations,* 1934 for a statement by Dearing which helps to clear up the *Aprista* position in this matter.
[50] *US Foreign Relations,* 1932, V, pp. 276-277.
[51] See Chapter 3.

hostile mobs of considerable size." [52] Stimson could not see that American lives were actually in danger and so he did not think it necessary to send a warship in the direction of Dearing's call.

The League of Nations was to play an important role in handling the border dispute. United States officials encouraged the League at the same time as it attempted to work for a settlement in other ways. Secretary of State Cordell Hull appealed to Brazil for aid in the matter. Washington refused direct aid to either Colombia or Peru in their preparations for further warfare, but Colombia was favored in the ensuing diplomatic maneuvers. Oscar Benavides, the new president at Lima, believed that Washington was partial to Colombia at that time. His beliefs were based on the fact that Colombia engaged the services of United States aviators for positions as civilian instructors. About the same time, April 1934, the Panama Canal Zone repair facilities were denied to a Peruvian naval vessel.[53] When the United States expressed its discontent with Peru's activities in Leticia, the natural result was a lowering of the popularity of "Uncle Sam" in Lima.

Peru's case was legally untenable, and with military conditions (both domestic and international) developing as they were, Lima was forced to back down. Negotiations taking place in Rio de Janeiro were concluded in 1934 with Colombia maintaining its hold on Leticia. The historian is prompted to review the broad scene and ask how much importance should be placed upon the fact that, from 1917 to 1930, Washington was anxious to mend fences with Bogotá, fences which had been badly damaged by the Panama Canal Zone acquisition. Was this one of the reasons why Peru believed that it stood at a disadvantage in the triangle? Ulloa believed that the United States aided Colombia against Peru in order to compensate for its Panama policy. He attributed Leguía's adherence to the Salomón-Lozano treaty to his desire to please Washington. And he further maintained that the Peruvian people never gave their approval to the treaty.[54] In any event, United States prestige languished because of the Leticia negotiations.

[52] *US Foreign Relations, 1933,* IV, p. 551.
[53] *US Foreign Relations, 1934,* IV, p. 385.
[54] Ulloa, *Posición internacional del Peru,* pp. 176, 186. Ulloa also believed that Peru was hurt over the Peruvian-Ecuadorian boundary negotiation because of a Peruvian desire to work for continental solidarity. In the long view this would not appear to be the case, for Peru did not suffer in the settlements reached. See *Revista Peruana de Derecho Internacional,* IV (Lima, 1944), p. 313.

Peru took a more aggressive stance with respect to its northern boundary following the Tacna-Arica settlement and its humiliation in the Leticia controversy with Colombia. The Ecuador-Peruvian boundary conflict, which again brought the United States into the negotiations, was first called the Oriente-Mainas dispute. This complicated problem involving 120,000 square miles of land, most of which was drained by the headwaters of the Amazon, has been troublesome on various occasions dating back to colonial days. In 1887 Ecuador and Peru submitted the dispute to the King of Spain. In 1910 rumors regarding the nature of the Spanish king's award resulted in both disputants mobilizing for war and concentrating troops along the frontier. Three nations, the United States, Brazil, and Argentina, studied the matter and suggested that the controversy be presented to the Permanent Tribunal at The Hague. Peru accepted this proposal; but Ecuador refused, and so a definite arrangement could not be reached. Peace was temporarily preserved, but it was a fragile peace at best.

Settlement of the Ecuador-Peruvian dispute made little headway under Leguía's second administration; the only actual achievement was the signing of a protocol. In the 1924 Ponce-Castro protocol the United States played a minor role. The disputants agreed upon four articles:[55] (1) They consented to submit the boundary question to arbitration in Washington, and even if a definite line could not be agreed upon, they were to try to determine the zones which each party reciprocally recognized and the zone which would have to be submitted to the arbitral award of the President of the United States. (2) When one or the other of the ends mentioned in articles one had been attained, then the delegations were to sign a protocol which would be submitted to the congresses of both nations. (3) The delegations were to meet in Washington immediately after the Tacna-Arica question—which had been submitted to the arbitration of the President of the United States—had been decided. (4) The two governments were also to try to anticipate settlement of the question.

Until 1934 little was gained by the Ponce-Castro protocol, since no further action toward its fulfillment was taken. In 1934 negotiations were resumed. Ecuador asked that the United States, Uruguay, and the ABC republics mediate the problem; Peru rejected this proposal. On July 8, 1936, Washington announced that, in accordance with the Ponce-Castro protocol, the President of the United

[55] *US Foreign Relations*, 1924, I, p. 305.

States would arbitrate the dispute.[56] Conferences of the disputing nations were held in Washington starting in 1936 but this negotiation broke off in 1939. Frontier clashes occurred in 1936, 1938, 1939, and 1940 with an undeclared war breaking out in July 1941.

The United States, Brazil, and Chile extended their assistance, but Ecuador delayed joining in inter-American pronouncements concerning a hemispheric position in the Second World War. The United States, supported by Argentina, Brazil, and Chile, discussed the matter with Ecuadorian representatives at the 1942 Rio de Janeiro meeting of the Foreign Ministers of American States, and some progress was achieved. On January 29, Peru and Ecuador signed a pact which provided the basis for settling the boundary question. Actual settlement was delayed, however, until the agreement of February 1945 was reached. The greater share of the disputed territory was then awarded to Peru, the country which had received the most support from the United States, Argentina, Brazil, and Chile. As expected, these developments directed Ecuadorian wrath towards Peru and the United States. Intermittently, 1946-1960, incidents and clashes continued to mar the border peace, and some of the discontent showed itself in OAS meetings.

As on various other occasions, it was made plain to Washington that part of the price for United States power and influence in Latin America was the acceptance of troublesome responsibilities. The officials on the Potomac had not ducked the problem, but Ecuador continued to feel it had been mistreated. As is often the case, the results showed that the weakest nation as measured in men, money, and machines had come out last at the negotiating table.

CLAIMS

The Landreau claim, after pending fifty years, was settled during Leguía's second administration.[57] Basing their claim on a Peruvian decree of 1865, the heirs of John Celestine Landreau asked $2,700,-000 for discovery of guano deposits. The United States had called the attention of the Peruvian government to the claim at various intervals between 1874 and 1919. A commission meeting in London in 1922 made an award of $125,000 in favor of the United States.

[56] Ireland, *Boundaries, Possessions and Conflicts in South America*, p. 229.

[57] For the Landreau Claim see: *US Foreign Relations* (various years 1874-1919); and Marjorie M. Whiteman, *Damages in International Law*, III (Washington, 1943), p. 1741. See fn. 41 of Chapter 2, which includes a reference to the Dreyfus claims.

When approximately eighty persons presented themselves as heirs or beneficiaries, Andrew W. Mellon, Secretary of the Treasury, filed a bill to have the Supreme Court of the District of Columbia determine the beneficiaries. The settlement of the Landreau matter was, by itself, insignificant, but it was indicative of two general characteristics of United States policy toward Peru in that period. First, Washington induced Leguía to treat certain economic interests in a friendly manner, although previous governments of Peru had refused to recognize these matters as definite obligations. Secondly, Washington encouraged Peru to settle Western Hemisphere problems without calling upon the international arbitration machinery of the League of Nations or The Hague Tribunal, even when Peru had requested that cases be submitted to The Hague.

A complete statement of claims, allegations, and trade complications would constitute a lengthy, monotonous record. For that reason, only the Landreau case and Peru's discontent over sugar marketing are being outlined here. The lean years of the 1930's found the smaller nation protesting that the Jones-Costigan legislation was particularly harmful to Peru.

Minister of Foreign Affairs Alberto Ulloa in 1936 requested a higher quota for Peruvian sugar imported by the United States.[58] The possibility of Peruvian restrictions on United States goods and a treaty designed to develop greater trade with the British were arguments used to bolster Peru's position. Ulloa pointed out that preferential treatment of Cuban sugar permitted Cuba to dump its product on the world market in a way which hurt Peru's trade. The foreign minister at Lima placed the major responsibility for the problem upon the United States. Peru's sugar problem, not so different from its cotton problem, was not alleviated in any appreciable manner until the rise of Fidel Castro. Peru's difficulties were increased with market shiftings of the Second World War era. Some indirect, temporary relief was afforded by Export-Import Bank credits, but Peruvian resentment stirred again in 1955 when the United States denied Peru an increased sugar quota.[59] Some import increases were allowed along the way, but it was not until the Castro-Washington break that Peruvian sugar benefited significantly from Cuban quota adjustments. Prior to the Second World War, Peru was deeply concerned with its sugar and cotton questions.

[58] US Foreign Relations, 1936, V, p. 920.
[59] Excelsior, Lima, July 1955, p. 11; and January-February 1956, pp. 5, 17.

7: INCREASED INTEREXCHANGE WITH THE SECOND WORLD WAR

The 1930's were years of relatively slack activity between the two countries. The northern nation's efforts toward the settlement of boundary disputes were not widely appreciated among *Limeños*, and, from 1932 to 1936, general commercial operations lagged. In spite of the notoriety focused upon the neatly packaged approach labeled "The Good Neighbor Policy," basic United States policies toward Peru changed very little, except for increased cultural activity. United States interest in Peru and the rest of Latin America received a generally favorable welcome as Washington began to concern itself more with personnel exchange programs. Latin Americans could say, "*Pues*, Columbus discovered America in 1492 and the United States discovered Latin America in 1942." But Secretary Cordell Hull's reciprocal trade overtures would not prosper in Lima, as they did in some places, until the Western Hemisphere was shaken by the European War.

While Europe was moving into war in 1936-1939, the United States was following its general Latin-American diplomatic line in Lima. National economic interests and national security were the prime concerns of the Department of State. At the same time Washington was concerned with general comity toward Peru, better understanding through good neighborliness, and hemispheric neutrality in the broad outlines. Care was taken by Roosevelt's "boys in the striped pants" to see that they did not risk being charged with intervention in Peru's internal affairs. The Secretary of State was seldom bothered with questions of grants-in-aid or matters of technical assistance. The northern nation did not appear to recognize any particular obligations or responsibilities to the Peruvian people. The relationship was not fundamentally different from that between Washington and any small European or Far Eastern nation in which there were heavy American investments.

Hemispheric matters did, of course, enter the Lima-Washington picture. Peru, although not particularly a prime mover or energetic actor, was host to the eighth Pan-American Conference at Lima in December 1938 at which "hemispheric defense" was emphasized. *Limeños* in general, along with most of the Conference delegates, applauded Cordell Hull's appeal for solidarity and defense against all foreign intervention. Washington's outmoded notions of United States, and even hemispheric, isolation—always a dream—was now an almost forgotten dream. The Good Neighbor Policy was paying dividends in Peru, but dissonance had not completely disappeared.

On the surface, and in most of the important facets, relations were good; but questions of market competition and the defaulted Leguía loans were points of disagreement in the late 1930's. Minor problems appeared to be developing around Japanese barter-trade offers and President Oscar Benavides' apparent friendship toward Hitler's Germany. After Hitler's designs on Latin America became known, it was imperative that the United States actively demonstrate its good neighborliness.

Peru was not content with the trade relationship existing between the two countries, complaining that tariffs eliminated most of Peru's major products from United States markets.[1] Lima negotiated a trade treaty with London but was not interested in signing one with the United States. The Peruvian sugar surplus presented the greatest obstacle, since Peru resented Cuba's preferential treatment, was unhappy about the dumping of sugar, and could not influence Washington to increase its sugar quota. Peru's need for a sugar market had been a factor in granting a favorable trade treaty to England. The United States chargé d'affaires credited the Peruvian National Agrarian Society with great power in these matters, attributing more power to it than the Society actually had.[2]

Another complicating factor was Peru's indifference to suggestions from Washington that the Leguía loan bonds be serviced. The president of W. R. Grace and Company, concerned about his firm's stake in the sugar question, reported that President Benavides believed Peru could improve its servicing of the debt if the United

---

[1] *Papers Relating to the Foreign Relations of the United States, 1936*, V (Washington), p. 932, hereafter cited as *US Foreign Relations*. See also Felipe Barreda Laos, *Hispano America en Guerra?* (Buenos Aires, 1941), p. 21.

[2] *US Foreign Relations, 1936*, V, p. 895. The statement in the dispatch from Peru, that the Society "overthrew" the Leguía regime through its support of Sánchez Cerro, is not supported in the record. A more complete study of the Peruvian National Agrarian Society is needed.

States would buy more of Peru's exports.[3] In any event, Peru would not go halfway on a trade treaty, and the Department of State let it be known that Lima's indifferent attitude on the loan debt was disconcerting.[4] In 1938-1942, Secretary of State Hull and others in the Department called Peru's attention—to no avail—to the debt.

Past financial transgressions rose to muddle the scene in those very years, 1938-1941, when considerable maneuvering was being conducted by both the Axis and the Allied powers in their relationships to Peru. As war spread in Europe in the late 1930's, the Benavides government gave Washington cause for worry by its friendship toward Italy, Germany, and Japan. An airline between Lima and Germany was opened. Benavides himself had a significant tie with Rome which dated back to 1917 when he was minister plenipotentiary there. According to the Peruvian newswriter, Genaro Arbaiza, Italian influence topped all others in Lima in 1938.[5] This was because of the local banking policies, the wealthy Italian colony, and fascist influence in sections of industry and agriculture. North American investors might make larger profits, but no United States citizen possessed influence in Peru equal to that of Gino Salochi, head of the *Banco Italiano*. Arbaiza claimed that no foreigner since Henry Meiggs had wielded more influence than did Salochi. Another insight into this facet of Peruvian thought can be found in the writings of José de la Riva-Aguero, best known for his *La Historia en el Peru* (Lima, 1910). *El Comercio* (March 12, 19, August 13, September 3, 1939) and *Mercurio Peruano* (March 1944) reported on Riva-Aguero's interest in Japan, his acceptance of much of fascism, and his lament at the collapse of Mussolini's regime. Peruvian interest in *Hispanidad* and its exaltation of all that which was Spanish seemed to be fed from antileftist and anti-Indianist movements. For this reason the *Hispanists* would decline in numbers as the *Apristas* grew.

Whatever the reason may have been, Peru did not appear willing to obligate itself to Japan. Early in the twentieth century there had been considerable Peruvian animosity engendered toward the Japanese workers brought in according to contracts with private agricul-

---

[3] *Ibid.*, p. 930.

[4] *US Foreign Relations*, 1939, V, p. 773.

[5] Genaro Arbaiza, "Benavides of Peru," *Current History*, XLIX (October 1938), p. 28. Also see, Jorge Basadre, *Chile, Peru y Bolivia independentes* (Barcelona-Buenos Aires, 1948), p. 732; and Luis Alberto Sánchez, *Haya de la Torre y el Apra* (Santiago, 1955), pp. 358, 361.

tural concerns. Over the years there was no way of telling exactly how many Japanese entered the country since there was also an influx of unauthorized entries.[6] At death, the *carnet* (permit for aliens) held by a Japanese was said to have been passed on to another waiting at the shoreline so that "a Japanese never died in Peru." Another cause of discontent arose over the dumping of textiles on the local market. Ill feeling on these matters reached a climax in 1940 when riots resulted in the smashing of Japanese stores in Lima.

For only a short time was there any danger of critical deterioration in relations between Lima and Washington. During the economic hassle of 1939, President Benavides at one point told the United States representative in Peru that if the United States did not appreciate Peru, the Peruvians could turn to Germany.[7] With the Japanese offering to buy more cotton on a barter basis at the very moment that German and Italian influence was growing, the generally harmonious relationship between the two Western Hemisphere nations appeared to be in for a drastic change. But in 1940 the war gave new life to Peru's economy and helped reorient trade with the United States. The election of Manuel Prado was also an important factor in helping to ease relations in late 1939. When Washington arranged for a loan in December 1940, Peru was satisfied that the United States intended to demonstrate more flexibility in its economic approach, and it became possible to work directly toward a treaty to facilitate trade. The man in the Lima street was not perturbed greatly with hostilities in Europe and likely took his cue from figures such as Haya de la Torre who was living in exile. From Buenos Aires in 1941, he wrote that both Americas must oppose totalitarianism even though the economies of the two were not on a solid basis of good relationship.[8] His stress was placed, instead, on the common grounds of interest in preserving democracy.

With Prado taking over the helm, it meant that a decidedly pro-Allied friend of the United States had stepped up to the presidency. Peru's foreign ministry issued statements to show that Peru strongly supported the position of unity and general neutrality of the Pan-

---

[6] Toraji Irie, "History of Japanese Migration to Peru," *The Hispanic American Historical Review*, Part I (August 1951), pp. 437-452; also, Part II (November 1951), pp. 648-664.

[7] *US Foreign Relations, 1939*, V, p. 773.

[8] Víctor Raúl Haya de la Torre, *La defensa continental* (Buenos Aires, 1941); and *Vision*, X (February 1957), p. 86.

American system.[9] In accordance with the foreign ministers meeting at Havana in July 1940, Peru stated that it would prohibit the dissemination of warlike propaganda.[10] About the same time, one of Peru's leading newspapers commented editorially that it was time for the United States to adjust its neutrality laws to a more realistic approach, one which would be more consistent with its outright aid to the Allies.[11] The ambiguity of the United States' so-called neutrality was apparent. In this same period, the German ambassador complained to Peru that some United States films were very damaging to Germany's interests and prestige.[12] Peru's film censoring board did prevent, for a time, the showing of films such as Charlie Chaplin in "The Great Dictator." These developments proved to be minor as Peru consistently aligned itself with the United States position, which in turn was more and more pro-Allied.

A Peruvian who was influential in improving relations between Washington and Lima was Pedro Beltran. Beltran, as a special Peruvian commercial delegate to Washington in 1940, made a real effort to clear up trading and financial problems. During the war he continued to work for close co-operation with the Allies. In July 1944 he took over the post of Peruvian ambassador to the United States and remained at this post until 1946. In 1959 President Prado called Beltran into his government as premier and minister of finance and he continued to act vigorously in those posts.

Also, well in advance of Pearl Harbor, Peru's economic interest had begun to direct its foreign policies. In October 1940, the Export-Import Bank of Washington extended a $10,000,000 loan to Peru to facilitate essential purchases in the United States.[13] The German *Compania Lufthansa S. A.* lost its permit to operate, and, at the same time, had its planes expropriated by Peru.[14] After several German ships left Peruvian ports without permission in March 1941 and were burned by ships' orders at high seas, the Peruvian govern-

[9] Alfredo Solf y Muro, *Memoria del Ministro de Relaciones Exteriores July 1940* (Lima, 1942), pp. ix-x.

[10] *Ibid.*, p. xiv.

[11] *La Crónica*, Lima, September 30, 1941, p. 2.

[12] Solf y Muro, *Memoria . . . July 1940*, p. xvi.

[13] Whitney H. Shepardson and William O. Scroggs, *The United States in World Affairs: An Account of American Foreign Relations 1940* (New York, Council on Foreign Affairs, 1941), p. 370.

[14] Solf y Muro, *Memoria . . . July 1941—July 1942*, p. xxi.

ment closed the German shipping concern, Transocean.[15] After Pearl
Harbor, Prado decreed the freezing of Japanese bank funds in Peru.[16]
As the war advanced and Axis hopes dimmed, the Peruvian government proceeded to take more definite action along the lines suggested
by Washington and London. In 1942, Peru and the United States
signed a treaty to facilitate trade.[17] A joint association was formed
by the two countries in order to carry out the rubber agreement of
April 1942, and a jointly controlled agricultural experiment station
was established in Peru's jungle at the same time. The Rubber Reserve Company (Peruvian Corporation of the Amazon), organized
in June 1942, was to concern itself almost entirely with the production, rationing, and distribution of rubber.[18] The United States was
also interested in securing copper, vanadium, petroleum, molybde-
num, cinchona bark and other jungle products. Another subsidiary
of the Reconstruction Finance Corporation, the Metals Reserve
Company, reached agreement to increase its Peruvian cotton purchases. A lend-lease agreement signed in March 1942 provided that
Peru was to repay 41.38 per cent of the "scheduled cost (about
$29,000,000) of armaments and munitions transferred by the United
States to Peru. . . ." [19] Lend-lease aid to Peru was considerably
more than that extended to the other northern Andean countries.
In various ways, then, the war acted as a spur to Peru's economy.

Peru increased its war participation in other forms. On January 24,
1942, Peru broke relations with Germany, Italy, and Japan, and, in
February 1943, affirmed its adherence to the principles of the At-
lantic Charter. During 1943 and 1944, the nation stepped up its
activities against Axis subjects living in Peru.[20] Some Axis citizens

[15] *Ibid.*, p. xxiv.
[16] *Ibid.* (annex), p. 3.
[17] *Ibid.*, p. 457. See also *El Peruano Diario Oficial*, Lima, October 3, 1941, p. 1;
also, *Cámara de Diputados, Diario de Debates* (1941); and *Cámara de Senadores,
Diario de Debates* (1941).
[18] *US Foreign Relations, 1942*, VI, pp. 665-673.
[19] *Ibid.* See also Solf y Muro, *Memoria . . . July 1941—July 1942*, p. 321.
[20] Solf y Muro, *Memoria . . . July 1942—July 1943*, p. vii. At the time of
Pearl Harbor, there were more than 30,000 Japanese in Peru. They did not constitute as great a problem as Alberto Ulloa had expected when he wrote that he
anticipated the necessity of sequestering them in a concentration camp: Ulloa,
Posición internacional del Peru (Lima, 1941), pp. 361-362. Also, *Revista Peruana
de Derecho Internacional*, IV (1944), pp. 307-308.
Carlos Sayan Alvarez, president of the Camara de Diputados del Peru, considered his country to be giving considerable spiritual and material aid to the

were deported—occasionally to the decided financial disadvantage of those being deported. In one instance 454 Axis nationals were interned in the United States. The United States embassy was interested in Peru's adoption of measures for economic control over Axis citizens.[21] Peru employed a widespread freeze on Japanese funds in banks and savings companies and ordered customhouses to clear no goods of Japanese origin without a special license from the Ministry of Finance.[22] The measures provided for the expropriation of property of Axis people if they engaged in subversive activities or propagandized for "systems contrary to democracy." [23] Early in February 1945 the nation declared that a state of belligerency existed between Peru and Germany and Peru and Japan.

The interexchange between the two nations became more diverse than it had been before the war. Late in 1941 Washington started negotiations to obtain permission for Army aircraft to use Peruvian airports and their facilities in the Talara area. The Talara Base (*El Pato*) was requested, partly because it provided a link in the defense of the Panama Canal, and partly because it offered protection for United States petroleum fields there. In order to provide security in these respects it was necessary to expand the airfields in the area. Official correspondence made it clear that Peruvian public opinion was reckoned with before use of the Talara Base was secured. With Peruvian co-operation, the United States constructed a temporary air base near Talara.

The Lima government co-operated further in the war effort by supporting the United States naval units which patrolled the Pacific coastline and offshore waters of South America. Washington followed a practice of inviting important members of the Peruvian armed forces for visits and tours in the United States.[24] Vice-President Henry A. Wallace visited Peru, and President Prado called upon leaders in the White House. In spite of the fact that the Peru-

---

United States in the struggle against totalitarianism, *Política nacional e internacional del Peru* (Lima, 1943), p. 40.

[21] *Medidas de Control Sobre Actividades Comerciales y Financieras de Nacionales de paises del Eja Establecidas por el Gobierno del Peru Durante el Actual Conflicto Mundial* (Peruvian Ministry of Foreign Relations: Mimeographed and translated at the United States Embassy, Lima, 1943).

[22] *Ibid.*, p. 3a.

[23] *Ibid.*, p. 54a. For law #9958, see *Revista Peruana de Derecho Internacional,* IV (Lima, 1944), pp. 307-308.

[24] Solf y Muro, *Memoria* . . . *July 1940—July 1941,* p. cxxviii.

vian public had become distrustful of "good will" tours, Wallace "reached the man in the street" and made a very favorable impression upon the people of Lima, according to Haya de la Torre.[25] The *Aprista* leader noted with satisfaction that the visiting vice-president recognized that United States economic imperialism had existed, but "the era of economic imperialism and dollar diplomacy" was ended forever. Out of respect for the president of the United States, April 15, 1945, was declared a day of national mourning for the death of Franklin Delano Roosevelt.[26] Probably the most significant influence of the war on relations was the increase in trade it effected between the two nations. The United States augmented its volume of earlier trade exchanges and picked up some of what had been German, Italian, or Japanese commerce.

Although most were friendly, not all Washington-Lima wartime exchanges were amicable. In September 1941 the Peruvian ambassador in Washington expressed strong disagreement when he heard that the New York collector of customs was holding up shipment of eighteen Douglas airplanes, model 8 A-5. A tenseness fell on Lima the next month when the news was released that the United States War Department had seized eighteen bombing planes which Peru had purchased in Canada from the Norwegian government.[27] The planes were ready to be shipped when the northern power commandeered them to meet urgent military needs. The United States military and naval attachés as well as the chief of the Aviation Mission to Peru were disturbed by the current of anti-United States feeling. Ambassador R. Henry Norweb also expressed alarm because the developments had afforded "totalitarian interests" [28] new possi-

[25] *Free World*, VI (July 1943), pp. 20-22, published a report of Víctor Raúl Haya de la Torre, entitled "The Impressive Oratory of Mr. Wallace." Also see Sánchez, *Haya de la Torre y el Apra*, p. 374.

[26] *Revista Peruana de Derecho Internacional*, V (1945), p. 212. *Excelsior*, Lima, January 1946, p. 19, referred to Roosevelt as the greatest figure in contemporary history in our continent. Because of Roosevelt's death (on April 12, 1945), April 15, 1945, was declared a day of national mourning for Peru.

[27] Solf y Muro, *Memoria . . . July 1941—July 1942*, pp. 125-127. Within a day or two all of Lima's newspapers gave the incident special emphasis, as did *La Crónica*, October 18, 1941, p. 1.

[28] *La Crónica*, October 18, 1941, p. 1. See also Alfredo Solf y Muro, *Memoria . . . July 1941—July 1942*, p. 128, and *US Foreign Relations, 1941*, VII, pp. 513-514, 517. The high respect held for President Roosevelt was probably a factor which encouraged Peruvian support of the Allied cause as well as restraint on the part of Peru when Washington commandeered the eighteen Douglas

bilities. All of Lima's daily newspapers carried bold headlines of protest. When Cordell Hull promised speedy compensation, Peru's Ministry of Foreign Affairs also insisted upon compensatory expenses for the ship, *Marañon*, which had been waiting in New York to transport the planes.[29] Washington authorities agreed to make total compensation to Peru in a payment amounting to $1,266,729.32. A satisfactory settlement was reached, but the entire matter had been complicated by the fact that the Peruvians had wanted the planes at that particular time because of bloody clashes with Ecuador over the boundary question.

For a long time the underlying problems were economic, but between 1938 and 1941 various influential Peruvians were critical of the United States on matters as diverse as the Ecuador boundary difficulty or the "Yankee" desertion of the Pan-American neutrality policy. One of Peru's best known scholars of international law, Alberto Ulloa, an influential diplomat himself, insisted that his country's efforts on behalf of continental solidarity had been harmful to Peru on the Ecuadorian boundary settlement.[30] Felipe Barreda Laos, Peruvian ambassador to Argentina and Uruguay from 1930 to 1941, accused Washington of supporting Ecuador's position so that, ultimately, the United States could obtain a base in the Galapagos Islands.[31] Others pictured *Tio* Sam as maneuvering to secure oil concessions in the disputed Amazon territory. In the early years of the Second World War, Barreda leveled written attacks at the United States which were the strongest of any to come from an official of the Peruvian government.

These were most sensitive points, but there were other lesser complications which grew out of wartime developments. Peru's foreign trade increased, to be sure, but the cost of living jumped at the same time. While the exchange rate between the sol and the dollar remained the same (about 6.50 to 1), the cost of living went up 101 per cent from 1939 to 1946. Following the war, the democratic gov-

---

planes. For example, see Alvarez's *Política nacional e internacional del Peru*, p. 14.

[29] Alfredo Solf y Muro, *Memoria* . . . *July 1941—July 1942*, p. 135.

[30] *Revista Peruana de Derecho Internacional*, IV (1944), p. 313.

[31] Felipe Barreda Laos, *Hispano America en Guerra?*, pp, 75, 77, 79 (see fn. 1 of this chapter). The Ecuadorian boundary problem caused a high nationalistic feeling at this time. It would be difficult to prove the Ulloa point, for in 1945 the United States did not stand in the way of awarding the bulk of disputed territory to Peru.

ernment of President José Luis Bustamante y Rivero suffered the loss of a strong export market for its most important items. As these items—principally those exported to the United States during the war—dropped in volume after the war, many Peruvians believed that they had been deserted as soon as their help and products were no longer needed.[32] In the five years following the war's end, only two of Peru's twelve principal commodity exports regained or held the volume of war exportation.[33] In the first fifteen years following the war, petroleum never regained its 1945 export volume; it was 1951 before copper reached its wartime figure; not until 1950 did cotton, lead, and wool attain the 1945 amounts; and coffee and sugar did not regain wartime dimensions until 1952 and 1953. Peruvian newspapers and magazines continued to complain of lack of United States concern for Peru's economy after the war was ended.[34]

Economic problems, although the most significant, were not the only ones. A minor incident at the temporary United States air base, El Pato, near Talara was handled discreetly by the United States officials concerned. Late in 1946 Peruvian officials suggested to the United States Embassy that it was appropriate to turn over control of El Pato to Peru.[35] The original agreement had provided for delivery of the base with its materials and equipment when the actual

[32] This discontent with trade policies after the war expressed itself constantly from 1946 to 1958 and, especially, shortly before Vice-President Nixon's stormy visit to Lima. Apristas, having supported the Allies and dropped their criticism of United States economic interests in Peru, were still prompted to declare themselves "anti-imperialists" on November 30, 1945, La Tribuna, Lima, p. 11. Other critical notes appeared in usually pro-United States papers such as La Crónica, August 10, 1946, p. 1, and Excelsior, January 1946, p. 3. The latter article complained that although Peru had co-operated and sold materials at low prices during the war, the United States wanted to collect earlier debts without taking note of the changed value of the dollar. At the same time that friction between United States soldiers in northern Peru with Peruvians was reported, there were front page news stories telling of Senator Theodore Bilbo's "Klan" membership and his proclamation favoring white supremacy.

[33] Those two were gold and zinc. R. F. Rodriguez, Market for U.S. Products in Peru, Department of Commerce (Washington, 1961), p. 14.

[34] Excelsior, January 1946, p. 3; El Comercio, Lima, May 9, 1958, pp. 5, 9; La Tribuna, May 7, 1958; Excelsior, April-May 1948, p. 5; and Excelsior, January-February 1956, p. 5. Part of the argument presented was that the United States wanted Peru to help build up Europe by selling Peruvian products at reduced prices.

[35] Revista Peruana de Derecho Internacional, VI (1946), p. 316; and New York Times, November 10, 1946.

state of war had ended. While negotiations were taking shape, a United States soldier on July 28, 1946 (Peru's Independence Day), interfered with a girl in the social set of a Peruvian naval officer, Alberto Rubio Watkins. The Peruvian officer said that he was menaced and, because of this, shot and killed Sergeant Oscar J. Eiland. The Peruvian government asked for prompt return of the base to Peruvian control.[36] On October 29, 1946, *El Pato* was turned over to Peruvian command.[37] There were no serious ramifications from this affair for, in the same month, the Peruvian and United States governments signed an agreement providing for the establishment of a United States Air Mission in Peru.[38] Also, in the same year the United States began providing technicians and consultants for Peruvian transportation services which included personnel to assist in air transportation matters.

In the years following the war, the Peruvian government purchased outright or secured under foreign surplus provisions through the Department of State various items of United States military equipment. Forty-two airplanes, two tugs, two minesweepers, four landing craft, a patrol frigate, some tanks, and ammunition were transferred to Peru in one year, 1947. For these items, Peru agreed to pay the sum of $868,915.[39]

In the years 1945-1948 a generally harmonious relationship prevailed, although the period was not one of ostensibly excellent relations as both earlier and later eras were often pictured. Evidence of this good feeling is ample, as demonstrated by the following examples: Peru's extending its highest award to Cordell Hull; United States aid to build up Peru's National Library after a fire; close cooperation in the establishment and early years of the United Nations; the signing of bilateral defense and technical aid agreements; and a greatly increased cultural exchange program. But, with an eye toward avoiding troubles in the future, where that can be accom-

---

[36] *Revista Peruana de Derecho Internacional*, VI (1946), pp. 314-315. During the tempest in the Peruvian press, the Senate at Lima asked the Peruvian office of Foreign Relations for a report: *Revista Peruana de Derecho Internacional*, VI (1946), p. 310.

[37] *Revista Peruana de Derecho Internacional*, VI (1946), p. 316. *Excelsior*, October 1946, p. 7, pointed out that the United States had lived up to its commitments as a good neighbor.

[38] *Revista Peruana de Derecho Internacional*, VII (1947), p. 123.

[39] *New York Times*, June 8, July 13, August 17, October 26, 1947. *Revista Peruana de Derecho Internacional*, VI (1946), pp. 182-184, 185.

plished, we should call attention to some of the events and developments evidencing less than harmonious relations in operation.

At times, Alberto Ulloa criticized the United States for wanting a "political" settlement of matters rather than a settlement of "justice." At the same time, he complained of the northern nation's attempts to dominate certain continental matters.[40] At the close of the Second World War, Peru was generally in accordance with the United States on hemispheric policies, but one point on which the two nations did not agree was the stand to be taken toward Argentina at the time the Department of State issued its anti-Peron *Blue Book*. First, it is pertinent that we note the background for this development, in which Peru and some other nations would not follow the leadership of Washington.

An amicable Argentine-Peruvian relationship was a well-established fact, and had been for many years, when havoc struck at Pearl Harbor.[41] In 1942 the two nations signed a commercial treaty which provided for "most favored" nation provisions and other trade exchange arrangements. Press reaction in Lima to this trade pact with Argentina was favorable, although not of signal importance. As official condemnation of German submarine attacks on ships of various American nations was made, an increasing concern over Argentine-United States negotiations became evident. The Peruvian *Journal of International Law* carried reports of the official requests and replies between Buenos Aires and Washington.[42] Argentina formally requested that the United States seriously consider the imbalance in South American armaments parity it was causing, asking that military aid of a proportionate amount be extended to the Argentine. Hull's response for the United States was sympathetically treated in the *Revista Peruana de Derecho Internacional*. Other published responses generally supported Hull's position when he denied arms aid to Argentina and when he rejected the Buenos Aires complaint that the United States stance hurt Argentina's relations with other American nations. An article published in the fall of 1944 admitted that Hull's stand might be exaggerated but did not object

---

[40] Ulloa, *Posición internacional del Peru*, pp. 381-384.

[41] Manuel A. de Elías Bonnemaison, "Historia de las Relaciones Diplomáticas entre Peru y Argentina," *Revista Peruana de Derecho Internacional*, III (1943), pp. 167-183, 303-311; IV (1944), pp. 70-79, 246-252.

[42] *Ibid.*, III, pp. 349, 355; also "La Nota Cordell Hull y el Canciller Argentino Storni," *Revista de Derecho y Ciencias Politicas*, VII (Lima, 1943), pp. 828-829.

to Washington's policy in general, not even when United States
ships were prohibited from going to Argentine ports. Attention was
focused on Hull's statement that Argentina's position in the war
encouraged Axis attacks in the Western Hemisphere,[43] and the
problem of espionage was also mentioned. Early in 1944, the Peruvian government claimed that Germans and Japanese had planned
a pro-Nazi coup at Lima. The conspirators were charged with proposing to stage anti-Jewish outbreaks and then take over during the
ensuing disorder. Very little evidence was offered to back up the
charges.

A skeptical note entered the picture in late 1944 and early 1945
with reference to Washington's strong stand and to Spruille Braden's
overtures toward "intervention" in Argentine domestic politics. At
the same time it was mentioned that several United States senators
were unwilling to back Braden in this. Luis Casalino Lancho, writing
in *Revista Peruana de Derecho Internacional,* could not envision a
completely satisfactory solution.[44] If the United States maintained
its rigid position and Argentina remained obdurate, the Argentine
would be excluded from regional activities. Although Casalino
tended to agree with Hull's pronouncements, he did not like the
prospect of Buenos Aires having to yield to Washington in order
to take its rightful place in the hemispheric circle. A more determined stand for Peruvian independence of Washington developed
out of the United States refusal to negotiate the Treaty of Inter-
American Mutual Defense with Peron's government. During the
war, the United States charged, Argentina had been a menace to
the security of the inter-American system. The Peruvian position
held that the conditions and circumstances treated in the *Blue Book*
were no longer existent in Argentina. Emphasis was given to the
fact that the Argentine elections of February 1946 had been strictly
legal.[45] Peru did not think that the new Argentine government of

[43] "Crónica International," *Revista de Derecho y Ciencias Políticas,* VIII
(1944), p. 413.
   [44] Luis Casalino Lancho, "En Torno a la Cuestión Argentina," *Revista Peruana
de Derecho Internacional,* IV (1944), pp. 265-267.
   [45] "Respuesta de la Cancilleria del Peru a la Consulta del Gobierno de los
Estados Unidos Sobre el Libro Azul," in *ibid.,* VI (1946), pp. 182-184. At
one point a Reuter's news report opined that the new government in Buenos
Aires would inspire principles of liberty and democracy. In 1943 there had been
publicity given to a questionnaire of the Argentine Institute of International
Law which might have set a positive tone. Questions dealt with the following:

Peron would be hostile to the inter-American system. Contrary to the policy suggested in Washington, Lima believed that confidence should be extended the new government. On this matter, the foreign ministry in the "City of Kings" refused to follow Washington's lead. By mid-1946, Peru and Argentina had signed agreements to facilitate travel and trade, and relations were rapidly returning to the same pleasant conditions which had existed before the war.

Because *Aprismo* had been critical of United States activities in the southern hemisphere before the Second World War, it is relevant to trace that party's views on the United States-Argentine difficulties during the critical period at the close of the war. A careful reading of the *Apra* Party newspaper, *La Tribuna*, for 1945 and 1946 shows a consistently pro-United States point of view and an over-all tone of criticism toward Argentina up until the time Peron was legally elected.[46] José R. Tamborini was upheld as the leader of democracy in contrast to the dictator Peron. According to *La Tribuna*, Peron's totalitarianism was identified with developments in Moscow, and Moscow was not to be trusted. Robert J. Alexander's *Communism in Latin America* does not support this *Apra* interpretation, since Alexander's account did not reflect a Peron appeal for communist support until March 1945.

Until March 1946, the stated position of *Apra* was one of commendation of Hull and of criticism of Peron, although José Gabriel, a bitter critic of Peron, did point out, as a guest editorialist, that United States businessmen had negotiated with Argentine tyrants when it was to their economic advantage.[47] Early in 1946 there appeared a note suggesting that Washington take care not to intervene in Argentina, and by April 1 Manuel Seoane believed it time to recognize Peron because he had been legally elected.[48] *Apra's* support

---

creation of a world organization after the war was ended; an international police force to prevent aggressive warfare; provisions for the new organization to develop greater financial and commercial exchange. See *Revista Peruana de Derecho Internacional*, III (1943), pp. 312-315. In 1947 Peru offered its suggestions for a system to stabilize prices, to standardize the monetary system, and to provide a hemisphere clearinghouse for products. See *ibid.*, VII (1947), pp. 243-245.

[46] *La Tribuna*, December 28, 1945, p. 5; December 29, 30, pp. 5, 10; March 2, 1946, p. 5; April 12, 1946, p. 8; April 13, 1946, p. 9; and many other issues.

[47] *Ibid.*, March 14, 1946, p. 5.

[48] *Ibid.*, January 26, 1946, p. 2; February 2, 1946, p. 4; February 8, 1946, p. 3; March 28, 1946, pp. 4-5; March 26, 1946, p. 2; and many others.

of Washington against Buenos Aires did not signify its backing in other international matters, although the support was there in most respects. In March 1946 Ciro Alegría lamented that American nations would defend democracy across the ocean and yet remain indifferent to the harsh tyranny of Somoza in Nicaragua.[49] Seoane, a Peruvian delegate at the United Nations, said in April 1946 that it was foolish for the United States to think it possible to lead Franco away from tyranny in Spain.[50] Later developments indicate that official Peru was less anti-Franco than its *Aprista* delegate had been two years earlier (*Revista Peruana*, 1948). At the same time that the *Aprista* newspapers of 1945 and 1946 were critical of communism in Moscow or Chile, they were laudatory of Rómulo Betancourt's successes in Venezuela. Peru's strongest political party was generally consistent in holding out a hand to democracy and turning a cold cheek to totalitarianism.

Within a few years other minor difficulties developed between the United States and Peru. The coalition government of President Bustamante (1945-1948) was faced with economic and political problems. This in turn set off moderate criticism of "Yankee" policies. Because of reduced purchases by the United States and lower world prices for exports, Peru's economy was hurt. Some generally "pro-Yankee" publications claimed that the United States wanted Peru to help build up Europe by selling Peruvian products at reduced prices.[51] Minister of *Hacienda y Comercio* Luis Echecopar García, and historian Jorge Basadre (a later minister of education and director of the National Library) have expressed discontent that the United States as well as Peruvian commercial financial interests did not lend their support to the democratic and civilian government of Bustamante.[52] At the same time, friction between the *Aprista* elements of the government and the Bustamante forces grew.

Apra had gradually come into the good graces of the United States government. During the Second World War the People's Party, as it was called, had supported the Allied nations and attacked the Axis cause. According to Luis Alberto Sánchez, Roose-

[49] *Ibid.*, March 2, 1946, p. 5.

[50] *Ibid.*, April 21, 1946, p. 4.

[51] *Excelsior*, April-May 1948, p. 5. *Aprista* papers in the provinces spoke well of United States aid operations and at the same time lashed United States economic imperialism, *Chan Chan*, Trujillo, October 18, 1946, p. 3, and *Hechos*, Chiclayo, August 21, 1947.

[52] Personal interviews: James C. Carey, Lima, Peru, April 26, 1962.

velt's Good Neighbor postures toward Latin America had inclined *Apra* in the direction of supporting the Allies as early as the close of 1938.[53] This, however, did not signify a renunciation of *Aprismo's* anti-imperialism which had, since 1924, protested "Yankee" political and economic aggression. Late in 1938, Haya de la Torre published in Chile a pamphlet entitled "La Buena Vecindad? Garantía Definitiva?" which professed faith in Franklin Delano Roosevelt, but proposed a wait-and-see attitude for the indefinite future. In 1941, *La defensa continental* by the *Aprista* chief encouraged both Americas to oppose totalitarianism for, even though the economics of the two (the United States and Latin America) were not on a solid relationship, they shared the common grounds of interest in democracy. Haya de la Torre declared that he had not been converted "into a friend of the United States from being a foe." "I have never been a foe of the United States but of United States economic imperialism." [54] Ambassador John Campbell White, sometime in 1944 or early 1945, began to look favorably upon *Aprismo*.[55] Ambassadors

[53] *La Tribuna*, and Luis Alberto Sánchez, "A New Interpretation of the History of America," *The Hispanic American Historical Review*, XXIII (August 1943), p. 445. Sánchez, influential *Aprista*, has had a distinguished record which includes his numerous writings and the administration of San Marcos University as its rector. This point is made also in Luis Alberto Sánchez's *Haya de la Torre y el Apra* (Santiago, 1954). In the same account, it is indicated that the United States officials were unofficially communicating with *Apra* as early as 1942.

[54] Víctor Raúl Haya de la Torre, *La defensa continental* (Buenos Aires, 1942), p. 135 (reprint of letter to editor of *Diario de Costa Rica*).

[55] In December 1944 Ambassador White expressed such a view to this writer during a meeting in Callao. *Aprista* international policy changed with changing conditions, and early in the war dropped its biting criticism of the United States economic policies and supported the Allies in general. Haya de la Torre said this stand was taken because the *Apristas* were pro-democracy and looked upon totalitarianism as a serious threat. See *New York Times*, December 25, 1942, p. 16, and August 15, 1943, p. 38; *La Tribuna*, November 28, 1945, p. 9, and November 29, 1945, p. 4. A lengthy article in *La Trinchera*, Lima (coalition paper: *Con el Frente Democratico Nacional*), August 4, 1945, pp. 1, 2, shows the softened attitude which had been adopted toward theoretical capitalism. *La Tribuna*, October 22, 1945, p. 1, and October 23, 1945, p. 1, demonstrated real enthusiasm for Rómulo Betancourt and his Venezuelan reform movement of the *Acción Democrática*. Manuel Seoane, *Aprista* leader, and Betancourt had been in exile together in Chile. The United States Department of State would have done well at that time to have noted the *Aprista* position toward Betancourt's program. Emphasis was given to Harold J. Laski's statement that communist expressions in favor of democracy were not genuine, *La Tribuna*, November 29, 1945, p. 4, but the United States nonintervention stance was appreciated,

W. D. Pawley and Prentice Cooper, June 1945 to June 1948, were sympathetic to *Aprismo*. One of the first of the conservative Peruvian writers to point out this rapprochement of the United States and *Apra* was a rightist and bitter anti-*Aprista*, Carlos Miró Quesada.[56] Miró Quesada wrote his views in the year 1945, and they went to the publisher in early 1946. Since Peruvians were accustomed to looking upon *Aprismo* in extreme terms of black or white, the rift which grew between Bustamante and Haya de la Torre tended to weaken Peru's government. In the long run, however, it was economic and not political difficulties which created the bulk of Peru's disappointment with Washington.

The reason for this is not difficult to find. Taking the two years 1936 and 1952 as years which were fairly representative of prewar and postwar trading conditions, we find that the war shifted considerable Peruvian trade into United States control and created a balance favorable to the United States. Statistics published by the United States Department of Commerce in 1961 show what happened. Between 1936 and 1952, the entire world's exports to Peru increased 22.2 times on a sol basis or 5.8 times on a dollar basis.[57] For the sixteen years following 1939, the United States percentage of Peru's total world imports was always someplace between 50 and 63.4 per cent.[58] Singling out the United States share of imports to Peru, we see that they increased, 1946 to 1952, 39.17 times in soles, or slightly over 10 times when figured in dollars.

In analyzing Peruvian export figures, it is important to keep in mind that, at that time, approximately 30 per cent of Peru's export business belonged to foreigners, chiefly United States citizens.[59] Peruvian exports to the entire world between 1936 and 1952 increased almost 11 times in soles or 2.88 times in dollars. On a sol

---

La Tribuna, December 2, 1945, p. 5. Headlines were provided for a State Department notice to United States companies to refrain from mixing in Latin-American politics, *La Tribuna*, November 29, 1945, p. 2.

[56] Carlos Miró Quesada Laos, *Pueblo en crisis* (Buenos Aires, 1946), p 173.

[57] *Foreign Trade of Peru, 1958-1960*, World Trade Information Service, Department of Commerce (Washington, 1961), p. 1.

[58] R. F. Rodríguez, *Market for U.S. Products in Peru*, Department of Commerce (Washington, 1961), p. 17.

[59] Memorandum which the Peruvian Minister of *Hacienda y Comercio*, Dr. Luis Echecopar García, sent to the American Bondholders (1947), a copy of which was directed to James C. Carey with an accompanying letter dated November 10, 1947 at Lima.

basis, the increase of Peru's exports to the United States, 1936-1952, was 15.83 whereas it was 4.2 times in dollar figures. A study of Peru's postwar economy in comparison to prewar times shows that it was beneficial to the United States even as the Peruvian economy was experiencing considerable growth. The index of real increase between 1942 and 1952 was from 100 to 143 in national income.[60] But, with decreased exports, increased cost of living, inflation, and a scarcity of dollar reserves, Peru found the period from 1946 to the outbreak of the Korean War to be a very difficult time.

In the years following the war, United States investments continued to grow, so that by 1953 the northern nation held 74 per cent of the direct foreign investment in Peru.[61] When Great Britain's 17 per cent was added to this figure, the total of the two Anglo-Saxon countries' investments stood at 91 per cent. In mining, United States interests owned $148,000,000 of $149,000,000 invested on long-term direct investment in 1953, and in petroleum it was $98,000,000 of $103,000,000 of foreign investment. For agriculture it stood at $12,-000,000 of $15,000,000. Portfolio investment gave the United States a margin of $85,000,000 of $110,000,000 of all foreign interests in that area.

At the end of 1954, as compared with the close of 1940, the wartime changes in amounts invested were significant. The following figures are shown in thousands of dollars for direct United States investments: manufacturing went from $4,998 to $19,000; trade jumped from $3,040 to $22,000; and mining and smelting increased from $20,182 to $171,000 (merely book value, not real value).[62] Agriculture, petroleum, finance and various other areas of investment also underwent a sharp increase in the period of the war and the years immediately following it.

The unpaid Leguía loans of the 1920's continued to plague relations between the two nations, as American bondholders tried to insist on a settlement of some sort at the very time that Peru was seeking additional credit. The New York Times (December 6, 1945) cited Ambassador William D. Pawley as saying that relations between the two nations had been complicated by the default on the

[60] Basic Data on the Economy of Peru, World Trade Information Service, Department of Commerce (Washington, 1960), p. 3.
[61] Investment in Peru: Basic Information for United States Businessmen, Department of Commerce (Washington, 1957), p. 5.
[62] Ibid.

debt. At that time, of a $150,000,000 foreign debt, some $66,000,000 was interest due. As early as 1946, *Excelsior* magazine had complained that there was pressure to collect the highly questionable Leguía loan debt.[63] In 1945 the *Ministerio de Hacienda y Comercio* had failed to move the Peruvian Congress to action when it tried to work out a settlement between the Peruvian government and the Bondholders Protective Council. In 1947, the *Ministerio* finally obtained congressional support for a settlement which, perversely, was turned down by the bondholders.[64] The main difficulty centered around the rate of interest to be paid on the outstanding principal. Most of the Leguía loans were still unpaid. Peru wanted the ultimate rate, to be reached in the seventh year, to be established at a figure no higher than 2.5 per cent. Bustamante's Congress had refused to accept 3 per cent in 1945, a figure which was acceptable to the Bondholders Council.[65] These loans, unsound and unethical in the 1920's, had originally called for from nearly 7 to 7.5 per cent interest.

Also complicating the matter were some slight differences over how to handle interest in arrears and a question of clarification of the service charge payments in dollars. The 1947 Peruvian offer of settlement would have allowed the bondholders, for the first year, 1 per cent interest on the face value of the bonds which, in turn, amounted to about 6 per cent on the then existing market value. Achievement of the 2.5 per cent on face value would have meant approximately 15 per cent on market value. Although these early negotiations were not successful of themselves, they were instrumental in leading to a settlement. Before an agreement could be reached, there was considerable debate in the Peruvian Congress. In 1952 a new fifteen-year loan was redrawn, at a low interest rate, to take care of the interest in arrears as of the end of 1946,[66] and, beginning on January 1, 1953, Peru agreed to pay 3 per cent on the face value of the foreign debt.

[63] *Excelsior*, January 1946, p. 3. This publication charged that when interest and exchange differences were figured, United States bondholders were trying to collect at the rate of 1,111 to 230 borrowed. For an English translation of the remarks of the minister of finance and commerce in the Chamber of Deputies and in the Senate, see "The Foreign Debt of Peru," *Andean Air Mail and Peruvian Times, Supplement*, Lima, June 13-20, 1952, pp. i-iv. hereafter cited as *Peruvian Times*.

[64] Memorandum which the Peruvian minister of *Hacienda y Comercio* sent to the American Bondholders (1947).

[65] *Ibid.*

[66] *Peruvian Times, Supplement*, June 13-20, p. iv.

Looking back upon the Leguía loans, we see that they proved to be a thorny matter of long duration. What had started in the 1920's as a contract between private United States investment concerns and the Peruvian government turned out to be a complex factor in international matters for some forty years.

We have already noted that economic action was one of the varied instruments of war used against the Axis. While wartime technical assistance was designed for Peru's economic development, it was also geared to fit Allied needs. Lt. Col. Edward A. Westphal, the first United States chief of field party in Peru, stated that "a considerable proportion of these cooperative activities were aimed at facilitating the extraction or the production of raw materials needed to further the war effort." [67] Two excellent examples of this kind of co-operation would be the Agricultural Experiment Station, which was located near Tingo Maria, and *Scipa* (Inter-American Co-operative Food Production Service). Another service, *Scisp* (Inter-American Co-operative Service in Public Health) was also initiated.

Although Scipa was formally established May 19, 1943, its real origin can be dated some thirteen months earlier.[68] When the Allied powers were cut off from the Far Eastern jungle products, the United States looked toward the Amazon region for rubber, barbasco, rotenona, quinine and such items. Near Tingo Maria, by agreement of the agricultural departments in Lima and Washington, an agricultural experiment station was established in April 1942. At the same time, the station was to engage in experimental work with the objective of increasing agricultural production in that region of the jungle.

Then in May 1943 The Institute of Inter-American Affairs (incorporated in the State of Delaware), in agreement with an agency of the Peruvian Department of Agriculture, signed a bilateral technical aid agreement which established the *servicio* known as Scipa. The purpose of the contract was explained in the title of the agency

[67] Lt. Col. Edward A. Westphal, "A Report on the Operations of the Servicio Cooperativo Inter-Americano de Salud Publica and on the activities of the Division of Health and Sanitation of the Institute of Inter-American Affairs in Peru from July 1942 to December 1945" (Lima: unpublished manuscript, 1946), p. 1; also quoted in the *Annals of the American Academy of Political and Social Science*, CCCXXXIV (March 1961), p. 16.

[68] *El servicio cooperativo interamericano de producción de alimentos* (prepared by the Information Service of the United States Embassy, Lima, n.d., but approximately 1958), p. 1 (hereafter cited as *El Servicio Scipa*). See also *Excelsior*, May- June 1949, p. 49.

122   Peru and the United States: 1900-1962

itself: "Inter-American Co-operative Food Production Service." The first agreement called for both the Peruvian and the United States agencies to furnish $300,000.[69] In addition, the Institute of Inter-American Affairs was to provide funds for salaries and travel of the members of the mission. Peru was to cancel out customs charges for Scipa importations of equipment, material, and accessories used in the program.

One of the first projects of Scipa was an attempt to bring about a widespread use of selected seeds, especially of potatoes, wheat, rice, and beans,[70] but early activity was limited to little more than encouraging the cultivation of Victory Gardens. In general, the *servicio* was favorably received by Peruvians, although there was considerable criticism of its specific operations and occasional misuse of funds.[71] Six and seven years after the program's inception, two Peruvian ex-ministers of agriculture wrote articles praising the program, but since both men were engaged, to some extent, in carrying out the project, their view was not entirely objective.

The other significant technical aid program introduced during the war was that of Scisp, established in July 1942. Scisp, the health co-operative *servicio*, comprised a program of training in public health and supervised the application of the training in a practical manner. The major purpose was that of providing Peruvians with greater experience in the application of more and better systems and methods of combating diseases. It was a joint *servicio*, but in the

[69] "Resolución Suprema, No. 286 (Peruvian) *Ministerio de Agricultura*" (Lima, May 20, 1943), p. 1, photostatic copy of which was provided this writer by the *Ministerio de Relaciones Exteriores*. Agreement signed by Peruvian Minister of Agriculture, Godofredo A. Labarthe, and United States Ambassador R. Henry Norweb.

[70] *El Servicio Scipa*, pp. 2-3.

[71] "Sample Survey of Public Opinion." In April 1962 this writer conducted a survey (questionnaire and interview of 200 Peruvians). A high proportion of responses reported Scipa as having been "very helpful to Peru in proportion to the time it has operated. . . ." Of the 181 questionnaires distributed, 157 were completed and returned. Of the 157 returned, 109 listed Scipa above cultural exchange activities and private businesses as having been helpful to Peru. All but two of the twenty persons interviewed reported Scipa "positive." This was not a random sample of Peruvian citizens. Probably one half of the persons responding had had (or their parents had had) a positive relationship with United States private business enterprise in Peru. Also, a majority had completed at least one half of the secondary education program. See also Chapter 8, and *Excelsior*, May-June 1949, pp. 5, 13.

first two years, 1942 and 1943, Peru contributed only a small part of the total budget.

As with Scipa, Scisp was first concerned with the jungle area because of military needs. One of the first great projects proposed was the creation of fifteen dispensaries in the Department of Loreto, which lay across the main Peruvian tributaries to the Amazon.[72] Due to the many difficulties and the high cost, only five of the fifteen were developed. In order to provide some service for the other river areas of Loreto as planned, nine medically-equipped launches were put into operation. Some of these launches were especially constructed in Iquitos, capital of the jungle department. Another project, which, although not entirely the work of Scisp, received great impulse from it, was the draining and swamp-clearing work around Chimbote, a coastal city situated midway between Lima and the border of Ecuador. During the war years, the *servicio* emphasized the northern coastal region as well as the jungle.[73] This may have been due either to the industrial possibilities of the area or to the fact that petroleum fields and an air base were situated in the north.

Postwar Peru, floundering from the loss of foreign markets, was hopeful that something similar to Marshall Plan assistance might be directed southward from Washington. Existing conditions encouraged the continuation and expansion of these extensive bilateral technical aid projects begun during the war, and other programs have been started since that time as well. Scipa, however, was the program which appeared to warrant the greatest emphasis in any projected continuation. It was not, therefore, permitted to lapse, and this co-operative service spent $12,595,627.20 from May 19, 1943, when it began, until July 30, 1958. Subtracting a figure equivalent to salaries and travel expenses, one would have approximately the amount expended by the Peruvian government for the *servicio* over the same period. (Further mention of the program is made in Chapter 8.)

Between 1943 and 1958 the following results were obtained under the Scipa program. Quarantine stations were established, farm

[72] *El servicio cooperativo interamericano de salud pública* (prepared by the Information Service of the U.S. Embassy, Lima, n.d., but approximately 1958), pp. 2-3; hereafter cited as *El Servicio Scisp.*

[73] *Fojas expositivas sobre el punto cuatro en el Peru* (prepared by the Information Service of the United States Embassy, Lima, n.d., but appears to have been printed in 1958 or 1959), p. 16 (hereafter cited as *Fojas Expositivas*).

machinery pools created, economic studies made, and storage facilities provided. Improved livestock breeds were introduced, and sanitary controls established for certain livestock groups. Encouragement was extended to a program of farm demonstration agents and an agricultural extension service, while aid to increase fisheries and livestock production was proffered. Attempts were made to help provide farmers with better seeds, tools, insecticides and equipment, and a diversity of agricultural experiments was conducted.[74] Up to the present, various experiments in agronomy and animal husbandry have also been conducted at the Tingo Maria experiment station, directed from its beginning to March 1946 by Dr. Benjamin J. Birdsall.

The activities of Scisp also continued into the postwar period. During the fifteen years after 1943, Peru assumed more and more of the cost required to sustain the projects until finally that aspect of the program cost Peru more than it did the United States.[75] From the program's origin up to mid-1958, the United States government had contributed $3,450,000.[76]

Over the years, the activities of Scisp have included local health demonstration programs, hospital construction and operation, health centers in back-country areas, and mobile health units. Reorganization and strengthening of the National Institute of Public Health have been instituted, and nutritional work and sanitary engineering have been undertaken. Nurses and personnel for various areas of public health have been trained.[77] Scisp's concern with the development of human capital was made plain early in its educational program.[78] Trainees under the health *servicio* up to the middle of 1958 included 166 professional personnel who had received training in the United States or other countries; some 468 Peruvians who had received for-

---

[74] *El Servicio Scipa*, pp. 3-23. See also Allen J. Ellender, United States senator from the State of Louisiana, *A Review of United States Government Operations in Latin America 1958* (Washington, 1959), pp. 284-285. This, a formal report, was submitted to the Senate Committee on Appropriations dealing with the foreign operations of the United States government (hereafter cited as *Ellender Report*).

[75] *El Servicio Scisp*, p. 15.

[76] *Ellender Report*, pp. 290-302.

[77] *Ibid.*

[78] *Ibid.*, pp. 302-303. Scisp received complimentary reviews, as in *Extra*, Lima, No. 149, January 21, 1958, p. 23; *Excelsior*, January-March 1948, pp. 12-13, 18; and *El Comercio*, Lima, October 18, 1960, p. 3.

mal training under Scisp facilities in Peru; and 34 persons from other Latin-American countries who had received formal or in-service preparation through Scisp in Peru.

It is difficult to determine how much impetus the war gave to the establishment of co-operative activities in general, or, how great their contribution was to the war effort. Scipa and Scisp were, of course, significant. A third co-operative *servicio*, Secpane (Peruvian North American Co-operative Education Service), was established in April 1944. Since the objectives of its program were not directly related to the war efforts, this *servicio* is discussed in Chapter 8.

It is evident that some independent agencies—those identified with unofficial United States general cultural interests—were more influential in making friends for the United States in Peru during the war than was Secpane. One facet of the Protestant and Catholic church activity sponsored from north of the Rio Grande was directed toward private schooling in Peru. These educational institutions, although not directly concerned with propaganda dissemination, were counterbalances to the educational institutions which the Axis peoples owned and operated in the nation. Schools like Callao High School, Colegio Andino, Lima High School for Girls, Santa Maria, and Villa Maria had an appreciable influence on Peruvian public opinion during the war, although it cannot be measured accurately. The thousands of graduates of these high schools and of other United States-oriented schools in Peru were more apt than not to be pro-United States in the period leading up to the war and, again, during the hostilities.[79]

A variety of other unofficial associations and agencies, such as the Y.M.C.A., medical businesses, and cultural organizations, had created some recognizable prestige. The Y.M.C.A., as well as the educational institutions, has often been considered a definite factor in improving relations between the United States and Peru. In a nation with a greater population and a stronger public school system, these factors would not have been as significant as they were in Peru.[80] In 1941 there were no public or official United States-sponsored li-

[79] "Sample Survey," Carey.

[80] *Ibid.* Under the question as to which foundations, associations, agencies, business concerns, organizations or other activities had achieved notable work in improving Peruvian-United States relations, the Y.M.C.A. was often listed, but it was not listed as frequently as were Point Four, educational institutions, and the *Instituto Cultural Peruano-Norteamericano.*

brary or library facilities in Peru for either English or Spanish-speaking people.[81] During the war, the *Instituto Cultural Peruano-Norteamericano* did start its library. The *Instituto* exerted a definite influence in various ways during the war period, but because of the later emphasis on cultural exchange and its ties to other general United States aid programs the *Instituto* is discussed later in this study.

On critical matters Peru and the United States had co-operated well during the great conflict. It appeared that the war might have helped draw the weak nation and the powerful nation into a closer understanding. Peru's economy had received not only a beneficial stimulant but also an adverse push toward specialization in minerals and in the direction of cotton emphasis. However, for the size of the country its economy was still one of the most diversified in all of Latin America. It gradually became evident that the "Yankees" had gained a greater share of Peru's regular peacetime market. After the war, *Limeños* seemed to think that Washington owed a bit more obligation to Peru's economy. It was not clear that Washington accepted any outright responsibility, but the evidence of the technical aid programs suggested such a possibility. It was possible that a little more concern (more than before the war) for Peru's economic welfare had developed in the Anglo-American government of the north. Only time could clear up the complexities of this relationship.

Political problems entered on the scene to pose new questions when Washington did not provide enthusiastic support for Bustamante's civilian democratic government. General Manuel Odría's rise to power encouraged domestic and foreign concerns, particularly United States interests and those Peruvians associated with them in the export of minerals. Luis Alberto Sánchez claimed that International Petroleum Company and other dollar interests benefited by the military coup.[82] There was some Peruvian criticism of the economic boost which Peruvians and United States "exporters" received from the Odría government.

The war gave rise to other developments which would later on

---

[81] The American Women's Literary Club and the Country Club in Lima maintained a small collection of books, but these were not widely used nor were they easily accessible to Peruvian citizens. See *Living Conditions in Peru*, World Trade Information Service, Department of Commerce (Washington, 1958), p. 7.

[82] Sánchez, *Haya de la Torre y el Apra*, pp. 460, 462; also *El Comercio*, December 1953 and January 1954.

be of concern to the United States. The Communist Party had given Prado's administration "full backing." According to Juan P. Luna, a very active Peruvian communist and "agent" of Vicente Lombardo Toledano, Prado's regime was supported because it had the correct stance toward the war.[83] Before the close of the first Manuel Prado administration, the communists were allowed to publish a small paper, *Democracia y Trabajo*. As communists worked to help defeat the Axis, their position in Peru improved—although not in comparison with the *Apristas*, who grew even more rapidly —and they gained more freedom of action. At the end of the war, then, there were various reasons why "Uncle Sam" could ill afford to ignore social and political matters in Peru to the extent that he had in the last half of the 1930's.

[83] Robert J. Alexander, *Communism in Latin America* (New Brunswick, Rutgers University Press, 1957), p. 230. Eudocio Ravines, *The Yenan Way* (New York, Charles Scribner's Sons, 1951), p. 314, claims that Luna was the agent of Lombardo Toledano. For a comment on *The Yenan Way*, see fn. 58 of Chapter 3.

8: THE UNITED STATES ASSISTANCE PROGRAMS

Preparatory to the discussion of technical assistance and financial aid programs, let us consider the conditions peculiar to Peru which clarify the amount of assistance it might expect, as well as its potentialities for the use of that assistance. The wartime tendency of the United States to encourage a concentration of Peruvian production in a few commodities has been mentioned earlier. More important was Peru's awareness of its dependence upon the United States economically and, to a lesser extent, in military affairs. Economic subordination was evident to anyone who understood the extent of United States private and public operations in Peru. That country's dependence upon the United States for exports and exchange for imports has already been demonstrated. Since 1925, the United States has been the main provider of foreign funds, both public and private. Military aid has been a significant prop to the government. For its size, the nation has received more military assistance in dollars than has any other nation in Latin America, as will be demonstrated in this chapter. Peru, in turn, has more often than not been a supporter of United States policies in hemispheric and world developments. Examples of this are: (1) Peru's rapid response in support of President Truman's actions in defense of South Korea; (2) Peru's support of the United States at the O.A.S. meeting in Caracas in 1954; and (3) Peru's motion in the O.A.S., July 1960, to consider Soviet relations with Cuba a "menace" to hemispheric welfare. In general, the foreign office at Lima has aligned itself with Washington on important issues brought up at Inter-American Conferences and at the Meetings of Foreign Ministers. By no means had the people of Peru agreed with their government's stand in earlier years on such matters as the United States Marines in Nicaragua or Lima's support of Washington at the Havana Conference in 1928. Ulloa, through the journal of international law, later let it be known that some resentment of Washington's aggressive, unilateral interpretation of the Monroe Doctrine always existed. Haya de la Torre's *A donde va indoamerica?* also made these points. But with the rise of European totalitarianism and the Second World War falling so close upon the heels of the Good Neighbor policy, *Aprismo* found itself championing United States causes as it had never done before.

Under these conditions of both official support and considerable popular support for the United States, it was not strange that Peru, as a matter of course, had expected aid to be forthcoming from north of the Rio Grande. Some Peruvians were inclined to check the figures, to note that their country was fourth from the bottom of the twenty-two hemispheric nations in terms of gross national product per capita, and look northward for relief.[1] Luis Rose Ugarte, Minister of Agriculture in June 1946, informed visiting former President Herbert Hoover that Peru was having a difficult time feeding itself and that farm equipment was needed to help with the task. Hoover was concerned with aid for Europe then, and Washington did not have a vital interest in the problems of Latin America. Although there has been some dissatisfaction with the amount of assistance received as compared with other O.A.S. nations, Peru has been granted aid about in proportion to its population figures.[2] In economic aid and total aid, Peru has ranked fifth in Latin America; in military assistance, Peru received the second highest amount— Brazil ranking first. During the fifteen years from 1946 to 1960, Peru has been granted over $283,000,000 in the form of grants and loans for economic purposes.[3] During the same period, Peru received over $94,000,000 for military grants and loans. (This figure may be too low, due to the fact that International Co-operation Administration funds also went to Peru's armed forces.) The net influence of both areas of aid must be reduced considerably when one considers

[1] George I. Blanksten, "The Aspirations for Economic Development," *Annals of the American Academy of Political and Social Science*, CCCXXXIV (March 1961), p. 11.

[2] Luis Felipe Guerra Martiniere, a Peruvian writer, has critically commented that the tendency of the United States to consider merely commercial interchange and military defense as the bases of relations between the two nations was too limited. He insisted that the two peoples had much in common in their outlook on political matters and in the general ways of life. See *Mercurio Peruano, Revista Mensual de Ciencias Sociales y Letras*, XXXIX, No. 372 (Lima, April 1958), pp. 161-162. For Rose's interview with Hoover, see *La Tribuna*, Lima, June 4, 1946, p. 7.

[3] *Operations Report*, International Co-operation Administration, F Y, Office of Statistics and Reports, Issue 1960, No. 4 (Washington, November 23, 1960).

that there were reciprocating conditions attached to part of it and that a sizable share of the loan credits were tied to the purchases of United States products or services.

In attempting to trace the over-all lines of the United States assistance programs to Peru, we start by noting that Peru has expected considerable aid and has received considerable aid. It is not simple, however, to determine just what this was, or what it has meant. Voltaire said, "It is a wise child who knows his own father." The United States aid program (AID, as it has been called recently) leaves equally unclear the question as to what extent it was Peruvian and to what extent United States needs which fathered the program's "children." To a degree, both were responsible for various projects. Technical assistance starting under the Institute of Inter-American Affairs, Point Four, Operations Missions, International Co-operation Administration (I.C.A.), and later the Alliance for Progress plan were "all alike and yet different somehow." They were all alike in that the purpose of each was to help the United States and the people of Peru at the same time. They differed in their means of achieving this and in the extent to which each would contribute to any significant changes within Peruvian society itself.

Because of the complexity of the issue there was some confusion as to the parentage of any one of the major programs. Security problems spurred the inauguration of technical assistance programs in the Second World War, when the question of Axis infiltration worried the two nations. The expanding influence of communism over the world and the growth of economic problems in the United States aided in the conception of Point Four. Those notions plus surplus agricultural and industrial products north of the border helped in the establishment of various aspects of Operations Missions. Part of the aim of aid to Peru has been that of selling American goods, arranging for credit, and maintaining United States influence over economic and defense matters in general. Hemispheric welfare and security questions are often closely bound up with financial or industrial developments. Castroism and a concern for Peru's basic social problems were both instrumental in fathering the Alliance for Progress scheme. Some of the changes in names and in emphasis over the years in each program can be traced to changes in personnel in Washington or in Lima and to political change-overs in the administrations of the United States. Peruvian problems, such as a rapidly increasing population and a growing social discontent, have also created pressure on the government at Lima to request help from Washington. This, coupled with the fact that Peru enjoys a diversity of undeveloped resources, encouraged the establishment of an aid program. The special interest groups of Peru —particularly the social elite, the economic oligarchy, and the military—often welcomed United States aid as one means of maintaining the conservative status quo from 1900 to 1960. The stated objectives of the Alliance for Progress may seriously alter this, if they are achieved, but that is a question of the present and the future— not one of the past.

Foreign aid to Peru in the Second World War and afterwards came into being under the Mutual Security Program. Early in 1942 the Institute for Inter-American Affairs was established under the Co-ordinator of Inter-American Affairs. This subsidiary government corporation had, as a purpose, co-operative health and sanitation programs to aid in increasing the production of vitally needed war materials. With the establishment of an experimental rubber station in 1942 came the introduction of a co-operative health program to fulfill some of the objectives of the Institute.

Between 1942 and 1960, total United States foreign assistance to Peru, obligations and commitments, came to approximately $336,000,-000, an amount covering most of the officially approved aid activities. It also included $235,000,000, or more, of loans which could not wholly be considered aid, due to the fact that United States agencies usually limited their financing to procurement in the States.[4] Various other facets of the assistance program resulted in a lessened net benefit to Peru because of reciprocating return clauses guaranteeing something to the United States or companies of the United States. The value of grants (the most outright form of aid) from 1946 to 1960 came to approximately $48,500,000. If one considers the net trade loss to Peru caused by the price decline of Peruvian exports to the United States as compared to the increases in importations from the northern nation (1946-1960), a new perspective is given for

[4] A Program for the Industrial and Regional Development of Peru (A Report to the Government of Peru) (Cambridge, Mass., Arthur D. Little, Inc., 1960), p. 29. Bedoya Reyes (fn. 72 of Chapter 11), El Mundo, Lima, August 1958, p. 11, did not look upon Export-Import Bank financing as meeting the needs of his country.

viewing the aid question. By weighing in the decrease in international exchange, the net effect of assistance to Peru is appreciably reduced.

The greater part of technical assistance aid funds extended to Peru was administered under the following categories: five *servicios* (joint United States-Peru) and a miscellaneous category covering a variety of projects. The five co-operative *servicios* dealt with agriculture, health and sanitation, education, labor, and rural development. As noted in the chapter, "The Second World War," three of the *servicios* were introduced during the war. Scisp (health) and Scipa (agriculture) developed serious programs, while Secpane (education) initiated very little work before the war's end.[5] Scipa was engaged in many active projects until April 1960, when the Peruvian government office, SIPA, took over the experimentation and development (largely agricultural) phases. The United States, through special projects of the United States Operations Mission (USOM), continued to engage in some of the earlier Scipa-type activities. The miscellaneous category included projects in transportation, industry, mining, technical education, and relief, with the addition of contracts with several universities of the States, loans for a variety of purposes, military aid, and other areas of assistance.

Secpane (*el Servicio Cooperativo Interamericano de Educación*) was established under a basic agreement signed April 14, 1944.[6] It was jointly financed by Peru and the United States. Under an agency of the Ministry of Public Education, this *servicio* was designed to give specific aid to rural, elementary, normal, and technical education. The initial impetus was directed toward "encouraging and developing a more dynamic system of education based upon the needs

[5] See Chapter 7 for a résumé of Scisp and Scipa work. *Aprista* newspaper *Chan Chan*, Trujillo, October 18, 1946, p. 3, was favorably impressed. At the very time that Lima's oldest and best known paper was energetically carping about the "Yankee" petroleum interests in the nation, it carried a complimentary article regarding Scisp's struggle to eradicate malaria: *El Comercio*, Lima, October 18, 1960, p. 3. *Extra*, Lima, No. 149, January 21, 1958, p. 23, complimented Scisp. *Excelsior*, Lima, numerous times, especially in 1949, praised Scipa: January-March 1948, pp. 12-13, 18; May-June 1949, pp. 5, 13, 25-26; September-October 1950, pp. 17-18; and for Scisp, see September-October 1950, pp. 38-39.

[6] Its operations got under way in 1945. *Fojas expositivas sobre el punto cuatro en el Peru* (prepared by the Information Service of the United States Embassy, Lima, n.d., but appears to have been printed in 1958 or 1959), pp. 18-19 (hereafter cited as *Fojas Expositivas*), reported Secpane founded in 1945, while p. 21 of same issue has it as of April 1944.

of individuals and communities . . . ," using improved school administration and organization.[7] One entire floor of the large modern building which was built to house the Ministry of Public Education was turned over to the *servicio*. On February 13, 1946, *La Tribuna* carried an article which was complimentary to the work then being done. From time to time other Lima papers, especially *La Prensa*, ran similar reports; but there has not been a heavy press coverage.

A variety of projects emanated from Secpane and the Ministry of Public Education, as the following list shows: revision of official programs; secondary reform movements; provision of tools and equipment for schools (part of the equipment coming from the United States); help on the construction of two normal schools; expansion of a vocational education program; development of training materials for technical education; establishment of an institute for English teachers; home economics emphasis; foundation of rural school facilities; publishing of numerous bulletins and booklets on educational theory, technical education and such matters; introduction of summer courses for vocational educators; training of personnel in the United States or other countries.

Starting in 1946, the *servicio* began preparing booklets for publication. In the years from 1954 to 1960, editing and publishing took a greater and greater proportion of the budget. From 1946 to 1957 some 225 different books or booklets (especially the latter) were prepared, and a total of 269,795 copies were printed.[8] These publications, some of doubtful value, dealt with a wide range of topics; some were concerned with teaching methods, programs of study, curriculum, educational reforms in Peru, subject matter questions, and educational theories along several lines. Toward the close of the tenure of Secpane, publications were issued that treated the topics of administration, guidance, orientation, evaluation, school planning, industrial education, and others.

Carlos Salazar Romero, Associate Director of Secpane and author

[7] Allen J. Ellender, United States senator from the State of Louisiana, *A Review of United States Government Operations in Latin America 1958* (Washington, 1959), p. 329 (hereafter cited as *Ellender Report*). *Fojas Expositivas*, pp. 21-23, would indicate that emphasis had been intended for the areas of normal training, rural education, and technical education.

[8] This figure includes the different editions. *El servicio cooperativo interamericano de educación* (prepared by the Information Service of the United States Embassy, Lima, n.d., but likely in 1958), p. 21 (hereafter cited as *El Servicio Secpane*).

of several of its publications, criticized the *servicio* as being too theoretical.[9] He claimed that the United States personnel sent to Peru were too often mere theorists, and that they were not able to apply their theories practically. He believed that this failure may have been due in part to a lack of understanding of Peruvian psychology and philosophy. In certain technical areas, Salazar Romero believed Peru needed scientists or technicians—but not theorists. He criticized some of the United States assistants for trying to implant United States theories and methods in cases where they were not adaptable to Peruvian conditions. He also considered the tenure of the United States personnel to be too short. In his opinion, the changing of personnel after a year or two was definitely harmful to the program. His conclusion, in part, was that Peru was wasting some of the funds (too much of them) which it put into the *servicio*.

On the other hand, two former ministers of public education were more inclined to see the beneficial sides of the program. Professor Jorge Basadre and General Juan Mendoza R. felt encouraged by the fact that two normal training institutions had been created and various other positive results attained.[10] Mendoza was particularly enthusiastic about the achievements of Secpane. The model normal school near Chosica was seen as one of the more important attainments of Secpane.[11] The *servicio* has reached a good many students and teachers in one way or another, and it will take many years to evaluate accurately the results of this influence.

From the beginning of the program up to 1960, the United States had expended an amount in excess of $3,656,180 on the education mission.[12] Washington's contributions amounted to about 45 per cent of the total in the joint fund. Certain personnel expenses would increase this percentage. Peruvian appropriations, apart from personnel salaries and travel, were larger than United States grants. A lesser amount of cash contributions was made by third parties. Completion date for Secpane was set for 1956, but the joint *servicio* continued until 1962.

[9] Personal Interview: James C. Carey, Lima, April 9, 1962.
[10] Personal Interview: James C. Carey, Lima, April 26, 1962 (both men were interviewed on that day). Juan Mendoza R. is the author of *Nuevo potencial para la educación peruana* (Lima, 1956). Both men have held the position of minister of education. For Mendoza's views, see *Excelsior*, September-October 1950, pp. 53-54.
[11] *El Servicio Secpane*, p. 8, and *Ellender Report*, p. 270.
[12] *Ellender Report*, and Carey interview of Salazar Romero, April 9, 1962.

In 1953 another joint *servicio* was created. Scep (*El Servicio Co-operativo del Empleo del Peru*) was established to provide an effective employment service which would serve both employers and employees. The objectives appeared to undergo various changes. A later report added the goals of interexchange between the two nations in the areas of knowledge, practices, and techniques related to labor and employment services. Also listed as an objective was that of encouraging good relations and understanding between Peru and the United States in the democratic ways of life.[13] At another point the functions of Scep were listed more specifically as follows: (a) find jobs for workers and workers for jobs; (b) maintain a program of information on the employment market; (c) maintain services of occupational information with data on jobs; (d) provide industrial service to help solve problems of personnel; (e) orientation and adjustment; (f) find and provide services for invalids, young people, old people who work, and those not adjusted or those who are handicapped; (g) keep all possible data on the job market.[14]

Scep was the minor *servicio* of the five, since it was never provided with as large a budget as the others. Scep's central office started out with ten employees in what was then the building of the Ministry of Labor and Indian Affairs. A report prepared by the co-directors of the *servicio* up to December 13, 1960, reported that Scep had been formed to "adequately plan" the orientation and utilization of potential human resources for the development of the country and "its economy." [15] In January 1955, Scep took a modest step toward this optimistic goal as it assumed the principal duties of the National Employment Service. This continued to be its main charge in the period.

From 1955 to 1960, Scep pursued the rather limited work of testing applicants, establishing norms, helping place people, aiding employers, and providing data. A manual of occupation analysis as well as occupational guides were prepared. Peru contributed an amount similar to that of the United States for support of the *servicio*. Through 1960, the United States had allocated approximately $290,-000 to Scep in addition to some personnel assistance. At this early

---

[13] *Fojas Expositivas*, pp. 25-26. The wording about "democratic ways of life" appeared in a carelessly prepared booklet, evidently arranged by the *Servicio* Scep itself (contains no date of publishing or data about publisher).

[14] *Ellender Report*, p. 271.

[15] Report of *Servicio* Scep (see fn. 13 above).

date it is difficult to measure the results of this labor service. Although the completion date for the agency had been set for 1960, it was later changed to the end of December 1962.

Another agency known as Scif (*Servicio Cooperativo Interamericano de Fomento*) was designed primarily to deal with rural development. This Point Four program started its operations in 1955 under a subdivision of the Ministry of Promotion and Public Works. Like the other *servicios*, it was jointly financed, each nation providing approximately the same amount of money. Through 1960, the United States had contributed about $1,000,000.

Scif's activities included the following: irrigation projects; drainage and development of land projects; construction help on a small dam at Maray for which the inhabitants of Maray furnished the labor; road work, especially in the Mantaro Valley; construction of bridges; and some help with industrial training schools. Some direct activities were carried out in co-operation with Peruvian communities. Senator Allen Ellender of Louisiana reported that Scif's intrinsic value rested in " . . . the fact that . . . it serves as training operations for Peruvian engineers, and the demonstration of the validity of providing technical engineering advice to self-help projects." [16] Part of the achievement of Scif was that of planning development projects.

From time to time a project would be administered by one *servicio* and then be shifted to another aid office. An example of this would be the Southern Peru Regional Development Project (for a time under Scif), a project directed primarily at relieving the serious drought conditions of southern Peru. USOM (United States Operations Mission) had the responsibility of providing technicians in the fields of social anthropology, economic geography, land planning and economics "in order to determine the potential of the area . . ." (its people and the terrain).[17]

Various relief programs were administered through ICA (International Co-operation Administration, commonly called Point Four). ICA activities in Peru were "directed at meeting the United States foreign policy objectives of maintaining in Peru a stable political and economic system." [18] ICA funds also went to further the *servicios'* activities in other ways. As in the *servicios*, the programs were pri-

[16] *Ellender Report*, p. 322. See also *Fojas Expositivas*, pp. 13-16.
[17] *Ellender Report*, p. 271.
[18] *Ellender Report*, p. 326, and *Fojas Expositivas*.

marily those of technical co-operation, complemented by Public Law 480 loans under Title I (Economic Development), Title II (Drought Relief in Southern Peru during 1956, 1957, and 1958), and Title II programs under the direct supervision of voluntary agencies (Catholic Welfare Committee and UNICEF). The southern Peruvian *altiplano* was threatened with famine in 1956 when John R. Neal, director of the technical assistance program, rushed in 47,000 tons of surplus food under Title II of Public Law 480, and some 10,000 tons of Peruvian potatoes from the central region of the country.[19] Criticism of the handling of the emergency relief is discussed later in the chapter.

Additional ICA projects, some of which involved considerable expense, were carried out in the areas of civil aviation (CORPAC), university contracts (textile engineering, sanitation engineering, chemical instrumentation, and agricultural research), public administration, mining and metallurgy, and a survey of the mineral resources of Peru under the direction of a United States Geological Survey Mission.[20] In comparison, Peru's share of ICA-administered programs under Public Law 480 up to 1960 was considerably lower in value than that of Brazil, but it was larger than that of Mexico.

The largest single loan project of a developmental nature for Peru —unless one includes the kind of Export-Import Bank loan arranged for private industry that was made to the Southern Peru Copper Corporation in 1959—was the Quiroz project, an irrigation and development enterprise involving about $8,000,000 of ICA funds in the years 1955-1958. The International Bank for Reconstruction and Development made an $18,000,000 loan to the project and ICA provided part of the local money through Public Law 480, Title I, loans.[21] Richard W. Patch claimed that Quiroz, contrary to declarations that it was intended for small landholders, "passed into the

---

[19] *United States Aid Operations in Peru,* Fourth Report by the Committee on Government Operations (Washington, 1961), p. 11 (hereafter cited as *United States Aid Operations in Peru*). See also *Andean Air Mail and Peruvian Times,* Lima, April 26, 1957, p. 13, hereafter cited as *Peruvian Times,* and *United States Aid Operations in Peru: Hearings* (before a Subcommittee of the Committee on Government Operations, House of Representatives, 87th Cong., 1st Sess., November 1960, March, April, May, 1961 (Washington, 1961), p. 422.

[20] *Ellender Report,* p. 326. For ICA figures see *The 14th Semiannual Report on Activities of the Food-For-Peace Program Carried on Under Public Law 480,* House Doc. No. 223 (Washington, 1961), p. 27.

[21] *Ellender Report,* p. 333.

hands of the few very wealthy men who own enormous haciendas in the Department of Piura." [22]

Loans made up the greatest proportion of our aid to Peru—that is if loans may be considered under the heading of assistance. Most of these loans were made with the object of increasing Peru's trade, but at the same time, most of the increased volume of trade was with the United States. If one considers loans, as such, to be aid, the question arises as to whether they were more aid to the United States or to Peru (or at least to certain United States private concerns). They may have been of little value to either nation, or they may have been of considerable value to both. In general, Hans J. Morgenthau believes the former and congressional committees of the United States believe the latter. In the main, the interest rates of United States loans were average or below average. Various loans were welcomed by the Peruvian press, but that could not be said of all. *El Mundo,* in August 1958, complained that the Export-Import Bank was designed primarily to help the United States sell its products and, as such, was not what Latin America needed. In 1955-1956, Prime Minister Pedro G. Beltran insisted that loans of foreign currency would "generate inflation" if the borrowing government lacked the funds in its own currency to take care of local expenses.[23] At that time he described the International Bank for Reconstruction and Development, as well as the Export-Import Bank, as lending for foreign purchases only.

During the period from 1946 to 1960, loans to Peru under foreign assistance categories totaled almost $235,000,000 as compared with $48,500,000 in direct grants.[24] Most of the loans were made with the joint objective of giving economic aid to the United States and Peru at the same time. In the assistance category, $198,600,000 was provided by the Export-Import Bank for trade expansion. Loans to the Peruvian military amounted to $15,700,000 dollars, in addition to the Export-Import Bank loan for submarines mentioned else-

[22] Richard W. Patch, "Peru Looks Toward the Elections of 1962," *American Universities Field Staff* (New York-Lima, May 1961), p. 6. The Quiroz facet of United States aid would appear to need more study than it has received.

[23] Pedro G. Beltran, "Foreign Loans and Politics in Latin America," *Foreign Affairs* (January 1956), pp. 297-304.

[24] *United States Foreign Assistance and Assistance from International Organizations; Obligations and Other Commitments July 1, 1945 through June 30, 1960* (International Cooperation Administration, Office of Statistics and Reports) March 31, 1961, p. 76 (hereafter cited as *United States Foreign Assistance*).

where. It is noted that outright grants for economic purposes were low as compared to the percentage of funds extended by loans, while for the military, grants were more than twice as great as loans.

Loan projects of a nature similar to the Quiroz irrigation plan went for the following items: land development in the area around Quiroz; expansion of the agricultural research station at Lambayeque; the Santa Rosa irrigation project; construction of the El Frayle Dam in the Department of Arequipa; aid to the Pedro P. Diaz Industries of Arequipa (in part for tanning hides and making leather goods); the Agricultural Production Program of Southern Peru, designed to increase production in the drought-affected areas; acquisition of railroad equipment (for southern Peru); and the Ayllu Fisherman's Co-operative at Chimbote. At least two of the above listed enterprises entailed the spending of $500,000 or more.[25]

Whether by loans, technical co-operation, equipment, or personnel, other forms of assistance were provided for development operations, common defense activity, voluntary relief agencies, emergency relief, educational projects, a variety of loan arrangements, and aid under the Mutual Security Program. The latter included $22,000,000 of funds through the ICA program. Other significant assistance projects under USOM supervision were those under Public Law 480, Title III, which entailed the sale of United States surplus agricultural products, or exchange, or some other form of distribution.

USOM supervised the handling of about $2,000,000 worth of milk and cereal products in the period of 1955-1957 and another $1,000,-000 or more in 1958, under the Peruvian agreement to purchase approximately 8,000,000 soles worth of wheat, rice, dairy products with transportation.[26] The funds from these sales, according to the 1958 agreement, were to be used by the United States to: (1) develop trade; (2) provide limited assistance; (3) make loans through Export-Import Bank channels (also to develop trade generally); and (4) make loans to Peru for economic development. The agreement between Peru and the United States also provided for these guarantees: (1) Peru was not to sell to other countries—or to make goods available to nations unfriendly to the United States; (2) the transfer of products was not to disrupt world markets; (3) the two governments were ". . . to seek to assure conditions of commerce permit-

[25] *Ellender Report*, p. 333. *United States Aid Operations in Peru*, pp. 9-10.
[26] *United States Treaties and Other International Agreements*, 1958, IX (Washington, 1959), pp. 695-696.

ting private traders to function effectively and will use their best endeavors . . . for continuous market demand. . . ." [27] The 1959 extension of the surplus agricultural sales plan provided that part of the income would be used for educational exchange. In 1960, an agreement for the sale of another 12,000,000 soles of products was completed. Conditions were similar to those of the 1958 agreement except that edible fats and oils were added to the list. Under the Mutual Security Program and following economic aid projects from the year 1942 through 1960, about $22,000,000 worth of surplus agricultural commodities were sold to Peru in accordance with Public Law 480, Title I, agreements. "Until 1955, the U.S. economic aid program to Peru had consisted of a comparatively small technical co-operation program, totaling in over-all amount only about $13,-000,000 in 13 years." [28]

In March 1956, United States Operations Mission Director John Neale called for extensive drought relief aid for Peru. Ambassador Ellis O. Briggs at Lima advised the secretary of state in Washington that, ". . . although the people in the drought area were not yet aware of the seriousness of the situation, some subversive elements were becoming increasingly active." [29] A grant of agricultural commodities, approximately $14,000,000 worth, was provided for the purposes of meeting food shortages. Under Title III of Public Law 480 some 30,000 tons of commodities, amounting to about $9,000,-000 in value, were donated to Peru for relief distribution. Authorization was given to use the grain in the following ways: (1) free distribution to drought victims; (2) distribution in payment for work performed on projects for the needy when jointly approved by the Peruvian government and the United States Operations Mission; (3) sale, with the proceeds to be used for financing public works projects, "which will be of permanent benefit to the area and which will provide employment for the inhabitants." [30]

Difficulties arose in the distribution of the grain. Less than 6 per cent of the food was "distributed free in the drought area (almost as much was lost or damaged from various causes)." [31] The State De-

[27] *Ibid.*

[28] *United States Aid Operations in Peru*, p. 11.

[29] *Ibid.* See also *United States Aid Operations in Peru: Hearings*, pp. 422-423.

[30] *United States Aid Operations in Peru*, p. 11.

[31] *Ibid.*, pp. 2, 13-15. ICA/W advised that a subsequent report from USOM stated this residue had been disposed of by March 7, 1960, bringing additional income.

partment claimed that total loss of foodstuffs was under 5 per cent for the program, but critics placed the amount much higher. "Almost 25 per cent of the food provided remained undistributed at the time the drought was officially declared over by the government of Peru; almost one half of this amount still remained in the warehouses a year later. However, as a result of Neale's failure to carry out his duties as USOM director, at least 60 per cent of the sales proceeds were used improperly, that is, contrary to the uses contemplated when this program was inaugurated." [32]

To some considerable extent, emergency food was sold at high prices although it had been intended as free relief sustenance. Mills charged four and five times the normal rates for grinding the grain. Of the 35,000 tons of grain sold to millers, 28,000 tons went to a single mill outside the drought area.[33] Dirt was mixed in with flour so that it would weigh more. In the starving town of Puno, 82 tons of grain were stolen, and it is believed that 350 tons of the barley were fed to Peruvian cavalry horses. Some of the influential Peruvians had luxurious houses built from food-financed public works. These were only a few of the accounts of the seamy business associated with stealing from the starving.[34] El Comercio called for prosecution of the Peruvian offenders involved in the scandal.[35]

The section of the United States act designed to permit "private traders to function effectively" may have been overworked by Peruvian as well as United States individuals. There is no way of determining how many persons profited unduly by the use of agricultural surpluses from the United States. The Congress in Lima was stirred

[32] Ibid., p. 2. Specific directions for disposing and handling of the commodities in Peru were not provided. When word reached Neale that the commodities were not reaching the people for whom they were intended, corrective action was not taken in any direct manner. There was, however, some confusion as to what office (ICA Director in Peru or ICA Director in Washington) should have taken the initiative in this case: United States Aid Operations in Peru: Hearings, pp. 271-273.

[33] United States Aid Operations in Peru, pp. 2, 13.

[34] "Y que ocurre con el 'Affaire' de la Sequía?" Caretas, Lima, June 15-30, 1961, p. 13. See also United States Aid Operations in Peru. Additional notes written in on the questionnaires of the "Sample Survey" called attention to the mismanagement of the relief project. Although relief was considered necessary and helpful, under that heading on the questionnaire "graft and corruption" was the most frequent comment where comments were included.

[35] El Comercio, May 29, 1961, p. 2. It will be noted that this came after the investigations in Washington.

to action in 1961, almost five years after the 1956-1957 famine relief aid had been handled in such an outrageous manner. News releases from Washington, based on congressional investigations, initiated "secret investigations" in Peru's courts and Congress. Some attention was drawn to the farming corporation, *Negociación Bazo Velarde, S.A.*, in which the director of the aid mission, Neale, was a principal stockholder. This enterprise was one which had been assisted by the aid funds. In 1958, ICA noted this fact, although belatedly and somewhat reluctantly, and on a "conflict of interest charge" [36] recommended Neale's separation from this duty as well as from government service in general.

The final conclusion of the Committee on Government Operations in Washington was that there had been great inefficiency in the handling and checking of the food relief program. The Operations Mission director in Peru, as well as the regional director in Washington's office of Latin-American Operations for ICA, were charged with not performing their functions properly.[37] The United States ambassador for most of the period concerned, Theodore C. Achilles, was poorly informed as to operations which took place under his supervision. According to the Committee on Government Operations, four different investigators of ICA personnel "demonstrated a peculiar disinterest in determining the validity of charges made concerning Neale's conflict of interest." [38] This writer has avoided making a judgment of Neale's activities in Peru, but even the casual student will note that the congressional investigation has revealed various acts of carelessness, inefficiency, and questionable business relationships.

Another area of aid to Peru in which it is difficult to determine usage is that of military assistance. The difficulties of gaining information were discussed by Senator Ellender in his report. While in Lima, the senator had attempted to obtain these data: (1) a

[36] *United States Aid Operations in Peru*, pp. 17-21. The matter was further complicated by Mrs. Bazo's position on the Mission payroll. She, a United States citizen, had married Juan Bazo of the farm corporation in which Neale was an investor. Juan Bazo was also on the Mission payroll. See *United States Aid Operations in Peru: Hearings*, pp. 58-61.

[37] *United States Aid Operations in Peru*, pp. 2, 4.

[38] *Ibid.*, p. 3. In evaluating the congressional committee report, the reader needs to keep in mind the fact that it is not the same administration in control in Washington in 1961 that had been in office in 1956. Although partisan political emphasis is not evident in the report, it is possible that such was a factor.

breakdown as to the personnel in each of the attachés' offices; (2) the motor vehicles assigned to their use; and (3) a brief summary of their functions. His questionnaire was returned marked "confidential." He did not think it a military secret as to how many automobiles were assigned to each attaché or as to whether or not their motor vehicles were pooled. He concluded, "In my judgment, this is an example of the armed services attitude, at times, that their business is their own and no one else's, and no one is supposed to even question what they are doing." [39] As Ellender discovered, the bulk of the United States military activities in Peru were administered under the following six heads: the air, army, and naval attachés at the Embassy; and the air, army, and naval missions to Peru. The naval mission has a long history, as we have noted earlier. The Military Aviation Mission (as adviser to the Peruvian Air Force) was established by basic agreements in 1939 and again in 1946. There was a provision for joint United States-Peruvian financing.[40] Since 1952, a very small Military Assistance Advisory Group has existed in Lima.

On occasion it has been difficult to distinguish between measures designed for mutual security and measures devised to bolster United States markets, especially at times when the sale of United States equipment was involved. These overlapping objectives are seen in broader arrangements of mutual security, for example, the Mutual Defense Assistance agreement of 1952,[41] in which Lima and Washington agreed to co-operate in "measures designed to control trade with nations which threaten the security of the Western Hemisphere." Who can say how much was defense and how much was pure profit for individuals? Some of the arrangements were clearly military provisions to make available to the other nation such assistance, equipment, materials, and services as the government furnishing them might authorize. In the interests of the common security of both governments, Peru was not to transfer the aid or items to any other government or to any persons or officers of another government.

[39] *Ellender Report*, p. 268.
[40] *United States Treaties and Other International Agreements, 1952*, III, Part 1 (Washington, 1954), pp. 352, 358-359. Also noted in *Ellender Report*, p. 269. For Peru's acceptance of the Air Mission, see *Revista Peruana de Derecho Internacional* (January-June 1947), p. 123.
[41] *United States Treaties and Other International Agreements, 1952*, III, Part 2 (Washington, 1954), p. 2897.

By purchase, lend-lease, loan, or some other form of transfer, considerable equipment went to Peru following the Second World War. The purchase of this equipment may not have been within the realm of economic wisdom for either the buyer or seller. Still, if Peru was determined to have more military hardware, Washington would readily conclude that it was better that the United States provide it. But, as some of the credit arrangements indicate, the United States was encouraging Peru to stock up in certain areas, especially in naval supplies. The Export-Import loan used to finance the purchase of submarines could hardly be construed as meeting the needs of internal security. The sale of such by the United States risked antagonizing both Chile and Ecuador.

Peru has generally co-operated in mutual defense maneuvers and other security exercises promoted by the United States or the Organization of American States.[42] The government at Lima agreed to operate a United States built minitrack missile-tracking system at a station near Ancón.[43] Co-operation in over-all defense matters appeared to have been fostered between Peru and the United States, and aid in the form of equipment may very well have come in the form of an assist.

Military assistance to Peru for the period from July 1945 to June 30, 1960, totaled something over the sum of $94,000,000, if loans are included.[44] As mentioned earlier, of all Latin-American countries, only Brazil received more. The source of military aid which is most difficult to determine is that which is listed under an ICA category. The form of aid which caused most bewilderment was a loan to Peru for help in purchasing two submarines which were ordered in 1955 and delivered in 1957. A renegotiated contract left Peru with a debt of $13,773,000 to the Export-Import Bank. This financing had taken the bank into a strange field. Not until 1961 did the Peruvian public works development budget show a significant contribution ($340,000) from the Ministry of War for a civilian project. This equipment for road construction apparently has been appreciated on

[42] New York Times, February 15, 1959, p. 4; March 6, 1960, p. 2; January 6, 1961, p. 3; a July 17, 1960, p. 1, Times account reports Peru's motion in the O.A.S. aimed at Soviet relations with Cuba which considered the developments a "menace" to hemispheric solidarity, security and democracy. For Peru's position on the United States defense of South Korea, see Revista Peruana de Derecho Internacional (1950), pp. 154-155.

[43] New York Times, March 8, 1959, p. 35.

[44] United States Foreign Assistance, p. 76.

a wider public front than has the rest of the military aid to Peru.[45] But, because of the very nature of defense problems and the confidential handling of security data, it is nearly impossible to draw precise conclusions in this general realm. When it is noted that funds for the armed forces constitute the single largest item of the Peruvian national budget, one wonders how wise it is for the United States to encourage this area of activity.[46] If the 1960 Peruvian national budget items of War, Navy, and Air are combined it is obvious that the armed forces receive upwards of 20 per cent. The figure of 1,531,774,764 soles does not include that part of the item "Government and Police" which is relevant to the armed services. As presented to the Peruvian Congress, the proposed 1960 budget was as follows: (Soles) Legislature-55,922,855; Executive-7,252,400; Judicial-74,121,000; Electoral Board-1,460,000; Government and Police-970,-195,000; Foreign Affairs-97,700,000; Justice-110,043,000; Labor and Indian Affairs-30,112,100; Education-1,397,162,100; Finance and Commerce-1,234,778,875; War-803,741,635; Navy-330,337,000; Air-397,696,129; Public Works-880,881,190; Health-1,059,596,800; and Agriculture-240,836,100.

There is no clear-cut view presented by the United States congressmen who have observed certain military aid activities in Peru. Some have written favorable reports, others have been dubious, a few have commented that it is easier to obtain funds for military aid than it is for economic assistance programs. Senator George D. Aiken, after a study mission to South America, had this to say under the topic, "Peru": "It is difficult, therefore, to make a military case for Latin-American military establishments beyond the kinds of national guards which are maintained by Costa Rica and Panama. From the economic point of view, it would seem that every Latin-American country could put to better use much of the resources now devoted to military establishments. . . . Parts of the military budgets of some Latin-American countries are in effect appeasement of the military—something to keep them happy so that they will not overthrow the government." [47] Edwin Lieuwen, although point-

[45] The road construction phase of military aid came in for ten favorable comments in the "Sample Survey." The survey showed that in general the opinion response was divided on the merits of military aid to Peru.

[46] *Peruvian Times*, April 14, 1961; January 8, 1960, p. 1. The February 19, 1960, issue carried the proposed 1960 national budget.

[47] *Latin America: Venezuela, Brazil, Bolivia, and Panama* (report of Senator George D. Aiken on a Study Mission to the Committee on Foreign Relations,

ing out that the Peruvian army has attempted to achieve positive economic growth, maintained that Washington's ties with Peru's military dictatorship resulted in considerable hostility.[48]

Although recent developments indicate that Peruvian military circles might encourage trends toward economic and political modernization, these developments are as yet too fragile to be accepted at face value.[49] Even with the possibility of a change in the Peruvian military and social systems, the past record is not encouraging. Under Sánchez Cerro, Benavides, and Odría the communists have acted more freely than they have under the civilian presidents. The fact that the military is antagonistic toward *Apra* must also be remembered. It is *Apra* which has prevented a greater growth of communism in Peru.[50] There is no evidence that the military has played any important part in checking the advance of the communists. If anything, the military has shown an interest in receiving communist political support, while quite consistently *Apra* has not welcomed that support.

One must conclude that liberal assistance, in a variety of forms, has been extended Peru. The training or education of individuals, by whatever means and in a diversity of fields, was a valuable phase in this assistance to Peru. Technicians, scientists, labor leaders, admirals, doctors, farmers, and many others were given special preparation in Peru or in the United States. In the fiscal year 1958-1959, there were ninety-some persons participating in the Fulbright and

United States Senate), 86th Cong., 2nd Sess. (Washington, February 2, 1960), p. 11 (see also pp. 195-196). Senator Aiken concluded that a reduction of military expenditures, which weakened the military, would work to strengthen the position of civilian governments. He suggested a gradual reduction of United States military aid, rather than an abrupt cut-off of such assistance.

[48] Edwin Lieuwen, *Arms and Politics in Latin America* (New York, 1960), pp. 7, 139, 236. See fn. 17, Chapter 1.

[49] Richard W. Patch, "The Peruvian Elections of 1963," *American Universities Field Staff* (New York, July 1963), pp. 4-5. The following study also suggests this positive approach: Juan Mendoza R., *Nuevo potencial para la educación peruana* (Lima, Peru, 1956). General of the Army Mendoza is a former minister of education. There has been some exchange of personnel and services between the official and unofficial assistance projects, from time to time. For example, Major Larry Montgomery, USAF Reserve, came to Peru with the Air Force Mission in 1946, and the following year was made superintendent of aviation of the Summer Institute of Linguistics (see Chapter 9 for SIL). *Peruvian Times*, November 1, 1963, p. 15.

[50] Robert J. Alexander, *Communism in Latin America* (New Brunswick, Rutgers University Press, 1957), pp. 220, 225.

Public Law 402 programs. The growth in this area of aid was especially rapid between 1940—when four Peruvians came to the United States—and 1960, when 120 Peruvians received grants or "official approval" from the United States government to study or do research in the States.[51] For a time in the early 1950's this phase of exchange lagged, but by the close of the decade it had prospered again.

The five *servicios* considered training of personnel as one of their main objectives. Toward the close of the 1950's, Peru increased its contribution to all of the joint funds at the very time that, in some instances, the United States was reducing its payment. When Washington cut its contribution, it did not necessarily imply a devaluation of the programs. It could have been considered the opposite. Some officials believed that our technical aid programs should "show the way," and then "gradually fade out" as the local national offices developed.[52] Senator Ellender concluded that many of the programs operating in Peru in 1958 were "doing untold good." But for reasons of economy, he wanted the administrative overhead costs reduced. Ellender criticized Ambassador Achilles for overstaffing and believed that the deputy director and the two assistant program directors of the USOM "should have been sent home long ago." He noted that of the aid budget ($2,400,000 for 1959) some $216,000 was designated for over-all administration, which did not include all administrative costs in the various *servicios* or other programs. The senator's conclusions were favorable to the aid efforts, but he wanted a more economical operation.

This writer's sample survey of Peruvian attitudes indicated that the over-all United States foreign assistance program was well received.[53] At the same time, discontent was registered because too

[51] These figures would not include other individual Peruvian students or researchers who were not listed "officially" in the Cultural Affairs office of the United States Information Service in Lima.

[52] *Ellender Report*, p. 269.

[53] "Sample Survey," Carey. Questionnaire responses showed that 109 of 157 considered the assistance programs to have been beneficial to Peru. Manuel Seoane, influential *Aprista* leader, believed that the assistance programs were well intentioned but deeply entwined in bureaucracy, and that they often fell short of being carried out: *El Mundo*, July 1958, p. 18. Bedoya Reyes doubted if the United States had enough knowledge and real concern with the needs of Latin America to meet the hemisphere's needs. He wrote this at a time when he opined that John Foster Dulles did not pay enough attention to Latin America, *El Mundo*, August 1958, p. 34.

often the aid was not distributed effectively at the local levels. Of 157 responses to the questionnaire, 114 believed that a greater propaganda effort was needed if Peruvians were to be well informed. Only ten stated that they were not interested in the aid program while 28 thought that adequate information was disseminated. A majority of 103 to 47 concluded that the United States should define more precisely the conditions of the aid and then supervise its operations with greater vigilance. The same number held that the United States needed to insist on social reforms accompanying the use of its funds.[54] In this survey, as in other reports, there was a feeling that the aid programs were well intentioned, but often became bogged down in bureaucracy (especially Peruvian) and fell short of being carried out.[55] There was a general impression that graft existed, especially where Peruvians were involved. The net result of the inquiry, however, demonstrated the positive effect of Washington's assistance projects.

In attempting any assessment of the assistance programs in Peru, one faces a maze of complications. For example, official correspondence tells of extended rivalry between two areas of United States aid programs. On the other hand, Eugene R. Black wrote the White House to inform President Truman's assistant of the successful work of Scipa in Peru.[56] In general, however, it appears that the assistance

[54] "Sample Survey," Carey. The question specifically asked: "When the United States offers economic aid to Peru, should it be agreed that Peru will attempt to amend its taxation system toward a more equal basis, to adopt a more active indigenous program, and speed up agrarian reform?" In this respect, 103 of 157 believed that Washington should be concerned enough to include a definite agreement on these points.

[55] El Mundo, July 1958, p. 18. Extra, January 21, 1958, No. 149, p. 23, carried an article which was very complimentary of the work of Scisp in its sanitation operations and the work of eradication of malaria in part of north-central Peru. On the other hand, United States congressional reports following investigation of a road building project and an irrigation program emphasized the inadequate planning and faulty supervision which were associated with the aid program. See United States Aid Operations in Peru, pp. 2-3. This evaluation was included in the same report which summed up the drought relief project as follows: "There is no competent evidence in the form of end-use checks, audits, or other documentary proof to support the claim of the Department of State and ICA, that a $14,000,000 drought relief program achieved the objectives which would normally be expected of a program of this nature." See also, El Comercio, October 18, 1960, p. 3.

[56] Keith Himebaugh correspondence, December 1952-May 1953; and Eugene R. Black to John R. Steelman, August 21, 1952, 212-A (Stanley Andrews Papers), Harry S. Truman Library.

programs have been beneficial to the United States in various ways as well as providing a support to our trading policies. It could be said that we helped ourselves while we helped Peru to help itself. The assistance tended to make friends for the United States—but possibly not as many as the output of men, money, and machines might have led our United States citizens to expect. If one considers the financial stability of Peru as a prime objective, then possibly it has had only limited success. For, although economic chaos did not take place, the sol lost in value, there was rapid inflation, and the cost of living greatly increased in the period 1945 to 1960.[57] The Julius Klein report of November 1949, recommending that Peru abandon the official parity of the sol, may have helped for a short time but, if so, it was at the expense of the many for the benefit of the few. And ten years after the Klein recommendation, the sol was not as strong as it had been in 1949, the cost of living had spiraled upward, and the economy was overly sensitive to world conditions. Still, the over-all picture indicated a slightly improved economy during the period of extensive assistance from the States. The aid provided in education and technical development will, in the long run, help both nations. As to military assistance, it appears that Peru has co-operated well in matters of hemispheric defense.

Even with the serious mistakes made by policy makers and administrators, it appears that the United States aid programs to Peru (1940-1960) have had a positive effect on relations, at least on a short-range basis. The question of when and how well Peru can move ahead without benefit of that help from the north must be determined in future years. However, there is little doubt that the years between 1920 and 1960 taught Washington something about the problems and the means of "exporting" culture. In 1920, a knowledge of the Spanish language had not been considered a requisite

[57] International Public Opinion Research, Inc., of New York conducted a study for Lima. Lima, although far above the rest of the nation, showed that only 1.6 per cent of the population could satisfy all their needs and enjoy the comforts and luxuries available in the community. While 3.6 per cent could enjoy the comforts except in time of serious economic crisis, they could enjoy only part of the luxuries available. Group C was that which, while holding jobs, could obtain its necessities, but who could obtain certain comforts and luxuries only with considerable sacrifice. The large group, consisting of 78.1 per cent, could obtain the necessities of life only through hard labor, and they were unable to enjoy most of the comforts of life. See Carlos A. Uriarte, "Un Ensayo en la Distribución de los Habitantes de Lima, Ciudad Capital, por Grupos Socio-Económicos," *Estadística Peruana* (March 1948).

for United States citizens making application for the highest advisory positions in Peru's national educational system, but by 1960 an effort was being made to secure personnel for the assistance projects who, in addition to the usual qualifications, knew the language and culture of Peru as well.

9: BINATIONAL CULTURAL CENTER AND UNOFFICIAL AID

The author's sample survey (see fn. 71, Chapter 7) of Peruvian attitudes included a question asking for suggestions as to what foundations, agencies, institutions, business concerns, and organizations had done the most to improve Peruvian-United States relations in the twentieth century. Sixty-four of 157 responses mentioned private aid projects. This chapter therefore treats those independent (nonofficial) operations which were most often named in the sample survey, and particularly the *Instituto Cultural Peruano Norteamericano* (ICPNA). This last organization has been singled out here since its purpose and scope are somewhat different from the activities discussed in the preceding chapter.

INSTITUTO CULTURAL PERUANO NORTEAMERICANO

Although neither an official nor an unofficial United States aid project, the *Instituto Cultural Peruano Norteamericano* had some objectives which would have been very similar to those of an official assistance program. This "house of culture," as President Prado called it, was engaged in the business of intercultural exchange. Begun informally in 1938, the Institute expanded and refined its activities until, in 1960, it involved 2,200 students and 50 teachers. Its operations in Lima entailed management of a 10,000 volume library, an art gallery, a record library and music room, a speech laboratory with recording facilities, a tearoom and small restaurant, and an auditorium for 500 persons. Since 1960, ICPNA has opened cultural programs and English classes in branches outside the capital city in addition to its other activities.

The ICPNA literature of 1960 dated the founding of its organization as June 1938, and attributed the work of establishment to a group of Peruvian and United States citizens.[1] The stated purpose

[1] "History of ICPNA," *Instituto Cultural Peruano-Norteamericano*, September 1960, Año XIV, No. 38 (*Impreso en los Talleres Gráficos de la Editorial Antonio Lulli*, Lima), p. 12.

was that of "increasing the knowledge and mutual exchange of the culture of Peru and that of the United States of America." United States Ambassador Lawrence Steinhardt attended the formal opening, and Dr. Alfredo Alvarez Calderón was the first president. Since that opening and up to the year 1960, about 20,000 persons have studied English or Spanish (especially the former) in ICPNA classrooms. Other thousands have viewed Peruvian and United States art and movies, listened to Peruvian and United States music and drama, attended lectures, and participated in recitals, conversation clubs, square dances, songfests, excursion clubs, and library visits. The Institute has co-operated with San Marcos University, the Ministry of Public Health, the Cultural Attaché Office and the United States Information Agency. It has assisted the Embassy and the International Institute of Education (New York) in screening and selecting candidates for scholarships open to Peruvian students in United States colleges and universities. It has taught English free of charge at the Diplomatic Academy of the Foreign Office and at the Ministry of Labor. Since December 1943 an English Teachers' Institute has been conducted by ICPNA with Peruvian government approval.[2]

When the United States developed its Binational Centers' program under the direction of the United States Information Agency, the Peruvian Institute was placed under its control. Individual Peruvian and United States citizens have, from the beginning, been active in keeping the work of ICPNA creative and progressive. The following list, although not complete, names the most active participants over a period of years: Jorge Basadre, Manuel Beltroy, Arthur Dewey, Luis Echecopar García, Albert Giesecke, Ples Harper, Leonard Hopson, Emilio Romero, Julio C. Tello, and Luis G. Valcárcel. In 1960, when a commodious new building was inaugurated, Robert L. Bancroft was the enterprising Director of ICPNA.

The stages of expansion of the Institute's operations have been reflected in the buildings which have housed it. Since its establishment, ICPNA has had four locations. In July 1960, the new six-story building with mezzanine and basement was officially inaugurated. Making the structure possible were a diversity of United States and Peruvian contributions, the largest being that from the United States government, which was presented by Richard M. Nixon in May 1958 while he was carrying out his stormy visit to Peru.[3] An ex-

[2] *Ibid.*, p. 13.
[3] *El Peruano* (*Diario oficial*), July 14, 1960, p. 1.

cellent location has been selected near San Marcos University, the National Library, and the ministries of public education and finance. The opening of this fine edifice represented the triumph of an important experiment in intercultural exchange.

ICPNA has exerted a definite influence toward good relations between the two countries.[4] The skeptic would argue, perhaps, that in general the Institute touches only those Peruvians already inclined toward the United States and that it fails to interest those with anti-United States inclinations. This may be broadly true, but there are still those in the middle, the large undecided group, who could be favorably impressed. Also, whatever the ICPNA can do to interest United States citizens residing in Peru in the history and culture of the country is highly important. This need was sadly emphasized in 1959, when distinguished Peruvians met to observe the centennial of the death of United States historian, W. H. Prescott, and "no representative of our ambassador and no prominent United States resident" attended the ceremony.[5] Conservative in many respects, Peru has long been proud of its rich cultural traditions. This is, no doubt, one of the reasons why a well-directed cultural exchange program such as ICPNA has been able to build important ties of friendship between the two nations. Upon returning to Washington from a visit to Peru and six other South American nations, a Senate Study Mission emphasized this important point when it reported that "our binational centers ought to be multiplied many times over." [6] Complimentary remarks of this sort, at one time or another, have been made in all of Lima's main newspapers.

VICOS

There were additional private United States aid projects, other than those singled out here, which have made a mark on Peru.

[4] *Ibid.* Also see "Sample Survey," Carey. ICPNA was listed along with Point Four projects as one of the activities which has been of considerable value in helping Peru. In 1962, ICPNA was publishing a four-page monthly bulletin (*Boletin*, ICPNA) which presented the affairs and activities of the Institute.

[5] William Benton, *The Voice of Latin America* (New York, Harper & Row, 1961), p. 155.

[6] *Study Mission to South America, November-December, 1961*, report of Senators Gale W. McGee, Frank E. Moss, Clair Engle, and Stephen M. Young (Washington, 1962), p. 14. See also *La Prensa*, Lima, June 2, 1963 (full page), p. 16. For *Aprista* opinion on this see, *La Tribuna*, Lima, January 23, 1946, p. 4; and March 25, 1946, p. 13.

Some of them are either not well known or have not as yet produced significant literature to study (as, for example, Catholic and
Protestant missionary work). There are also many small isolated
private aid projects—too many to treat within this brief study. The
American Society of Peru, the Y.M.C.A., International Basic Economy Corporation (a private activity of the Rockefeller brothers),
various philanthropical associations, and a variety of missionary
medical and educational work all deserve more space than this study
allows them. Three important projects (Vicos, the Summer Lin-
guistic Institute, and Tournavista) are selected for treatment here
because they are dynamic rural operations in the mountain and
jungle regions. Since most official United States aid has been confined to urban centers, there is a need to ponder the assistance directed to rural areas, even though in the main it has been unofficial.

The nonindigenous population of Peru has long wavered between
attitudes of indifference and resignation to the tremendous, feudal
"Indian Problem"—the fact that approximately one half of the
country's population has not been incorporated into the modern
life of the nation. Much has been written about the difficulties involved, and in recent decades the political parties have made many
promises about the Indians' plight, but up to 1960 very little had
been accomplished. An achievement which most definitely pointed
up the possibility of doing something of permanent significance
about the great Andino enigma took place at Vicos, an *hacienda* in
a canyon-like valley just south of the 21,000 foot mountain, Huascarán. Vicos lies in the department of Ancash not far from the town
of Huaráz.

Vicos was one of the field stations established, through a grant
from the Carnegie Corporation, to carry out studies in technological
and social change. The project began as an unofficial enterprise
under the direction of Allan Holmberg, Professor of Anthropology
at Cornell University. Later, it became a joint project with the Peruvian Indigenous Institute co-operating with Cornell. This move gave
Holmberg the invaluable assistance of Carlos Monge, Manuel Ve-
lasco Nuñez of the Indigenous Institute, and Mario Vásquez, an
anthropologist who spoke the Quechua language of Ancash. A particular objective of the station was to study closely the process by
which "technical changes" were accepted or rejected by Vicos inhabitants, and to understand why the changes were viewed with
suspicion, and "how previous anthropological experience . . . could

be marshaled to make innovations attractive to the community." [7]
To some extent, the experiment was an attempt "to establish a pilot
community which would stir the imagination of outsiders, and encourage others to imitate the changes accomplished in Vicos. . . ."

In 1951 the *Instituto Indigenista Peruano* and Cornell reached an
agreement by which the Peru-Cornell project leased Vicos for a
five-year period. Vicos had been a tremendously large *hacienda* of
19,000 acres under the supervision of the Huaráz "public benefit
society," a high-sounding name for a group which produced little
in practice. The "public benefit society" had been accustomed to
leasing the community (land and people) to the highest bidder.
The person or company (highest bidder) to whom the *hacienda*
was leased had exploited the inhabitants in an effort to make Vicos
profitable. Its inhabitants had grown to fear outsiders, since outsiders (Peruvians or foreigners) had usually come only to exploit
labor in exchange for pitifully low wages and some coca drug for
chewing.

It took nearly a year before the project administrators could gain
even a smattering of confidence or respect from the downtrodden
Indians of Vicos. The experiment moved carefully and slowly as it
attempted to encourage the inhabitants to talk of their problems and
ask questions. Introduction of a new and better type of seed potato
helped open the door to important contacts. Insecticides and fer-
tilizers were made available to the interested farmers. In the second
year of the project, a new school was constructed for which the government of Peru later provided seven teachers.[8] A potable-water
system and an electric plant came into being. In order to emphasize
the value of the program, the inhabitants were encouraged to help
in the construction of these tangible improvements.

At first, some doubts and skeptical questions were raised. Even
a United Nations commission thought the changes were "superficial." [9] Nearby *hacendados*, fearful of losing a cheap labor supply,

[7] Richard W. Patch, "An Hacienda Becomes a Community," *American Uni-
versities Field Staff* (New York-Lima, October 4, 1957), pp. 5, 12. Allan R.
Holmberg (co-director at Vicos), "Changing Community Attitudes and Values in
Peru: A Case Study in Guided Change," chapter in *Social Change in Latin
America Today* (New York, published for the Council on Foreign Relations,
Harper Bros., 1960), pp. 78-100.

[8] Patch, "An Hacienda Becomes a Community," *op. cit.*, p. 8; and Holmberg's
"Changing Community Attitudes and Values in Peru," *op. cit.*, pp. 91-92.

[9] Patch, "An Hacienda Becomes a Community," *op. cit.*, p. 9.

looked upon the experiment with misgivings. But the inhabitants of Vicos gradually developed a new spirit of independence and hope. They looked toward the abolition of the *hacienda* system and set to work to make Vicos a community of small landowners and co-operative farmers. Through their own community government provision was made for all who so wished to work the common land on a share basis, in addition to working their individual allotments. President Prado proclaimed the expropriation of Vicos from the public benefit society of Huaráz and awarded it to the members of the Vicos community, but stipulated that the *Vicosinos* must pay the benefit society for the land. A group of men left the community temporarily for employment on the coast—their wages to be used on the purchase price—while the government of Peru provided a loan to aid in the purchase of the nearly 19,000 acres. Thus was this community of free citizens born about 1956 or 1957. In April 1962, the representatives of Vicos traveled to Lima to make an all-important payment on the community.[10] An example for the rest of Indian Peru, Vicos stood as a model for all people who could read or understand.

Learning how to read in Spanish had been one of the requisites of success for indigenous Vicos leaders. In health matters, the United Nations UNICEF had been of help. The United States Scipa (Inter-American Co-operative Service for Food Production) also assisted the program. Richard Patch commended the Peru-Cornell project for its wisdom in "limiting its success" rather than continuing to expand activities and services. The project withdrew its North American personnel and made the community responsible for itself. The results at Vicos are encouraging, even if not yet widely influential. Manuel Seoane, a political leader who was critical of some United States official aid programs, had the highest praise for this community project.[11] In summary, it can be pointed out that if the achievements at Vicos have not been particularly dramatic, at least they are real.

[10] *La Prensa,* April 5, 1962, p. 10.

[11] *El Mundo,* Lima, July 1958, p. 18. The Peruvian government set about to launch five projects in other communities along somewhat similar lines. See Holmberg, "Changing Community Attitudes and Values in Peru," *op. cit.,* p. 96.

THE SUMMER INSTITUTE OF LINGUISTICS

Another unofficial aid activity (unofficial from the United States point of view, but not from the Peruvian) was directed at Peru's Amazon basin area. Since the early days of the Republic there have been laws which recognized the problems and needs of the jungle Indians but, up until 1945, transportation and communication obstacles practically limited Peruvian government activity in this area to theoretical developments. Peru's government, in moments of concern, was baffled by the lack of teachers and text books adequate for dealing with the forty-five distinct tribal groups of interior Peru. In fact, these tribal peoples did not even have the "paper that talked," or a language reduced to writing. From 1945 to 1960, the Summer Institute of Linguistics, SIL (*Instituto Linguistico de Verano*), was the most dynamic force in transcribing spoken words to writing and in teaching the aborigines to read and write.[12] This Institute had originally begun in an abandoned farmhouse in the Arkansas Ozarks in 1934. In 1942 it moved its home base to the University of Oklahoma campus.

The United States' William Cameron Townsend, with many years of experience in Latin America (especially in Mexico and Guatemala before Peru and Ecuador), was the guiding spirit of the work. The Wycliffe Bible Translators (incorporated in California), the University of Oklahoma, and the Peruvian Ministry of Public Education co-operated in the organization, research, teacher training, direction and teaching involved in this complex project.[13] In the summer of 1945, with the encouragement of President Prado, Townsend visited and surveyed that part of the Peruvian jungle where he was planning

[12] Efrain Morote Best, "Tres Temas de la Selva," *Revista Peruana de Cultura*, Lima, January 1957, Año VII, Nos. 19-20, 4. See also, Olive A. Shell, *Grupos Idiomáticos de la Selva Peruana*, Publicaciones del Instituto de Filologia de la Facultad de Letras de la Universidad Mayor de San Marcos, Estudios, No. 7 (Lima, 1959); and "New Light in the Jungle," *Andean Air Mail and Peruvian Times*, Lima, June 13, 1958, pp. 6, 8, hereafter cited as *Peruvian Times*.

[13] The Wycliffe Bible Translators Mission was founded in 1942. It was dedicated to making the Bible available to all the Bible-less tribes of the earth in their own language. The Summer Institute of Linguistics teaches language analysis to 500 students annually at the Universities of Oklahoma, North Dakota, and Washington and has branches in England, Australia, and Canada.

to commence his work.[14] In June 1945, Townsend and the energetic minister of public education, Enrique La Roza, signed an agreement which provided that SIL would import specialists to study the tribal languages, establish vocabularies, make recordings, and compile scientific data concerning the indigenous tribes. At that time, various of those tribes, destined later to become interested in reading and writing, were still fearful of outsiders and inclined to shoot at sight. Some of them still practiced the art of head shrinking.

The 1945 agreement was amplified by another in April 1951, and supported by Supreme Resolution No. 909 (November 28, 1952), which provided for a course of study to prepare and certify native teachers who would then return to their own peoples and teach in their own languages. These actions and needs gave rise to the foundation of the main base of SIL, the Yarinacocha school, hospital, radio station, and center of scientific study. A precursor of the work to follow had been the medical missionary activity of Dr. Kenneth Altig at Yarinacocha in 1949. This center was located about eight miles from the Ucayali River port town of Pucallpa. By 1958, Ralph Eichenberger, then in charge of a crowded twelve-room clinic, likened his work to that of a city's public health service, except that his city ". . . covers a quarter-million square miles, our visiting nurses are hundreds of jungle miles apart, our consultation is by radio, our ambulances are balsa rafts and jungle-hopping planes." [15]

Very important for the jungle educational project was the establishment in 1953 of the government training school at Yarinacocha, a project suggested by the minister of education. During the first three months of each year, the most likely teacher prospects were chosen from the different tribes to embark on a study of Spanish, advanced academic subjects, and teaching methods. It was discovered that the selectees from the sixteen different tribes were eager and curious students. When accredited, they returned to the jungle as government-paid teachers. By 1956, forty bilingual schools (Spanish and an indigenous tongue) had been founded in Peru's Amazonian world.[16]

[14] Ethel E. Wallis and Mary A. Bennett, Two Thousand Tongues To Go (New York, Harper, 1959), and (London, Hodder, 1960).

[15] Clarence W. Hall, "Two Thousand Tongues To Go," Reader's Digest (reprint, August 1958), p. 10.

[16] Best, "Tres Temas de la Selva," op. cit., p. 8. See also Peruvian Times, June 13, 1958, p. 6.

Activity increased as funds from the government of Peru and private sources in the United States were received. The annual budget for SIL exceeded $1,000,000.[17] A twenty-four-hour radio control tower became the nerve center for the vast jungle operations of the field workers. Yarinacocha created thatched-roof accommodations and dormitories for 207 workers and their families, and a cafeteria with dormitories for tribal participants. Townsend began by sending his United States personnel out in pairs, that is, husband and wife, two single women, or two men, as recruiters and missionary workers. It was his policy to have a trained nurse as one of the two if it were at all possible. The single women have been unusually successful in interior Peru, particularly in places where it might have been very dangerous for men. Hostile chiefs, curious and at the same time less apprehensive of mere girls, have permitted the linguistic worker-nurse-missionaries to contact their people. The short-wave radio and/or airplanes have been, on occasion, the salvation of Peruvian and United States personnel as well as of ailing indigenous inhabitants. SIL had nine or more airplanes at its disposal during the period of its greatest activity (one of the planes having been a gift from the people of Mexico).[18] The air arm of SIL came to function as a subsidiary of the Peruvian Military Air Transportation system. In some years, SIL planes flew more than 1,500,000 air miles over the jungle.

In 1956 United States personnel working for SIL in Peru totaled fifty-five or sixty. Considerable time was consumed in reducing the spoken languages to written symbols. Numerous dedicated and talented Peruvians directed the expansion of the work in certain areas. In 1957, Efrain Morote Best was appointed by the Ministry of Public Education as supervisor of the jungle schools. His work has been outstanding.[19] SIL personnel have attempted to preserve legends, folk songs, anthropological data, and even the drum-beating messages (tambores) of some tribes.[20]

By 1960, the project had established close contact with twenty-nine tribes of Peru's "Green Hell." The Ministry of Public Education

[17] Hall, "Two Thousand Tongues To Go," op. cit., p. 15.

[18] Best, "Tres Temas de la Selva," op. cit., p. 7.

[19] La obra del instituto lingüístico de verano en el Peru (pamphlet with no date or place of publication listed), Edificio Ministerio Educación Pública, 14 piso. This pamphlet is handed out to interested persons at the Institute office.

[20] Ibid.

was actively aiding and financially supporting the training and up-
keep of teachers, preparation of books, and the establishment of
schools in jungle huts or in any other available place. The office of
Indigenous Affairs (of the Ministry of Labor and Indigenous Affairs)
participated actively in research, organization of material, and other
activities. The Ministry of Public Education and the Peruvian government turned over the fourteenth floor of the new public education building to SIL.

Conservative elements of traditionally reactionary Peru—reactionary insofar as general cultural matters are concerned—were appre-
hensive of the influence of this organized foreign movement which
conducted Bible reading and missionary medical work with the indigenous tribes. In 1953, a Lima newspaper released several articles
by a prominent Roman Catholic which charged SIL workers with
being "Protestant Wolves," engaged in work "sectarian and proselyting in nature." [21] Townsend answered with an explanatory letter.
A Catholic authority applauded Townsend's letter as a "masterpiece
of Christian love and reconciliation." [22] Townsend contended that
SIL represented no one religious body, that it co-operated with all,
believed in Christ, and, being nonsectarian, did not teach rituals or
ecclesiastical systems. He considered himself to be serving God and
humanity at the same time that he was engaged in scientific work.
Later on, the Papal Nuncio in Lima asked God's blessing upon the
work.[23]

Luis Valcárcel, one of Peru's most noted workers in indigenous
affairs, paid SIL a high tribute on the occasion of its tenth anni-
versary. Normally cautious in his use of words, Valcárcel said that
"never in our country has there been such an extraordinary case of
social action and scientific work realized by a group of foreigners.
. . ." [24] The minister of education in 1955, Carlos Gonzales Iglésias,
praised the work highly in a public address.[25] The President of Peru
demonstrated that he shared in this respect for SIL and its director

[21] Hall, "Two Thousand Tongues To Go," op. cit., p. 14.
[22] Ibid.
[23] Ibid., p. 15.
[24] Best, "Tres Temas de la Selva," op. cit., p. 5. Some of the interior indigenes
(like the Shapras) have, since starting to work with SIL, ventured into lumber-
ing and cattle-raising activities. John Tuggy of SIL has helped with these enterprises, Peruvian Times, October 4, 1963, p. 3.
[25] David Torres Calle, Ciencia lingüística, alfabeto científico para veinte lenguas
de la selva (Lima, n.d.), p. 13.

when Townsend was decorated with the Order of Merit for Distinguished Service, a rare honor for a foreigner. Whether fish or fowl (humanitarianism or science), SIL has continued to raise questions as to its nature, but up to 1962 it appeared to be working for the improvement of relations between the United States and Peru.

TOURNAVISTA

Another attempt to civilize one of the gateways to the jungle has been made at Tournavista. This was also complex in origin; a combination of motives—profit for individual enterprise and missionary zeal—were at work on a frontier. An agreement made in 1953 and approved by the government of Peru in 1954 contracted for missionary-minded Robert G. LeTourneau, United States industrialist, to construct thirty-one miles of road (later extended another five or six miles) from a point in the jungle off the Lima-Pucallpa road. LeTourneau had had experience with pioneer agriculture in the African jungle. He disagreed with both the usual individual-enterprise usage of raw materials (namely, withdrawal of the raw material from the country), and governmental aid by outright extension of money. Instead, he believed that firms with a sufficient world-trade basis should set up machinery in undeveloped nations and work toward the development of industries.[26]

In return for the construction of the road, LeTourneau was to be granted ownership of nearly 1,000,000 acres of land (an area larger than the state of Rhode Island). The United States industrialist obligated himself to "divide into lots for colonization purposes a part of the lands allocated . . . ," to build a "permanent landing field," and, among other things, to supply for rental or sale modern machinery in the colonization zone. In return, Peru exonerated LeTourneau for ten years from import duty on "all machinery, spare parts, implements, supplies and other articles and materials" used in the construction and colonization program.[27]

Opposition to the LeTourneau project came from the Consortium of Catholic Engineers who charged that LeTourneau's plans for de-

[26] LeTourneau Tech's NOW, January 1, 1961, XV, No. 1. This is a four-page news bulletin (LeTourneau activities) prepared at LeTourneau Technical Institute at Longview, Texas.

[27] Peruvian Times, February 12, 1954, p. 22. An English translation of the contract was included in this issue.

veloping the Peruvian hinterland "would set up a 'Protestant nucleus' in that region. . . ." [28] LeTourneau's statement that his "partner" was God led the Catholic group to fear that his chief goal was proselyting among the Indians. Apparently, LeTourneau was not surprised by this opposition, but was confident that he would be allowed to carry through on the project because of the written contract with Odría and the oral assent of other officials. In response to the charges of the Catholic group, LeTourneau stated that he "wanted to come down there and develop that land and see that the people get a better standard of living, and that probably the church—that means the Catholic Church down there—would get more money as a result." [29]

Construction work was started, as per agreement, within one year of the signing of the contract. The road was not completed within the first five-year contract period, but the concession agreement was renewed for an additional five years. Due to the many obstacles encountered, this extension was also too short a period for completion of construction and development. The enormous undertaking involved considerable agricultural experimental work, the development of equipment to turn back the jungle and hold it in check, the establishment of radio and air service, and educational and evangelical work with the jungle Indians.

This vast pioneering project was many-sided. At one time, the Mennonite Central Committee provided fifteen young men for work on the development of Tournavista and the construction of the road. [30] Timber and beef production were found to offer the best market potential for the area. The herd of cattle consisted of Charbray, Brahman, Brown Swiss, and Cebu-Criollo stock. Other food and livestock crops for man and beast were soon developed.

At this early date it is difficult to judge the long-term results of the Tournavista project. The LeTourneau family think of it as somewhat of a "God-and-LeTourneau-Family Point Four program." [31] There have been discouraging aspects even as the big machines (brought from the United States and up the Amazon) have temporarily destroyed the jungle and prepared it for road and crops. By

[28] Sam Pope Brewer, "Catholics Protest Texan's Peru Plan," *New York Times,* October 1, 1953, p. 11.

[29] *Ibid.*

[30] LeTourneau Tech's NOW, April 15, 1955, IX, No. 8.

[31] *Time* (Latin American ed.), March 25, 1957.

1957 the project had taken $1,500,000 of LeTourneau's own money,[32] and before the close of 1961, some $5,000,000 had been expended for operations.[33] The Institute of Linguistics, sixty miles away at Yarinacocha, was able to provide some valuable medical and dental aid to the project. That such aid was not always readily accepted by the local Indian populace was a surprise to some of the LeTourneau family.[34]

By 1960 it appeared that, at last, a town had been permanently established on the banks of the Pachitea River and that corn and rice and vegetables would probably continue to grow where once the jungle had ruled supreme. A 5,800-foot air strip and two-way radios in four stations were in operation. By the close of 1958, more than 1,700 acres had been cleared and the first settlers were coming from the United States. Up to 1961, however, only two United States citizens had purchased land.[35] The new town had the advantage of nearness to the Pucallpa-Lima road, but progress was difficult and slow. The future holds the important keys to the lasting influence of all these achievements. There is a wealth of raw materials (including petroleum) in the region, but these as well as the other potentials around the town of Tournavista await further development.

MISCELLANEOUS ACTIVITIES

Numerous other associations, business enterprises, foundations, or organized scientific and fine arts groups have been engaged in some type of formal or informal assistance activity in Peru. A few of these activities are here listed: Rockefeller Foundation work with libraries and with antimalaria operations; the British-American Hospital's contribution to Peru's health-sanitation needs as well as the training of nurses; church missionary operations; private United States di-

[32] *Ibid.*

[33] *Peruvian Times*, March 22, 1957, p. 2; June 14, 1957, p. 2; July 26, 1957, p. 3; April 11, 1958, pp. 3-4, 6; and December 22, 1961, p. 3. See also, *Business Week* (February 13, 1954), pp. 102-104; *Fortune*, XLIX (February 1954), p. 52; "Mover of Mountains," *Barron's* (April 23, 1956); and *Peru*, Pan-American Union (Washington, 1957).

[34] LeTourneau Tech's *NOW*, January 1, 1958, XII, No. 1.

[35] *Peruvian Times*, December 22, 1961, p. 8. For agricultural advancement, see LeTourneau Tech's *NOW*, November 1, 1954, and February 15, 1961. Periodic reports are carried in *NOW*, 1954-1960.

rected schools; the American Businessmen's Club and the American Women's Literary Club, which have, on occasion, conducted an aid project; Carnegie Institute's aid for Peru's *Instituto Geofísico;* the United States Geological Institute of Peru; various projects of universities and colleges of the States; the National Institute of Public Health of the United States which has provided grants-in-aid; the work of the International Basic Economy Corporation; scholarships for Peruvians from a variety of United States sources; and housing or other development projects sponsored by United States business interests.

Most Peruvians have not seen fit to classify the essentially non-profit-making activities of United States business concerns in Peru under the head of assistance to Peru. The relative value of the enterprises has been a point of spirited debate among Peruvians, and even when some value has been accorded the particular enterprise, this has not meant admission that its existence in Peru had worked toward good relations. There has been some very definite resistance to the economic strength of United States private enterprise.[36] Periodically, resentment is shown toward the preponderant position held by United States concerns. But it is admitted that, on occasion, International Petroleum Company (I.P.C.), Cerro de Pasco, and W. R. Grace and Company have been concerned with attempts to improve the standard of living of their employees. These giant corporations as well as some small ones have directed part of their efforts to housing needs. The results of such endeavors are not readily interpreted.

I.P.C. has given the greatest attention to housing, as demonstrated by its operations at Talara, where it has, literally, built a town. The only serious study of this project known to the writer raises some doubt as to whether or not labor problems can be diminished or solved by improving living conditions. Patch's conclusion was that "an improved standard of living may be necessary for good relations but it is not sufficient." I.P.C.'s housing aid was in effect the nur-

---

[36] See *El Mundo, Excelsior, Extra, Caretas,* Peruvian magazines, and *La Tribuna* and *El Comercio* newspapers. In addition to these moderate publications, one finds the extreme opposition in communist publications (see page 222). Some Peruvians who admit that United States concerns do more for their employees than do the national businesses still find it difficult to reconcile themselves to the dominant economic position of foreign capital. They picture Peru as a helpless subject under an absentee landlord. This foreign strength appears to be an affront to national aspirations and national pride.

turing of a town at Talara. The facilities have also induced relatives and friends of petroleum workers to use the housing. Unfortunately, the community does not provide many additional sources of income other than those of the petroleum industry. Housing has been only one of the many problems. It appears that I.P.C.'s good intentions regarding housing and community needs have created "greater expectations and dependency." [37] Although Patch's study is far from definitive, it is the best one available.

A business which was started by a United States citizen and, though expanding and flourishing, has not particularly concerned itself with employee benefits is the Faucett Aviation Company. Elmer J. Faucett of New York attracted attention in 1922 when he made the first solo flight from Lima to the Amazonian port of Iquitos.[38] In 1928 he started a small airline in Lima. Since then the business has extended its operations to many interior points of Peru. While prospering, Faucett has gained the respect and admiration of Peruvians in general.[39] This company, Peru's oldest domestic airline, has always identified itself with national needs and interests. A Faucett Foundation has been established for the purpose of providing scholarships for young Peruvians and United States residents in Peru who wish to study for a career in aviation.[40]

As has been noted above, there is no simple formula for classifying what should be considered foreign aid (official or unofficial). Nor is there any quick, easy way of determining the value of any assistance program. It is evident, however, that the amount of aid or assistance for Peru which was originated in the United States or by United States citizens has been large in amount and varied in nature. The more important assistance projects (both official and private) are not without admirers among those Peruvians competent enough to judge. On numerous occasions this writer was informed that assistance in living, and in making a living, is appreciated when offered in a sincere, friendly manner—but that Peruvian friendship cannot be purchased with mere money.

[37] Richard W. Patch, "An Oil Company Builds a Town," *American Universities Field Staff* (New York-Lima, March 12, 1958), pp. 1, 2, 12.

[38] *Excelsior*, August-September 1942, pp. 15-18.

[39] *Ibid.*, and *Peruvian Times*, November 13, 1959, p. 20.

[40] *Ibid.*, and *Peruvian Times*, September 21, 1962. An avenue connecting with the Lima-Callao International Airport is named in honor of Faucett.

10: THE MIGHTY DOLLAR AT WORK

Peruvians and North Americans hold varying points of view toward the need for and the benefits of United States private investments in Peru. The opinion of most informed Peruvians seems to be that Peru has long needed outside capital and technical know-how to best employ its raw materials and domestic labor force. Carlos Miró Quesada, who insists that his country has not had the wealthy individuals found in Argentina, Chile, Venezuela, Cuba, and Brazil, claims that Peru's many powerful *hacendados* have not had large capital reserves.[1] This may have been the case, but there have been many moderately wealthy Peruvians who have chosen Europe or the United States, in preference to their homeland, as the place to invest their funds. Those Peruvians who have been willing to invest at home have done so only on terms extremely favorable to themselves. This has been an important factor in making their nation dependent upon outside capital and thus subject to high interest rates on money borrowed from private sources.

The merits of United States investments have constituted a source of disagreement. Some Peruvians would like greater investment and some would wish for less. However, there has been a general feeling that since the United States, in one way or another, has had such a great influence in Peru, Washington must accept responsibility commensurate with that strength. The contention is that where there is power there should be obligation.[2] The "Yankees" have been the principal foreign creditors for Peru ever since the Leguía loans. Interest rates of 18 to 28 per cent (1940-1960) in Peru were considered, by those who thought them high, a part of the responsibility of their

[1] Carlos Miró Quesada Laos, *Pueblo en crisis* (Buenos Aires, 1946), p. 223.
[2] Francisco Miró Quesada, "Estados Unidos: realidad y problema," *El Comercio*, September 25, 1960, pp. 6-7. In a series of special articles, September-October 1960, this position was clearly stated in this established, conservative paper which has for years belonged to the family of the author of the article. These articles dealt with social questions also. In one of them, October 23, 1960, p. 6, the point is made that the United States cannot correctly call itself a democracy as long as the race question remains unsolved.

principal buyer-seller-creditor, the United States, both publicly and privately.

At the close of the Second World War, an atmosphere of optimism briefly prevailed in Peru before it dissipated in a clash with the hard facts of economic realism. The hope and talk of a *Peru Nuevo* rose when the man in the street elected Bustamante to the presidency.[3] However, it soon became evident that Bustamante could not solve the pressing economic problems. *La Tribuna*, the *Aprista* paper which continued to support almost all of Washington's international positions, began to express discontent with the economics of private United States investment.[4] In January 1946 Alberto Ulloa, head of Peru's delegation to the UN, said that foreign capital would be accepted in Peru but that it must be conditioned to the needs of the nation.[5] Some dissatisfaction was expressed concerning United States firms operating in Peru and the pressure which the dollar brought on the exchange rate of the sol. Earlier in the war, Luis Alberto Sánchez put the argument in a scholarly fashion:

> Many American politicians and financiers consider Latin America only a source of raw materials, purchased, of course, at a very low price. That means that we have been reduced to a very low standard of living and cannot, as a result, be consumers. In consequence, the powerful industries of the United States have lost many millions of buyers in Latin America. This is a contributory factor in the social failures and unemployment among certain workers in your country.[6]

It seemed that the need for outside capital and technological know-how was being recognized in Peru. However, the discussion continued more and more to center on the question of what prices should be paid for these.

Prior to Nixon's visit in 1958, resentment was apparently felt because it was believed that Washington did not assume the responsibility commensurate with its superordinate influence. This emphasis

[3] *La Tribuna*, Lima, December 29, 1945; December 30, 1945, p. 5; January 26, 1946, p. 5.

[4] *Ibid.*, December 28, 1945, p. 5; February 7, 1946, pp. 13-14; March 21, 1946, p. 13; March 28, 1946, p. 5.

[5] *Ibid.*, January 18, 1946, p. 2.

[6] For this statement of Luis Alberto Sánchez, see L. S. Rowe, *Latin American Viewpoints*, lectures on Latin America delivered at the Wharton School, University of Pennsylvania, in the fall of 1941 (Philadelphia, The Academy of Political and Social Science, 1942), p. 6.

was greatest in hard times, as in 1938, 1948, and 1958. Prior to 1958, the official United States position was that it did not intend to provide regular public credit for development south of the Rio Grande. Private investment was supposed to handle the needs. Latin Americans protested. When, in 1958, foreign markets (especially those tied to the United States) declined, Peruvians looked to the United States for relief and, when the northern nation did nothing but talk of the possibility of further reducing the markets, *Limeños* found their temperatures rapidly rising. Following Nixon's rough reception, Washington changed its attitude. Part of that changed attitude was reflected in the flow of public credit to the South.

Since the Second World War, United States interests, public and private combined, have dominated the Peruvian economy to an extent uncommon for a nation of Peru's size and diversity. Total direct investments by these interests have climbed to $446,000,000 while the total foreign portfolio investments in 1956 reached another $250,-000,000, most of the latter also deriving from "Yankee" capital.[7] It is not easy to determine precisely to what degree and in what manner this domination has come about. The United States Departments of Commerce and State have been of little value to scholars who have searched for a comprehensive explanation of this phenomenon.[8] According to the *Hispanic American Report* (January 1957), new United States investments in Peru during 1955 amounted to $28,500,000, double that of 1950. We are not told, however, the direct nature and make-up of that increase.

[7] Hubert Herring, "Peru in Serious Trouble," *Current History* (February 1963), p. 117. Also, *Analyses and Projections of Economic Development, VI, The Industrial Development of Peru*, United Nations, Department of Economic and Social Affairs (Mexico, D. F., December 1959), p. 26. Investment amounts cited in this manner usually include merely the book value, which is considerably lower than the real value.

[8] The Department of Commerce, 1947, informed this writer that the material required "does not appear to be readily available here in Washington. . . ." In the same letter several Peruvian offices of an official nature and United States regional offices of the Department were suggested: letter from George Wythe, Chief, American Republics Division, Department of Commerce, February 10, 1947. A follow-up of these suggestions also proved nearly fruitless. In 1962 this writer interviewed United States Minerals Attaché John Burgess, Jr., in Lima, and found him unwilling to provide significant factual data for research. Additional correspondence and interviews in Washington, Denver, and Lima, 1959-1962, have demonstrated how very difficult it is to obtain vital statistics in this area, and of what little assistance the United States government is in securing definite information on specific companies.

In one way or another, as the main buyer, seller, and financier, the northern nation maintains a strong hold over the southern one's international exchange position. A considerable share of exports and imports fall under the direction of the dollar. United Nations' publications (1959) show that, for 1955, per capita exports placed Peru in an unsatisfactory position as compared to other Latin-American countries.[9] The foreign exchange regulations, which prevailed in Lima during the 1950's, have made it difficult to determine the significance of increased prices for goods imported from the United States as compared with a lower rate of increase for Peruvian exports to the northern country. There are two rates of exchange, "the 'certificate rate,' which is used only in merchandise trade transactions and for certain specified invisibles, and the 'draft' or free rate, which can be used without restrictions." [10] Tourists usually convert foreign exchange on the basis of the draft rate. With such practices as are followed in certain other nations—i.e., double invoicing of imports, smuggling, and illegal export of capital—the corrupt, or at least questionable, methods employed by both Peruvians and United States citizens may provide part of the explanation as to why the Departments of Commerce and State can claim—honestly or dishonestly— that they do not truly know the extent or nature of United States concerns operating in Peru.[11]

About 35-40 per cent of Peru's gross national product came from foreign enterprises, mainly United States-controlled. In the early 1950's, nearly 10 per cent of Peru's national income was accounted for by the mineral industries.[12] Most of Peru's mineral production has been and is owned by outsiders. By 1960 about 96 per cent of the direct foreign investment in mining came from United States concerns. Approximately 98 per cent of petroleum production has been

[9] *Analyses and Projections of Economic Development* (United Nations—see fn. 7 of this chapter), p. 14.

[10] *Living Conditions in Peru*, World Trade Information Service, Department of Commerce (Washington, December 1958), p. 3.

[11] Gary MacEoin, *Latin America: The Eleventh Hour* (New York, P. J. Kenedy and Sons, 1962), p. 202. MacEoin's discussion of this is related to the general Latin-American scene and is not confined to Peru, but this writer has found it to be valid in the case of Peru.

[12] *Investment in Peru: Basic Information for United States Businessmen*, Department of Commerce (Washington, 1957), p. 49. See also *El Rol de las Inversiones Norteamericanas Dentro de la Economía Peruana* (printed in Lima by the Information Service of the United States, no date, ca. February 1958). Received at the Peruvian National Library, March 25, 1958, n. p.

controlled by International Petroleum Company since the 1957 merger with the British Lobitos interests. In addition, United States businesses have come to own two thirds of all foreign direct investments in manufacturing. In agriculture, the United States share amounted to considerably over one half of all foreign ownership; however, both agriculture and manufacturing are areas where Peruvian ownership predominates.

Principal United States mining interests as of 1960 were as follows: the Cerro Corporation,[13] Utah Construction Company, American Smelting and Refining Corporation, Phelps Dodge, Martin J. Heller (*Cia. Administradora de Minas*), and the Vanadium Corporation of America. Because of liberal legislation concerning depletion allowances, mineral investments have paid high profits. A liberal mining code has maintained foreign capital quite free of any special legislation in this area of development (see *A Statement of the Laws of Peru*, Washington, D.C., 1962). The Cerro Corporation's consolidated net income for 1959 was $9,100,000. Consolidated sales during that year amounted to $158,280,000.[14] In addition to mining and smelting, the corporation managed extensive agricultural interests in the Peruvian sierra and assumed the fabrication of its metals into mill products in the United States. The 1950's were three times as profitable on an average annual basis as had been the prosperous 1940's.[15] The Cerro concern accounted for 84 per cent of the copper, 36 per cent of the gold, and 55 per cent of the silver produced in Peru in the years from 1906 to 1938. The Vanadium Corporation of America was, for a long time, the owner of the sole vanadium mine in Peru. From 1907 to 1931, its mine supplied approximately 44 per cent of the world's total. The years from 1935 to 1939 saw it turn out about 45 per cent of the total for the world, and by 1946 it had dropped to 30 per cent.[16]

Cerro was the single giant in the mining field until 1960 when American Smelting and Refining, with a $115,000,000 loan from the

[13] For a long time, the name of the company was the Cerro de Pasco Copper Corporation. In 1961, the name was shortened from "Cerro de Pasco Corporation" to the "Cerro Corporation."

[14] *Andean Air Mail and Peruvian Times*, Lima, February 19, 1960, p. 1; hereafter cited as *Peruvian Times*.

[15] *Ibid.*, April 29, 1960, p. 1.

[16] *The Peruvian Economy, A Study of its Characteristics, Stage of Development and Main Problems*, Division of Economic Research, Pan-American Union (Washington, July 1950), p. 101.

United States government, joined Cerro, Newmont Mining Corporation, and Phelps Dodge in the rich copper mines under the heading
of Southern Peru Copper Corporation at the Toquepala project.[17]
This is the largest copper mine to be opened anywhere in the world
since the Second World War. Not even African copper could be
produced as cheaply—just over ten cents a pound.[18]

In the past petroleum has also been produced at low cost figures,
with the bulk of it being pumped along the Pacific coast or near the
coast. Ganso Azul, a holding company for Texas Gulf Producing
Company interests, has been a successful, if small, recent pioneer of
the interior jungle country. Peruvians themselves have played a very
small part in the development of the oil industry. Through the International Petroleum Company (I.P.C.), a Standard Oil Company of
New Jersey subsidiary which started operations in 1914, the parent
firm has long remained the dominant figure in the field of oil drilling
and refining.[19]

Since 1957, I.P.C. has been the lone giant in the production and
distribution of petroleum. In that year I.P.C. purchased the British
Lobitos oil fields. The Lobitos concern, small but nevertheless the
second largest in Peru, had been organized in 1901. This merger gave
I.P.C. a monopoly and ignited a political and popular controversy
over the entire question (see Chapter 11).[20] In 1959, at the Talara
refinery alone I.P.C. handled 98 per cent of all crude oil refined in

[17] *Peruvian Times*, February 12, 1960, p. 2. Under loans and credits of the
Export-Import Bank, as of March 31, 1956, the sum of $100,000,000 to Southern
Peru Copper Corporation for Toquepala copper project was listed, *Investment
in Peru: Basic Information for United States Businessmen*, p. 4. The same
source shows that in 1950, Cerro had borrowed $20,800,000 for a zinc refinery.

[18] *Peruvian Times*, April 1, 1960, p. 6. The same issue of *Peruvian Times*, in a
section entitled "Toquepala Supplement," carries considerable detail relevant to
this mine. The point is made that there were open-pit removals of 120,000,000
tons of overburden.

[19] *Peruvian Times*, November 13, 1959, p. 15.

[20] *Ibid.*, and *El Comercio*, Lima, which gave headlines and feature articles to
the increase in gasoline prices. The Chauffeur's Federation of Peru declared a
general strike in 1958 in order to protest the increase of gasoline prices: *Caretas*,
Lima, April 15-30, 1958, p. 9. The Peruvian press carried numerous articles
dealing with the petroleum controversy. I.P.C. purchased a full-page advertisement in *Extra*, Lima, February 4, 1958, p. 11, purporting to answer the question whether there was a petroleum monopoly in Peru. In the main, the matter
of production was avoided in that advertisement. In *Extra*, March 11, 1958, p.
31, I.P.C. took exception to information printed in *El Comercio*, February 2,
1958, concerning the increase of gasoline prices.

Peru, and it was noted that the new cracking tower had treated an average of 44,200 barrels a day during the year 1958. (For a brief discussion of the housing services provided by I.P.C. see Chapter 9.) I.P.C. is easily one of the leading examples of private United States capital controlling a Peruvian industry; it dominated oil, that industry so sensitive to national feelings.

It is difficult to obtain exact information as to the amount of capital which I.P.C. has invested in Peru. From the company's statement for 1958, we learn that the figure was "more than" $180,000,-000.[21] How much more we do not know. And if this is book value, we do not know what the amount would be in real value, although most likely it would be considerably higher than this. On the other hand, United States Department of Commerce figures list a mere $86,000,000 for direct investments in petroleum in Peru.[22] Debates in the Peruvian Congress questioned the accuracy of the $217,000,000 figure for I.P.C. investments when its Lobitos holdings were included.[23] The company claimed to have had very low profits in the 1950's. One reason that its income would have been considerably lower than its earnings was the fact that reinvestment of earnings appears to have been high during the years between 1953 and 1958. At least part of the reason for reinvestment can be attributed to the effort made to stimulate production by intensive prospecting and the application of secondary methods of recovery.[24] Extremely low-cost production may be less likely in the future because the highest hopes for prospecting lie in the interior (Eastern) provinces. We could conclude that, unless good discoveries are made on the continental shelf, the production increment which might be made by 1965 is not a particularly promising one. I.P.C. estimated, albeit conservatively, that Peru would produce 17,100,000 barrels in 1959 and would consume 16,500,000.[25]

[21] Peruvian Times, May 15, 1959, p. 14. This figure, book value, is not necessarily representative of the real value. In 1954 the value of the output of crude petroleum and natural gasoline (I.P.C. held a virtual monopoly of this) amounted to $51,000,000. See Investment in Peru: Basic Information for United States Businessmen, 1957, p. 56.

[22] "United States Private Direct Investments in the Latin-American Republics, by Country and Major Industries" (mimeographed), Department of Commerce (Washington, 1955-1961).

[23] Peruvian Times, November 13, 1959, p. 15.

[24] Analyses and Projections of Economic Development (United Nations), p. 14.

[25] Peruvian Times, May 15, 1959, p. 15.

In recent years there have been strikes and other expressions of opposition shown toward the foreign petroleum interests although domestic products have carried low prices. Discontent was expressed, especially by the Peruvian Federation of Chauffeurs and *El Comercio* newspaper, concerning the La Brea and Parinas concessions which I.P.C. held. Charges of excessive profits, the draining of Peru's richest fields, and maintenance of monopoly over production were leveled at the United States petroleum interests. The debates carried on in the Peruvian Congress were heated. Influential *El Comercio* called for nationalization of the industry and pointed to Mexico as an example to follow.[26] It is indicative of Peruvian opinion to note that Belaúnde Terry—who later became president—injected into the campaign the matter of recovering Peru's subsoil rights.

One of the largest general concerns still active in Peru is that of W. R. Grace and Company. (For a brief history of its early period

[26] *El Comercio*, September 8, 1960, pp. 2, 5; September 25, 1960, pp. 1, 2; and November 20, 1960, pp. 1, 2. During 1959, 1960, and especially 1961, *El Comercio* carried out a campaign attacking the United States petroleum interests. See Chapter 11 which deals with Vice-President Nixon's visit. The debate over the petroleum reserves is a complex one. See *Cámara de Diputados, Diario de Debates* and *Cámara de Senadores, Diario de Debates*, especially 1959, 1960, 1961; also *La Tribuna*, April 4, 1946, p. 9.

Alberto Ulloa initiated the I.P.C. controversy in 1932, when as a young law professor at the University of San Marcos he stated that the company's claims were not founded on legal rights. Since that time there have been some bothersome questions (part of the time they were raised merely for political reasons), but as late as 1960 it appeared that most of Peru's congressmen were not willing to declare against the legality of I.P.C. in Peru. See *Peruvian Times*, April 15, 1960, p. 1. For fuller statements representing the I.P.C. point of view in this controversy, see the *Peruvian Times*, March 11, 1960, pp. 14-15; May 20, 1960, p. 9; and June 16, 1961, p. 2. Leading the attack against I.P.C. has been Peru's oldest, and usually conservative, newspaper, *El Comercio*. For criticism of I.P.C., combined with requests for nationalization of petroleum, see the following issues of *El Comercio*: August 14, 1960, special Sunday section; September 8, 1960, pp. 2, 5; September 16, 1960, pp. 1, 3; September 25, 1960, pp. 1, 2; October 1, 1960, pp. 1, 7, 9; October 5, 1960, pp. 2, 4; October 12, 1960, p. 3; October 15, 1960, pp. 1, 4; October 16, 1960, p. 2; October 18, 1960, p. 19; October 20, 1960, p. 2; October 23, 1960, p. 2; November 5, 1960, p. 2; November 9, 1960, p. 2; November 11, 1960, p. 2; November 20, 1960, pp. 1, 2; November 21, 1960, p. 9; November 25, 1960, p. 18; December 2, 1960, p. 2; January 1, 1961, p. 5. Criticism of Pedro Beltran, premier of Peru and owner of *La Prensa*, Lima, appeared on various occasions in *El Comercio*, as on September 8, 1960, p. 2, and October 23, 1960, p. 2. From time to time a counterprotest was registered in *La Prensa*, as, for example, October 4, 1960, pp. 1, 2.

see Chapter 4.) With a record of continuous operations since 1850, W. R. Grace has the longest history of all United States firms. As shipper, air transporter, importer-exporter, sugar grower, manufacturer, and paper and textile producer, Grace has played an influential and varied role in the Peruvian economy. At "Paramonga," near Trujillo on the coast, the company's 17,000-acre sugar *hacienda* has long operated a refinery and paper mill, and has produced by-products, as well.[27]

The Grace policy of identifying itself with Peruvian national interests appears to have been a relatively effective measure for good will. This policy is reflected in its adoption of the name, "Casa Grace," and in its tendency to employ Peruvians at levels of administrative responsibility. Of course, it has often had the advantage, as compared to mineral investments, of being engaged in areas of production of goods or services which were not as sensitive to popular hostility.

Important United States private concerns not already mentioned but operating in Peru include the following: the First National City Bank of New York; Anderson-Clayton and Company; Goodyear; Marcona Mining Company (Utah Construction); Panagra airways; International Telephone and Telegraph; Frederick Snare Corporation; United States Steel Export Company; Wessel Duval and Company; and Westinghouse. In recent years, International Basic Economy Corporation and Sears, Roebuck and Company have developed extensive retail operations.

What about net profits? Although it is nearly impossible to secure detailed information, the above reports from the principal companies demonstrate that earnings have been high. How high depends on how one interprets the amortization figures, interest rates, and reinvestment of earnings. In many basic products for export the pro-

[27] The first half of the year 1959 showed W. R. Grace reporting a net income of almost $7,250,000 for that six months. This included interests outside Peru. In Peru, Grace is associated with Texas Gulf Producing oil interests also: *Peruvian Times,* September 25, 1959, p. 3.

For a complimentary report, see Eugene W. Burgess and Frederick H. Harbison, *Casa Grace In Peru* (Second Case Study in an NPA Series on United States Business Performance Abroad), National Planning Association (Washington, 1954). See also *Papers Relating to the Foreign Relations of the United States, 1930,* III (Washington), pp. 752-753, where Ambassador Dearing is quoted: "I am reliably informed that Sánchez Cerro told the manager of Grace Company that he was entirely satisfied with the company and it could expect his support as it had never dabbled in politics."

duction costs have been low. At the same time taxes have remained low. According to the United States Department of Commerce figures, the earnings for direct investments of $301,000,000 in 1955 were $41,000,000.[28] This figure of between 14 and 15 per cent is not far different from the one estimated by a United Nations group.[29] However, there are various ways of making the net profit appear to be lower than it actually is. One method is explained in engineer Luis A. Pflucker's article, "Politica de Oro" (*La Tribuna*, March 27, 1946) which shows how *barras de blister* would appear on the record as copper, zinc or such exports while actually there would be a much more valuable mineral in them. In that way a copper exporting concern can hide considerable gold in the ingots or ore which are shipped to the United States and elsewhere for refining. There are other ways which depend more directly upon bribery or simply upon unique accounting methods. With many of the concerns being heavy importers and exporters in a position to use the two rates of exchange, double incorporation (United States and Peru), and other devices such as double invoicing and illegal export of capital, there is good reason to believe that net profits run considerably higher than the figures provided by the Department of Commerce in Washington. Amortization requirements of long-term foreign capital in Peru had increased to nearly $36,000,000 by 1955 and to $45,500,000 in 1956. (Over the last quarter century, inflation and other causes of depreciation of the real value of national currencies have not been especially significant in the case of the sol. At least the loss of real value of the investment dollar, due to these, has not made it as important to have as high a rate of interest in Peru as in many countries of the world. The record of the sol compared to the dollar is not a poor one when all matters of international exchange are considered. The dollar has been hurt by inflation in the United States and it could hardly expect to escape the same fate in Peru. Yet, the value of the dollar has been well maintained in relation to the sol over the last twenty-five years. The sol suffered a four to one decline, for the exchange rate was 6.48 soles to the dollar in 1940 and by 1964 it took four times as many soles to purchase a dollar. This difference, in terms of real value is not badly distorted.) It is

[28] *Investment in Peru: Basic Information for United States Businessmen*, p. 5. This is figured as the sum of income and undistributed subsidiary earnings, probably at book value rather than real value.

[29] *Analyses and Projections of Economic Development* (United Nations), p. 26.

well to remember that often the companies are reporting only the book value figures and not the real value figures.

Are profits too high? Not according to the people providing the capital. But what is a fair price for capital and technological know-how? This cannot be answered without determining what is a fair price for natural resources and labor. The investor, domestic or foreign, speaks of the risk involved. The nationalistic Peruvian replies in this vein, "What risk? Your large concerns have operated here for forty years and had little risk of nationalization, governmental interference, effective competition, or high taxes."

Capital has its many critics in a society such as has been in existence in Peru during the twentieth century. Especially will foreign capital be singled out for critical examination.

The investor is inclined to refer the critics to such matters as the industries started, the number of people employed and, in vague terms, to the tax payments. In the significant area of minerals, including oil, we note that foreign concerns alone employed 20,613 persons[30] in 1946 and that the great percentage of these were Peruvians. Cerro Corporation employed 8,990 to head the list of United States interests and I.P.C. followed with 6,169. It is worth noting that the lucrative extractive industries contributed 7 per cent toward the national income—even with a great amount of the nonferrous metals being exported—but that they employed less than 2 per cent of the active population.[31] Cerro's working force, mainly Peruvian, had increased to 14,700 by the year 1959, while the total number of employees of United States companies had passed the 46,000 figure.[32] The United States Department of Commerce figures show that companies operating in Peru in 1955 paid out $39,000,000 in wages and salaries, $14,000,000 in income taxes (most likely including payments of royalties), and other taxes amounting to $9,000,000.

What positive long-term gains has Peru made as a result of the influx of outside capital and industry? United States companies often mention that they have provided better working conditions and higher wages than have the domestic employers. In 1960, I.P.C.

[30] *The Peruvian Economy, A Study of its Characteristics, Stage of Development and Main Problems*, p. 107.

[31] *Analyses and Projections of Economic Development* (United Nations), p. xxiii.

[32] *Peruvian Times*, May 6, 1960, p. 10.

stated that it had pensioned more workers than any other company in Peru.[33] The fact that it has also provided good housing does not mean that such accommodations necessarily work for good relations between the company and nearby citizens or even between the people of Peru and the people of the United States.[34] Private companies have claimed that they were training technicians for the future development of Peru—a sort of private technical assistance program. But nationalists have often pointed out that foreign interests were paid well through profits for any service they might have provided.

Although no carefully collected and arranged data have been assembled, it is evident that many Peruvians, probably the majority, do not consider the United States private investments to have worked as a positive factor in the over-all relations between Washington and Peru. In the author's "Sample Survey" the two largest concerns, Cerro and I.P.C., were most often listed in reply to the question: "What United States enterprises (foundations, associations, agencies, institutions, business concerns, organizations) have caused the most damage to Peruvian-United States relations in the twentieth century?" [35] Only seven of the 157 responses failed to provide answers. Many replies listed one of the other businesses. Two questionnaires carried the information that the "superior attitude" held by United States persons toward Peruvian employees was harmful to relations. In write-in suggestions, fourteen charged that restricted salaries or wages and the ceiling as to the rank which Peruvians might hold in United States concerns were causes of discontent. Replies to the following question were suggestive as to opinions held toward major areas of United States operations in the country: "II. Which has been most helpful to Peru in proportion to the time it has operated here? Check one: (a) International Petroleum (here for about 48 years) _____. (b) *Instituto Cultural Peruano-Norteamericano* (here for about 22 years) _____. (c) Scipa on U.S. aid in food production (here about 18 years) _____." I.P.C. was listed

[33] *Peruvian Times*, April 29, 1960, p. 17.

[34] Richard W. Patch, "An Oil Company Builds a Town," *American Universities Field Staff* (New York-Lima, March 12, 1958). See Chapter 9 for a statement on the I.P.C. housing project.

[35] "Sample Survey," Carey. This is the survey mentioned in Chapter 7 (fn. 71) where 157 of 181 questionnaires were returned. The survey was made by this writer in Lima and Callao in April 1962.

two-ninths as many times as was the Cultural Institute, and only two-seventeenths as often as Scipa.[36]

On occasion the major concerns have been subjected to violent outbursts. Peruvian authorities and United States management have tended to blame the violence upon communist agitators. There may be some truth in this charge, but it is not the complete explanation. In 1957, police shot eight demonstrators, killing two, in the strike against the Utah Pacific Company at the port of Ilo where work for the Southern Peru Copper Corporation was centered.[37] With capital from an official agency in Washington (Export-Import Bank) being provided for this private enterprise, the situation reflected the complex relationships existing between public interests and private interests in the mining of copper.

The year 1960 was one in which bitter clashes between dollar investors and Peruvian workers arose. Three Andino Indians were killed and twenty-five policemen injured near the city of Cerro de Pasco when the Indians, reportedly led by the mayor of the city, moved onto one of the farms occupied by the Cerro Company. The rioters claimed the farm as their property. Later, in a group numbering 2,000, they attacked the police station and secured the release of four of the rioters.[38] (Thirty years earlier, in 1930, Cerro de Pasco

[36] *Ibid.* This information is all the more significant since a large number of responses came from people who should have had favorable relationships with United States businesses or whose parents had had that association.

[37] Richard W. Patch, "Testing Time For An Experiment in Freedom," *American Universities Field Staff* (New York-Lima, November 9, 1957), p. 16; and *New York Times,* November 9, 1957, p. 11.

[38] *Peruvian Times,* May 6, 1960, p. 1. Mountain Indian farmers in the area have attempted to take and hold lands now claimed by Cerro de Pasco. This "Communal Movement of Peru" (*Movimiento Comunal del Peru*) has attempted to gain land from various great landowners of central Peru. The movement caused Cerro de Pasco to make a full-page statement in the *Peruvian Times,* December 8, 1961, p. 9, in response to what had been published in *Expreso,* December 1, 1961. A small part of Cerro de Pasco's statement follows: "The Cerro de Pasco Corporation is owner of a group of farms in the highlands of the Departments of Pasco and Junín, whose extension does not arrive remotely at the figure given in the advertisement of the *Movimiento Comunal.* . . . On the farms of the Corporation there is no system of peonage or other form of servitude, all workmen and employees being on a wage basis with the social rights provided by law. . . . Although the Corporation has full legal right to own and exploit its cattle farms, it has no objection to selling part of them to the Government, to private parties or to the *Comunidades,* retaining only sufficient extensions for the production of meat for its workmen and employees." The Federation of Bank

had been the scene of another bloody riot when the Peruvian government sent troops to protect the personnel and property of the Ameri-
can company.) In 1941, the residential area occupied by United
States citizens was guarded by armed employees of this mining com-
pany. *Hacienda Paria*, a Cerro de Pasco sheep farm in the central
Andes, was the center of one of several attacks upon that company.
La Prensa (October 25, 1960) claimed that a band of organized
and militant Indians (possibly of the dissident *Aprista* faction,
Aprista Rebelde) employed funds from Cuba to aid the agrarian
Indian forces. At the same time, *La Prensa* charged Luis Miró
Quesada's *El Comercio* with being hypocritical since, while claim-
ing to dislike Castro's government, it was simultaneously the "main
mouthpiece of Fidelismo" in Peru. A violent outbreak in 1960 at
W. R. Grace's Paramonga sugar estate resulted in three deaths and
sixteen injured when workers fought a pitched battle with police.[39]
Two thousand workers had been on strike for three and one-half
weeks, and part of the discontent was alleged to have been caused
by the installation of time clocks. The National City Bank of New
York has been the object of strikers and stone-throwers on more
than one occasion. With this evidence, one is forced to conclude
that the mighty dollar is not always appreciated.

The government of the United States has loaned appreciable
amounts to Peru and to United States companies in Peru. Loans
and credits of the World Bank and the International Development
Association have usually totaled fifth or sixth highest for the Hemisphere between 1948 and 1960. Public capital aid for agriculture in
Peru has been proportionately higher than that extended to any
other Latin-American country.[40] United States public aid has also
been extended for the following: electric power, highway improvement, port improvement, and a cement plant. I.C.A. and Mutual
Security programs in Peru have always been among the largest for

---

Employees of Peru, in protesting the casualties brought about when troops and
police sought to remove members of *Comunidades*, went on strike early in
March 1962. A scuffle between National City Bank officers, on the one hand,
and an agent of the Federation of Bank Employees, on the other, took place
March 8, 1962. For a copy of the Bank's position in this incident, see a translation of the letter sent by the Bank to the Minister of Labor: *Peruvian Times*,
March 16, 1962, p. 3.

[39] *Peruvian Times*, May 6, 1960, p. 1.

[40] *The World Bank and IDA in the Americas: A Summary of Activities*
(Washington, January 1962, and earlier issues).

the Latin-American nations.[41] In general, United States public loans and credits were more openly welcomed than was the inflow of private capital. The simple explanation for this rests on the fact that Peruvians did not pay the high price for public money which private capital required. This does not mean that the Export-Import Bank loans were always popular.[42] Usually, the World Bank called for international procurement of goods purchased through its financing, while United States government agencies usually limited their financing to United States procurement. In this way, United States public capital for Peru was beneficial to the United States private interests operating there.

As might be anticipated, a study of Peruvian newspapers and periodicals reflects some resentment of the influential United States capital holdings. General news stories favorable to the investments are also common. In addition to this, various companies have published their own periodicals in either English or Spanish; and some in both languages. An examination of the critical press reveals that criticism comes from a variety of sources. On occasion it is mentioned that natural resources are exploited in the regions where low-cost production can be carried out. Critics point out that, although there are transportation and communication developments made by outside capital, these are usually of primary benefit to the people exploiting the resources and are not designed to meet the needs of the national economy. The normally moderate *Excelsior* opined in 1956 that the United States was made up of very ambitious people looking for ways to enrich themselves under the "Republican regime" in Washington.[43] From 1956 to 1960 there appears to have been an increasing tempo against outside capital. Trade policies were described as acts of "El Imperialismo Yankee." The Aprista newspaper, *La Tribuna* (1958), expressed the opinion that it was not a source of pleasure to have Samuel Waugh, president of the Export-Import Bank, accompany Vice-President Nixon.[44] Another newspaper, *Ultima Hora*, protested that the Peruvian economy was

[41] *Operations Report*, International Cooperation Administration (Washington, 1959, 1960, 1961).

[42] *El Mundo*, Lima, August 1958, p. 11, reported Bedoya Reyes as saying that the Export-Import Bank was not what Latin America needed. See also *El Mundo*, November 1958, p. 3; and *La Tribuna*, May 7, 1958, p. 1.

[43] *Excelsior*, Lima, January-February 1956, p. 5. Also *Hechos*, Chiclayo, August 21, 1947, p. 1.

[44] *La Tribuna*, May 7, 1958, p. 1.

suffering heavily.[45] Extremist papers like *Libertad* attacked the Cerro
Corporation holdings of mines and *haciendas* as "feudalistic." [46]
Communist, or at least apparently communistically-inclined Solo-
mon Bolo (vitriolic unfrocked priest), journalist Genero Carnero
Checa, and peasant leader Hugo Blanco have in recent years kept
up a cry of complaint against United States capital operations in
Peru. Nobody would seriously suspect Archbishop Juan Landázuri,
O.F.M. (later a Cardinal) of Lima, of communist leanings, yet he
is reported to have said: "The Church condemns capitalism and
also the miserable situation to which it has led innumerable workers." [47] Although he was not singling out United States investments,
and the word capitalism was not defined, this reference to the social
injustices in that vein has meaning for one trying to understand
national and international problems.

Influential Pedro Beltran (see Chapter 7), representing the
moderate conservative financial segment, expressed confidence in
"Yankee" private capital. He saw his country, with respect to its
need for outside capital, in the same condition as the United States
of some 100 years earlier. In his opinion, the United States government should insist that Peru set its house in order (primarily control
inflation and arrange for sound investment conditions) and then
turn much of the task over to private foreign capital.[48] Beltran was
not very explicit on just how this should be done. When he was
premier and minister of finance, his efforts to free the sol in the
open markets were looked upon with favor by domestic and foreign

---

[45] *Ultima Hora*, Lima, April 29, 1958, p. 8. This account stated that it was
time that the United States responded to Peru's friendliness with acts and not
merely with words.

[46] *Libertad*, Lima, April 25, 1962, pp. 1, 6-7. This appears to have been a
small *Aprista* paper at one time, and one that was later taken over by the *Apra
Rebelde*, communists or some extremist group of the left. For the capture of one
of the agrarian rebel leaders, Hugo Blanco, see *El Comercio*, May 31, 1963. For
a listing of the extremist press, that which can be counted on to attack United
States business interests *per se*, see pages 222-223 of this book.

[47] MacEoin, *Latin America: The Eleventh Hour*, p. 135. In 1962 at the age of
forty-eight, Archbishop Juan Landázuri Ricketts became the youngest new member of the College of Cardinals when Pope John XXIII elevated him to that
post. The name Ricketts comes from his mother's side of the family where
Cardinal Landázuri is a descendant of an English merchant, William Ricketts.
Peruvian Times, February 23, 1962, back page.

[48] Pedro G. Beltran, "Foreign Loans and Politics in Latin America," *Foreign
Affairs* (January 1956), p. 300.

businessmen. It is not likely that the ordinary citizen appreciated his efforts as was implied by his failure to gain support for the presidential nomination in the 1962 campaign. In 1961, Beltran reportedly was opposed to 8 per cent interest on Alliance For Progress money to Peru, saying it was too low a rate.[49] Some people would have the dollar play one role; others would have it play another.

There is no simple way to determine the degree of popularity or unpopularity of North American capital in Peru. An experienced observer and highly respected author on Latin-American affairs, Hubert Herring, has generalized on the matter as follows: "United States capital is too omnipresent for the tastes of (Peruvian) nationalists. . . ."[50] In the Peruvian Congress all shades of opinion are reflected. There are those numerous representatives who would not think of criticizing United States investments because of the danger of upsetting the apple-cart. This "apple-cart" is one which protects their own favored rights in the prevailing situation, wherein free and honest elections are the exception rather than the rule. Then there are those who genuinely support United States capital investments because they view them as having been very beneficial to Peru. Others, like Alfonso Benavides Correa in the Chamber of Deputies, have bitterly decried Peru's economic "subjugation" to foreign economic interests.[51] Author César Levano has taken a left-wing position in calling for the national protection of natural resources so that foreign interests will not subvert them.[52] Another writer, Jorge del Prado, suggested a more moderate middle-of-the-road position for Peru which would be between the United States and the Soviet Union.[53] And so the arguments go back and forth. Herring com-

---

[49] *Hispanic American Report*, XIV (October 1961), pp. 720-721.

[50] Herring, "Peru in Serious Trouble," *op. cit.*, pp. 99, 117.

[51] Alfonso Benavides Correa, *Interpelación a la cancillería* (Lima, 1958). See various of his Chamber speeches as reprinted in this work, here cited.

[52] César Levano, *Por la nacionalización del petróleo* (Lima, 1960), pp. 50-83. For other expressions of discontent with economic matters, see *Excelsior*, July 1955, p. 11, and October 1955, p. 19; *El Mundo*, April 1957, p. 3; *La Tribuna*, May 7, 1958, p. 1, May 8, 1958, p. 3; *El Comercio*, May 7, 1958, p. 3; *Ultima Hora*, April 29, 1958, p. 8; and many others of the moderate press. For extreme criticism, see Chapter 12. *Excelsior*, July 1955, stated that mere words such as "Good Neighbor" and "American Co-operation" were entirely inadequate. New economic policies were wanted.

[53] Jorge del Prado, *Una tercera posición* (Lima, 1960), p. 205.

mented that, "no matter how truly foreign investment may serve the national economy, its presence is always irritating." [54]

It is evident that there is no simple formula for determining to what degree private foreign economic power aggravates citizen Juan (Doe) Gonzalez of Lima, any more than there is of knowing how much responsibility the government in Washington should accept for segments of Peruvian economy where United States citizens have such a great hold. It appears that Peruvians have become quite sensitive to market fluctuations and tariff changes. A representative of the Peruvian Mining Association, Edgardo Portaro, told the Tariff Commission in Washington that a United States tariff raise on lead and zinc "would not only disconcert our people but also disillusion them about the ideals of Americanism." [55] At that time, 15 per cent of Peru's foreign earnings came from exports of lead and zinc, and production of those two items accounted for 4.5 per cent of the nation's gross national product. Would the government of Peru have turned away from the United States leadership on other things simply because of market difficulties in lead and zinc? The answer to this can only be determined by a study of power and pressure politics in Peru, and possibly an understanding of the relationship of those forces with those of United States private investors.

If Peru follows the trends already taken in Mexico, Argentina, and Brazil, this would suggest more discontent with the power of the mighty dollar and ultimately more regulation or some move toward nationalization. A United Nations study predicts that a greater percentage of earnings will be taken from the country by 1965, thus leaving Peru in need of capital in any event, even if the 1945-1955 trends are projected.[56] This is all the more reason to ask if the long-range public interests of the United States are being best represented by policies which have as their sole primary goal the protection of dollars invested in Peru.

Various aspects of this study bring to the forefront the complex question of what is the "public interest" and what is the "private interest" of the United States in its dealings with the government in Lima. In discussing the entire field of Latin America, W. S. Woytinsky had this to say:

[54] Herring, "Peru in Serious Trouble," op. cit., p. 117.
[55] New York Times, November 27, 1957, p. 30.
[56] Analyses and Projections of Economic Development (United Nations), p. 26.

To sum up, investment of U.S. capital in foreign countries is neither hidden aggression nor a blessing for the receiving nations. It has nothing in common with the U.S. mutual security program. Neither encouragement nor discouragement of the outflow of U.S. capital should be an objective of our foreign policy in any part of the world—least of all in Latin America. . . . Thus, the goal of the United States in Latin America is *not* to extend the cold war, to promote the U.S. exports, to protect and build up U.S. investments, to befriend and support pro-big-business governments or any particular economic doctrine. . . . The pattern of development in that area will be determined by its peoples, their governments and their intellectuals.[57]

Woytinsky asks to what extent the United States should be "interested in promoting the outflow of capital—and occasionally the flight of capital—from this country to the happy lands where there is no profits tax and payment of other taxes is left to the discretion of capitalists?" He questions the merits of foreign aid objectives which suggest extending aid to other countries in order that United States exports might be thereby increased.

H. W. Balgooyen, vice-president of The American and Foreign Power Company, saw the matter of "national interest" and "individual advantage" of private investments in Latin America from a different perspective:

Here is a three and one-half billion dollar market for our goods— a market at the very beginning of its growth and development and expanding in terms of purchasing power at a rate much faster than our own. It is entirely in our national interest and to our individual advantage that this growth and progress should continue—that resources should be further developed, that industry should expand and flourish, and that a more prosperous and satisfying way of life should be achieved. Every individual whose productivity can be raised above the subsistence level is a potential customer; and every person with a peso in his pocket after providing for minimum living need can, with others of his kind, broaden the markets for American goods, increase the opportunities for American workmen, and make for closer commercial and cultural ties among all the American nations.[58]

[57] W. S. Woytinsky, *The U.S. and Latin America's Economy* (New York, n.d.), pp. 50-51. This 66-page booklet was published under the sponsorship of the Tamiment Institute, following an eight-month trip the author took to Latin America in 1957-1958.

[58] Clement G. Motten, Virgil Salera, Richard L. Davies, H. W. Balgooyen, *Latin America: Development Programming and United States Investments* (Philadelphia, University of Pennsylvania Press, 1956), p. 51.

The difference of opinion is great, then, between the points of view of Woytinsky and of Balgooyen. The present writer believes that the government at Washington would do well to clarify its position and long-range objectives relating to these divergent points of view.

Private investment, United States government investment, and foreign aid programs are intricate parts of the network of Peruvian-United States relations. United States government loans will have the effect of making the dollar more responsible for the Peruvian economy unless those loans can be amortized in such a way as to leave Peru more the master of its own household. Economic aid and technical assistance should not be viewed as, primarily, a way of opening new outlets, or maintaining old, for United States capital and products. Long-range policies of Washington should aim at development of the Peruvian economy, a stabilization of that economy, and a wider distribution of the economic product among Peruvians. If these goals are not set forth as important, there is an even greater danger that the United States government will become more and more involved in the complexities of responsibilities for Peruvian economics without possessing the authority to deal adequately with the problems that are sure to arise.

11: A VICE-PRESIDENT AND THE UNIVERSITY

Vice-President Richard M. Nixon's Latin-American tour of early 1958, in itself only one of many hemispheric incidents of the day, has provided us a window through which we can view the broader developments and problems of that period. Because of the great publicity given the event by both the United States and Peru, it is a well-lighted window opening directly on Washington-Lima relations. It afforded an important perspective for judging the strengths and weaknesses of *Apristas*, communists, and other critics of United States policies during that hazardous time. The incidents of the Nixon tour turned out to be a pivotal point for Washington in its approach to postwar Latin America. The nations to the south were demanding more attention, and the violent demonstrations at Lima and Caracas, especially the latter, added considerably to that demand. The visit of Nixon is meaningful if it is viewed as part of the larger course of developments which transpired after the Second World War.

After Nixon had been insulted and spat upon during his stay in Lima, there were immediate outcries which tended to blame the communists for the incident. Some dedicated communists were probably involved (possibly very active in organizing the anti-American forces), but this does not wholly explain the fury which confronted the Vice-President in May 1958. The facts behind the chain of events extending back more than a year before the visit and the developments after it make it evident that the cry of "Communism" was far from adequate in explaining what happened, or more important, why it happened. Nixon's Latin-American tour, primarily because of the violent protests which occurred in Peru and Venezuela, was an eye-opener to Washington. In mid-1958 only a fool would deny that United States policies were failing to achieve their purposes. Between 1948 and 1959 the government of the United States and various of its independent and quasi-independent foundations had expended considerable time and money in Latin America, but in spite of this effort a tide of ill will had piled up there. Because of poor counsel, Nixon innocently walked head-on into this wave of resentment.

At first, the stock explanation—one totally lacking any depth of understanding—was that Latin Americans were unhappy because the United States had neglected them for Europe and Asia.[1] In a very superficial manner, the answer indicated the correct approach; but it failed to show in what respects Latin America had been neglected and, therefore, just what were the causes of its unhappiness. The case of Peru was lumped loosely with that of the rest of Latin America. Before it was over, the "Affaire Nixon" forced Washington to take a more searching look into matters.

The causes of the discontent were varied and widespread. Looking at the Lima-Callao population centers alone, it was evident that the causes of discontent were deep and complex. In the rural area there were many additional causes. The voices of unrest were all the more vocal because in May 1958 Peru was experimenting with democratic procedures. Political parties, labor unions, the press, and Peruvian citizens as individuals had seldom if ever known such freedom from restraint or fear of reprisal. By using force, dictator Odría had been able to prevent discontent from rising into the open during his tenure (1948-1956), but the Prado government which followed him permitted considerable freedom of expression and was unwilling to use strong measures to stamp out opposition.

Yet for various reasons other than the backlog of anti-Odría feeling, there were potent forces at work. For one thing, Fidel Castro was rapidly becoming a hero in Cuba as well as over much of Latin America at the very time that many Peruvians were saying to themselves that they knew there was a better way of life in which they were determined to share. Much of this combination of rising hopes and growing discontent centered in Lima and Callao or the other urban centers of Peru, but it was starting in the rural area. As in other countries, many people in Peru thought that deep social changes were contingent upon the success of some such movement as the one proposed by Castro.

Another point of unrest was that, in many respects, the economic

---

[1] Just prior to Nixon's unhappy Peruvian experience, the New York Times (April 28, 1958), in discussing the tour, stated that there existed in Latin America "a general conviction that the United States has been holding back aid while being overly generous to Europe."

interests of Peru and the United States appeared to be in conflict. From the end of the Second World War, with the exception of the Korean interlude, economic relations with the United States had been generally unfavorable. This unsatisfactory relationship, from Peru's point of view, had also extended from the ousting of Leguía up to the semi-active participation of the United States in the Second World War in about 1940. The Korean War had boosted Peru's export volume and value and in this way improved the economy in general. Thus when the Korean War and the two world wars were viewed in perspective, the opinion in Peru was that only in time of extreme emergency did the United States pay serious attention to the Peruvian economy. The point of view was expressed that since the Export-Import Bank's primary purpose was to sell the products of the United States, it did not fit Latin America's needs.[2]

Throughout the twentieth century, one of the most active reform centers in all Peru had been the University of San Marcos. And of all Latin-American university student federations in 1958, few if any had as close a relationship to national politics as had the San Marcos student organization.[3] A writer in El Mundo, in April 1957, opined that the United States should talk less lyrically and act more forcefully with respect to an economic program to help eliminate misery in Peru so that the chances of communist growth would be lessened.[4] Other writers made the same point, but it would remain for the student federation of San Marcos to emphasize this in a dramatic manner.

During the most critical period in 1958, the San Marcos Federation of University Students went on record condemning the powerful influence which United States interests held over Peru's natural resources, particularly its minerals.[5] The United States concerns had, under Odría, continued to extend their control over Peruvian mines, and in 1957, Standard Oil of New Jersey (International Petroleum Company) had, by taking over control of the British Lobitos interests, become literally a monopoly of petroleum production.[6] In No-

[2] El Mundo, Lima, July 1958, p. 18b; August 1958, p. 11.
[3] This writer was a student at San Marcos University in 1942 and had a class under Víctor Andrés Belaúnde, later president of the United Nations Organization.
[4] El Mundo, April 1957, p. 3; August 1958, p. 11.
[5] Richard W. Patch, "Nixon in Peru," American Universities Field Staff (New York-Lima, May 20, 1958), p. 5 (hereafter cited as "Nixon in Peru").
[6] Caretas, Lima, April 15-30, 1958, p. 9.

vember 1957 serious strikes hit the United States copper investment areas. The government suspended the constitution for thirty days in an effort to control the difficulty. During the November strike against the Utah Pacific Company and the Emcee Company in Toquepala, the police shot eight demonstrators, killing two of them.[7] The next month Peru's postal workers were out on strike, as were the workers on the Grace and Company's sugar hacienda of Cartavio. The strike of Lima's transport workers presented a particularly difficult problem. The Federation of Bank Employees (relatively strong) held Lima in a bank strike during the first half of May 1958.[8] This same federation had struck in 1957, an action which many interpreted as a demonstration against the United States copper interests. May 1958 was a tense period, as is shown by the threat of a general strike if the government went ahead with its warning that it might dissolve the federation of bank workers.[9]

A labor dispute which had significant implications regarding attitudes toward the United States was the one directed at the International Petroleum Company (I. P. C.). The Chauffeurs Federation of Peru (a well-organized group) declared a general strike in April 1958 to protest the increase in gasoline prices. In Cuzco there were acts of open violence.[10] The seriousness of the petroleum problem in general was reflected in Peru's sales abroad. In the year 1958, petroleum and its derivative exports dropped to 702,779 metric tons from the 1,040,291 of the preceding year. The 1958 figure was the lowest export amount since the Second World War.[11]

There is no simple explanation of why I. P. C. has aroused the feeling of nationalism in Peru as much as it has.[12] A nationalistic spirit can, it seems, be aroused regarding petroleum in almost any underdeveloped nation where foreign interests are powerful. From time to time in 1957 and 1958 I. P. C. was criticized by various seg-

[7] Richard W. Patch, "Testing Time for an Experiment in Freedom," *American Universities Field Staff* (New York-Lima, November 9, 1957), p. 16.

[8] *Ibid.*, and *Caretas*, April 15-30, 1958, p. 9.

[9] *Ultima Hora*, Lima, May 7, 1958, p. 2.

[10] *Caretas*, April 15-30, p. 9.

[11] R. F. Rodríguez, *Market for U.S. Products in Peru*, Department of Commerce (Washington, 1961), p. 14.

[12] "Sample Survey," Carey. I.P.C. was cited more times by Peruvians as having caused "harm" to Peruvian-United States relations. Although this was not a scientific or widespread sampling, it was indicative of an upper-middle-class expression of opinion.

ments of the press, which raised questions concerning "monopoly conditions" in production, labor conditions, the value of I. P. C. investments in Peru, and the loss of Peruvian control over future petroleum developments.[13] I. P. C. attempted by both paid and unpaid press releases or advertisements to present its position to the public. When there appeared to be a variance between I. P. C. investment figures as reported in the government's Auditing Department of the Tax Office and those cited in congressional debates, I. P. C. issued an explanation. No definite value was established which satisfied the various points of view. I. P. C. used figures between $154,000,000 and $217,500,000 for estimating the company's Peruvian investment in 1959. Some informed Peruvians believed that the figure should have been considerably higher, and said it was maintained at a low level as a tax evasion tactic. This is a maneuver often used by both domestic and foreign-owned business concerns.[14] The best known daily of Peru, the powerful *El Comercio*, was very active in its attacks upon I. P. C. and upon the government for permitting one company to gain such strong control over the industry. This newspaper, usually conservative or even reactionary (at least not normally identified with social change), was to increase its attacks during 1959, 1960, and 1961. Part of the explanation for *El Comercio*'s stand is the fact that Prado's government had invited and received *Aprista* support in the 1956 election. The owners of *El Comercio* had for many years been bitter enemies of the *Apristas*.[15] Also, there was a feud between the Miró Quesadas of

[13] *El Comercio*, Lima, October 1, 1960; *Extra*, Lima, No. 154, March 11, 1958, p. 31; *Andean Air Mail and Peruvian Times*, Lima, March 15, 1957, hereafter cited as *Peruvian Times*, November 13, 1959, May 15, 1959; and *El Comercio*, August 14, 1960.

[14] Over the years, *La Tribuna*, Lima, has made this point or hinted at it. Influential Peruvian bank officials told the author this and then asked not to be quoted. On the other hand, the *Peruvian Times*, December 8, 1961, p. 6, carried a two-column article written by the manager of I.P.C. which made the tax item appear to be a large item of expenses.

[15] In 1935, Carlos Steer, a fanatical young *Aprista* (son of a British ship officer and a Peruvian woman) had assassinated the elder editor, Antonio Miró Quesada. This writer interviewed Steer in the National Penitentiary in 1945. Steer related that he was a wild idealist with a hope of helping Peru; that Mrs. Miró Quesada was killed accidentally as she tried to protect her husband. Steer then shot himself several times in the mouth but failed to end his life. Evidence of *El Comercio*'s rivalry with Pedro Beltran's paper *La Prensa*, Lima, cropped up as of September 8, 1960, and October 23, 1960, in *El Comercio*. *La Prensa* replied in a similar tone, October 4, 1960, pp. 1, 2.

the *El Comercio* and Prado's Premier Pedro Beltran, publisher of *La Prensa*. This, when added to the other factors already mentioned, would account for much of the fury over United States-owned petroleum in Peru.

Other factors had damaged Peru's foreign exchange and internal economy. Many Peruvians had become concerned with the threat of increased United States tariffs on lead and zinc. Congressman Alfonso Benavides Correa had a great deal to do with this apprehension. His 1957 speeches in the Chamber of Deputies decried Peru's economic "subjugation" to foreign interests, singling out the United States as the nation which hurt Peru the most because of lead and zinc tariffs.[16] He suggested that Peru should look toward ways of opening trade with communist countries as well as with Latin America. Secretary of State Dulles was well aware of the Peruvian point of view on this matter, and at the American Foreign Minister's Meeting in Washington in September 1958, noted that the Peruvian minister did not spare words on what he thought of the United States quotas and threatened cut-back on lead and zinc.[17] In 1958, zinc prices were lower than they had been in 1953, and the volume of export was the lowest that it had been for four years. Although lead exports were up in 1958, they were headed for a serious decline in 1959. As approximately 15 per cent of Peru's foreign earnings derived from the two metals, there was real concern with the United States' treatment of these metals—a concern which had been very much alive for at least two years before Nixon's visit. People in a powerful nation such as the United States, with its wealthy, diversified economic system, have difficulty in appreciating the worries of a small, weak nation when it comes to market adjustments pertaining to one or two items. The average man in the United States might find it incredible that Peruvian citizens were actually concerned with the United States lead and zinc tariffs or quotas.[18]

All five of the principal newpapers of Lima demonstrated a real uneasiness and disappointment with Washington over the lead and

[16] Alfonso Benavides Correa, *Interpelación a la cancillería* (Lima, 1958).

[17] Hollis W. Barber, *The United States in World Affairs: An Account of American Foreign Relations 1958* (New York, Council on Foreign Relations, 1959), p. 366.

[18] While this writer and Mrs. Carey were residents of Peru between 1940 and 1945, they had a teen-age Peruvian lad living with them. He expressed a feeling of resentment because the United States had such a powerful influence over economic developments in his nation.

zinc question in 1958.[19] Their feeling against the United States was expressed in terms such as "economic aggression," and "the end of the Good Neighbor Policy." [20] *El Comercio*, May 7, carried an article which quoted Ernest Baertl, president of the National Mining and Petroleum Society, to the effect that Peru and the United States needed to concern themselves with the fact that Peruvian miners were receiving such a small amount for their efforts in the production of lead and zinc. *Ultima Hora*, May 7, 1958 (at the time that Nixon was visiting Lima) reported that a pound of lead cost twelve cents. Of that, the United States duties and charges took seven cents, which left Peru five cents for production and land freight charges.[21] At this same time, the student organization of the Engineering School expressed discontent with the United States political-economic policies.[22] The *Apra* student officers of San Marcos University also protested against "imperialism." [23] They claimed that because of United States policies the Peruvian and United States oligarchies had a "stranglehold" on Peruvian economy.

The minerals question was by no means the only commercial difficulty, but because Peruvians had concentrated on mineral production during the Second World War and the Korean War there was a feeling that their assistance deserved greater appreciation. Especially did that seem the case when they could not find sufficient markets for their products after the wars had ended. A widespread notion also appears to have existed in Peru that the United States should and probably would take over the major problems of the country. This was associated with the belief in Peru that the United States was definitely the important key to Peruvian welfare in many respects.[24] In 1958, Peru complained that the United States mer-

[19] *El Mundo*, October 1958, p. 7.

[20] *Ibid.*

[21] *Ultima Hora*, May 8, 1958, p. 8.

[22] *El Comercio*, May 9, 1958 (this letter addressed to the editor was written at an earlier date), p. 9.

[23] *La Tribuna*, May 8, 1958, p. 3. *El Comercio*, May 9, p. 9. The *New York Times*, April 28, 1958, had reflected that "Nixon's mission was made more difficult when the United States Tariff Commission issued . . . its recommendations for raising tariffs on lead and zinc and imposing import quotas."

[24] Ray Josephs, *Latin America, Continent in Crisis* (New York, Random House, 1945, 1948), p. 190. Peruvian willingness, both private and public, to accept "Yankee" recommendations is notable in many respects. A variety of United States missions, including those educational and economic in nature, have often been given a relatively free hand in these sensitive areas of national life.

chants were underselling Peru on cotton and taking over part of its market in Argentina, Chile, and Colombia; at the same time, United States coffee prices were held down, and a preferential sugar treatment for Cuba (or United States owners in Cuba) worked to the disadvantage of Peru. Resentment mounted when the United States refused to increase Peru's sugar quota.[25] In the same vein, a complaint was made that Japan received preference on the United States fish market while Peru did not.[26] Peru's problems were not just those of reduced exports or lower prices in a few commodities; in value, Peruvian exports were at the lowest point in 1958 of any year since 1956, and imports followed the same downward course.[27] In 1958 both the gross national product and the national income were under the figures for the preceding year. Justly or unjustly, the United States was held responsible for Peru's trade decline. Plagued by a rising cost of living, many strikes, political unrest, falling bank reserves, and decreased exchange, Peru's prospect was bleak. Some Peruvian writers who looked hopefully toward the idea of a Latin-American common market were critical of the United States for not being more encouraging in that respect. Warranted or unwarranted, there was widespread discontent with the United States.

It is manifest that a significant and underestimated backlog of displeasure awaited Nixon upon his arrival. If communists or professional rioters were looking for an incident to use to their advantage on May 8, it was not difficult to find widespread anti-United States feeling upon which to build. It was not that any one single point of discontent was particularly great; it was rather that there was a great diversity of points of resentment. But there were nonetheless clear warnings. Various publications hinted that the general reception awaiting the Vice-President might not be entirely pleasant. An article in *Semanario Peruano*, April 30, 1958, suggested that measures be taken in Lima to prevent any unpleasant incidents which might cause Nixon's visit to result in harmful relations between the two countries.[28] *Extra*, another magazine issued just before the visitor arrived, expressed concern that the welcome might not be entirely

[25] *Excelsior*, Lima, July 1955, p. 11.

[26] "Posición del Peru Ante el Impuesto del Atún—Defensa de las Aguas Territoriales," *Revista de Derecho y Ciencias Políticas*, XV (1951), pp. 573-576.

[27] Rodríguez, *Market for U.S. Products in Peru*, p. 15.

[28] *Semanario Peruano*, IX, No. 6 (Lima, April 1958), p. 5. Because of its tendency to sympathize with the Moscow party line, some people considered this publication to be communist.

friendly and polite.[29] The newspaper, *Ultima Hora*, in its first lead editorial on Nixon's proposed visit, made note of the resentment along the coasts of Latin America.[30] The editorial commented that Nixon would find a friendliness of Peruvians for the United States, but added that he would also observe that it was time for the great northern nation to respond to this friendliness with acts, not mere words. The claim was made that Peru's economy was suffering. The nation had been neglected by the United States, but Peru wanted satisfactory commercial transaction rather than charity.

There were some writers who believed that the way for a nation to get Washington's attention and be placed on the "needy list" was to wave the communist flag on high. *Ultima Hora*, May 7, charged that the United States would show an interest in Peru's hungry masses and miserable living conditions only when the local governments denounced the growth of communism. The writer asked, "Do we have to hope for the growth of communism in order to make the United States change its policies?" This was followed by the comment (with apparent levity) that nations expecting to be visited should mobilize the masses in order to have them welcome the visitor at the airport with communist banners in their hands.[31] The suggestion was, "appear to be communist," and then Washington will listen to your complaints and consider your needs.

In addition to economic stresses, political strains on Peruvian-United States relations were also evident. At times it was difficult to distinguish between the opposition to Prado's government and the discontent identified with the United States. On March 4, 1958, the government had decreed that all general political meetings involving an assembly of people were to be held in the Campo de Marte. Three days later, the Party of Christian Democrats called a "silent march" demonstration to protest the decree. After police intervention, with the use of force and tear gas, there was a mob outburst which resulted in an attack upon the newspaper office of *La Crónica*, the National City Bank (of New York), the Banco Popular, and public transports.[32]

[29] *Extra*, Lima, No. 159, May 13, 1958, p. 4.

[30] *Ultima Hora*, April 29, 1958, p. 8.

[31] *Ibid.*, May 7, 1958, p. 9.

[32] *Extra*, No. 154, March 11, 1958, p. 11. In March 1962, the National City Bank was involved in a serious controversy with the Federation over matters which were, in part, personal controversies. Nearly 10,000 workers over the nation went on strike.

Early in May, less than a week before Nixon's visit, rambunctious students, while demonstrating in favor of "University Reform," crashed into a member of the *Guardia Civil* and smashed him to the ground.[33] This sort of thing was new for usually "disciplined" Peru, and it reflected a growing discontent with the military prerogatives and prestige of the police of the *Guardia Civil*. Ex-dictator Odría had depended upon the military. Some people, particularly university students, resented the military assistance which Washington had extended Odría as well as the pact made with him for future aid to Peru.[34] By coincidence, the United States was cast in a doubtful role as far as the antimilitarist students were concerned. Odría had been residing in the United States during a time when he was most unpopular. This discontent was demonstrated in Buenos Aires on May 1, 1958, while President Prado was visiting there.[35] Persons who had been exiled under Odría threatened Odría's former government leader, Alejandro Esparza Zañartu, while he was in Argentina. Numerous Peruvians resented the fact that the United States government had decorated Odría and applauded his government.

Throughout his administration, dictator Odría had enjoyed the full support of Washington and the United States financial-industrial-commercial interests. Odría in turn had shown a friendly attitude toward United States investors.[36] In various ways Odría had received military assistance. One of the most surprising means of aid was through the Export-Import Bank, which loaned Odría money to use for ordering the construction of two submarines in the United States.[37] In June 1953, Ambassador Harold Tittman, acting on President Eisenhower's instructions, had decorated Odría with the United States Legion of Merit in the rank of commander. Although numerous Peruvians had earlier been happy with Odría's achievements in economic and educational affairs, there was in 1958 a widespread feeling of ill will growing toward him. His tenacious persecution of the *Apristas* had earned him the bitter enmity of Peru's largest and best organized party, as well as the opposition of various other factions with inclinations toward either democratic or civilian government.

[33] *Ultima Hora*, May 3, 1958, p. 2.
[34] "Nixon in Peru," p. 5.
[35] *Ultima Hora*, May 2, 1958, p. 3.
[36] Tad Szulc, *Twilight of the Tyrants* (New York, Henry Holt, 1959), p. 196.
[37] *Ibid.*, p. 197.

This matter of the United States and Odría was wrapped up in the broader problem of Washington and dictators in Latin America. For at least twenty years prior to Nixon's visit some discontent had been evidenced with the United States policies of "liking" and assisting a dictator if he professed himself to be friendly to the United States and "disliking" and withholding aid from one who was not inclined to follow Washington's lead. The editor of *Caretas*, a popular magazine of the time, claimed that John Foster Dulles preferred to close his eyes to reality when it came to tyrannies.[38] On the day of Nixon's troubles in Lima, the newspaper *La Tribuna* (*Apra*) referred to this United States approach as "Your double standard." [39] The lashing stated that Eisenhower had decorated or helped dictators such as Batista, Trujillo, Stroessner, Odría, and Pérez Jiménez. This denunciation had been presented in the form of an open letter to Nixon on page one. Some displeasure was shown because the Vice-President had not bypassed dictatorially-governed Paraguay on the tour, and with the fact that arms aid was going to Batista.[40]

More conservative Peruvian writers wanted it known that they also resented the friendliness-to-dictators "policy" of the northern power. Some United States writers were criticized for failing to observe that revolutions in Latin America were often struggles for liberty against dictatorships and for attempting to justify "Yankee" interventions on the basis of internal revolutions and anarchy within Latin-American nations.[41] A few Peruvian intellectuals joined with other Latin Americans in February 1958 in a manifesto which called for mutual defense against dictators.[42] On the very eve of Nixon's visit, a Lima newspaper carried a United Press account of "Himmler-type" Marcos Pérez Jiménez and the well-guarded, luxurious Florida mansion

[38] *Caretas*, June 1-15, 1958, p. 5.

[39] *La Tribuna*, May 7, 1958, p. 1.

[40] Nixon's scheduled visit to Paraguay prompted some questions from students at Montevideo's University Law School to which Nixon paid a surprise visit. Nixon said that the United States did not back dictatorships because it approved of them, but because, if discrimination were shown, "we would be charged with interfering in the internal affairs of other countries and with trying to impose our system of government on them." *New York Times*, April 30, 1958.

[41] *Mercurio Peruano: Revista Mensual de Ciencias Sociales y Letras*, XXXIX, No. 372 (Lima, April 1958), p. 161.

[42] *New York Times*, February 20, 1958, p. 51. See also E. Ramírez Novoa, *America Latina y Estados Unidos Las aventuras de Mr. Nixon en Latinoamerica* (Lima, n.d., but obviously after Nixon's visit).

which he owned and in which he lived at the time.[43] A minor note of this sort was unimportant in the broader relationships over a period of time, but considered in the atmosphere of May 7 it may have been more significant than it first appeared.

There also was a dispute over the question of control of the Pacific coastal waters which dated back to 1952. This also contributed to the general unrest. Chile and Ecuador agreed with Peru in the contention that the South American nations held jurisdiction over the waters to a point 200 miles out from the coast.[44] The United States protested, and refused to recognize any claims beyond the three-mile limit. Washington had suggested the matter be turned over to the International Court of Justice.[45] The question was further complicated when in 1956, over strong protests from the United States, the Inter-American Council of Jurists approved the resolution that each state was "competent to determine its own territorial waters." This issue, although not especially brittle, was very much alive in 1958. Historically, such questions were important to Peruvians. Peru had been sensitive about maritime and naval matters ever since the catastrophic defeat by Chile in the War of the Pacific. Both the guano industry and the fish industry, important to Peru's economy, had long called attention to the importance of the coastal waters. In May 1958, ". . . United States boats made up a large proportion of the fleets fishing in the undefined waters." And a number of United States tuna boats had "tried to avoid paying the Peruvian license fee of $2,500." [46] Further complicating the matter was the criticism charging that Japan enjoyed benefits in the United States fishing industry which Peru did not have.[47] In prosperous times, the questions of coastal waters and fishing rights would probably have received little attention in Peru. These were not prosperous times.

Perhaps no one issue by itself would have stirred a mass protest against Nixon. But the many small issues, when grouped together, contributed to a general condition of mind which reflected adversely

[43] *Ultima Hora*, May 7, 1958, p. 21.

[44] *El Comercio*, May 9, 1958, pp. 3, 9.

[45] Barber, *The United States in World Affairs, 1955, 1957*, p. 223.

[46] "Nixon in Peru," p. 9.

[47] *Excelsior*, January-February 1956, p. 17. E. Ramírez Novoa's (see fn. 42 above) criticism was directed at the "new dollar diplomacy," especially at United States activities in Peru's mineral industry, pp. 38-39.

upon the United States from many angles and from various social groups. News releases in Peruvian newspapers of early May suggested minor points of criticism related to immediate details of the visit. *El Comercio* commented that the appearance of numerous beggars on the streets of Cuzco was a distasteful sight for tourists.[48] *Ultima Hora* carried a caption on page five which read, "Nixon and Company Will Occupy Twenty Suites in the Grand Hotel Bolívar." Mention was also made that Jinx Falkenburg, Hollywood and television star, was to help with the press coverage while the Nixons were in Lima. Nixon's newspaper "entourage" of more than forty newsmen was referred to on the same page that carried news of the lead and zinc problems. There was the suggestion, also, that the United States needed to understand Peru and other Latin-American nations better.[49] A last-minute comment stated that although Latin America might not be great in a military way, it did have a great economic, spiritual, cultural, and human force.[50] The latter point seemed to be aimed at emphasizing this question to Washington: "Do you see any value in our culture, or are we to be considered only a geographic block in your defense plan?"

Earlier developments in Uruguay, Argentina, and Bolivia should have given the United States Embassy and Nixon adequate warning as to what to expect in Lima. Shortly after his arrival on May 7, demonstrators expressed some anti-United States feeling. The police were prepared to curb any excesses. A second-year law student was detained by the police. The whistles and shouts deriding Nixon and/or the United States while he was on the way to the banquet at the Embassy were indicative of what could happen. A news story hinted that, because of the situation, Nixon might not go to the University of San Marcos.[51]

On the morning of May 8, Nixon attempted to visit the University of San Marcos, but because of the hostility of a rock-throwing crowd assembled outside the gates, he had to abandon the project. The official student organization had, a short time before, passed a motion declaring Nixon unwelcome at San Marcos. This strongly-

[48] *El Comercio*, May 8, 1958, p. 15. On May 7, 1958, *El Comercio* reported that United States mining concerns were planning to explode great amounts of dynamite in welcome of Nixon.

[49] *Ultima Hora*, May 3, 1958, p. 5; and *El Mundo*, August 1958, p. 34.

[50] *Ultima Hora*, May 7, 1958, p. 9.

[51] *Ibid.*, May 8, 1958, p. 2. The writer in *Ultima Hora* may have been hoping to dissuade Nixon from attempting to visit San Marcos.

worded motion (using some doctrinaire communist terminology) presented many of the complaints which Peruvians held against the United States at that time. For this reason, if not for others, it is an important piece of literature.[52] In the following resolution-type statements, the student action closed its case:

1. To ratify the anti-imperialist position of the students of San Marcos in particular and the students of Peru in general, and to express our fraternal salute to North American students and to the North American people, whose democratic virtues we recognize, and who have been so often sacrificed in imperialist wars;
2. To declare *non grata* the presence in Peru of the Vice-President of the United States of North America, Mr. Richard Nixon, because he embodies the plutocratic and imperialist interest of the North American government;
3. That the visit of Mr. Richard Nixon to our University is without the approval of any student organization.[53]

The evidence leads one to conclude that on the morning of May 8 the Peruvian government, the United States Embassy, and Nixon himself all knew that the spokesman for the university students had declared that the Vice-President was not welcome at San Marcos. Nixon's account, *Six Crises*, fails to mention this significant fact. That omission, on Nixon's part, should not be overlooked by the students of history or international affairs.

Nixon's visit brought out the fact that ill feeling was widespread, but actual violence was quite limited. Lima turned out to be a dress-rehearsal for Caracas (Ecuador was bypassed). Ambassador Achilles warned Nixon of the temper of the masses, and when the Vice-President retired late at the Grand Hotel Bolívar, in the center of the city, he heard the chant of the crowd, "Nixon, get out!" About 10:00 A.M., May 8, the United States official party placed a floral decoration at the base of the monument to José de San Martín. A silent crowd, numbering close to 1,000, watched this. At the University Park, about three blocks distance from the Plaza San Martín, a noisy mob shouted, "Nixon, get out! Go home!" And an occasional, "Muera Nixon (Death to Nixon)," was thrown in. Nixon later described the mob as numbering 2,000—mostly teen-agers—led by tough, case-hardened communist operatives. He thought he saw fear, not hate, in the crowd's eyes. The visiting party attempted to

[52] See Appendix.
[53] "Nixon in Peru," pp. 6-7.

enter the university grounds, but was blocked by the mass of humanity before it. When Nixon insisted on debating with student leaders, angry voices rose and stones were thrown in his direction. John T. Sherwood, head of the Secret Service detail, had one of his front teeth broken off by a flying rock. Nixon's account in *Six Crises* suggested that he retreated from the San Marcos crowd, not with colors flying, but with words sailing as he tried to get in a parting shot.[54]

> I could not resist the temptation to get in one good lick. I stood up on the rear seat as the car moved slowly away and asked Sherwood to brace my legs so that I would not fall. I shouted, with Walters translating in rapid-fire Spanish, "You are cowards, you are afraid of the truth! You are the worst kind of cowards." I felt the excitement of battle as I spoke but I had full control of my temper as I lashed out at the mob. Those nearby us who heard me quieted down but the rocks from the rear continued to fly.

From San Marcos Nixon's party went to the Catholic University, and shortly after that it returned to the Hotel Bolívar. Meanwhile, a small group of rioters tore out the flowers which represented the United States flag in the floral display at the Plaza San Martín. When Nixon appeared again in the plaza, stones and tomatoes were thrown and he was greeted with shouting and spitting. While he was returning to the hotel, a man spat directly in the Vice-President's face (Nixon claimed that he kicked the man a solid blow).[55] The violence ended in the same way that it had started, suddenly.

Semanario Peruano claimed that Nixon had been desirous of appearing the martyr in order to gain support for his presidential nomination.[56] E. Ramírez Novoa thought that Nixon was a deliberate provoker in the way he defied the students and sought out meetings with hostile groups.[57] The question has been raised as to why Nixon insisted upon visiting San Marcos University; he was not taking part in a cultural tour, and he had been warned of the feeling against his visit. Nixon maintained he was determined to appear because he felt it important that he demonstrate to the "anti-American Peruvians" that they could not intimidate him. He has also said that he thought he could face the mob down. However, Novoa and others

[54] Richard M. Nixon, *Six Crises* (New York, Doubleday, 1962), p. 202.

[55] *Ibid.*, p. 204.

[56] *Ibid.*, p. 11. This article states that Peruvians did not intend "spitting" upon the United States but rather upon a degenerate economic system.

[57] E. Ramírez Novoa (see fn. 42 above), pp. 24-25.

believed that Nixon was, in part at least, conducting a political tour on the "road toward the White House." The distinguished historian, Basadre, asked this writer if it had not occurred to United States citizens that Nixon sought publicity in conflict. Nixon was desirous of further contact with students even after one of the flying stones had hit Sherwood, and even though Ambassador Achilles was visibly shaken by the fury outside San Marcos. After being turned away from San Marcos, the vice-presidential party paid a visit to the Catholic University. Student officials of the Catholic University informed the newspapers that they resented the uninvited, unannounced, and inopportune visit of Nixon.[58] They were unhappy that he had entered a "private assembly" where student elections were taking place. Nevertheless, after going to another room with part of the student body, a polite question and answer period was held.

In the discussion at the Catholic University, questions of arms aid to Batista, lead and zinc tariffs, the 200-mile ocean zone, the Latin-American common market, United States agricultural surpluses, and other economic matters were presented. Nixon admitted that the United States could do more economically to help underdeveloped countries. He opined that it was "not sufficient to demonstrate that communism is bad; we must also prove that liberty and democracy are better." [59] In general answers, Nixon presented a flexible approach on the part of the United States government in the face of the criticism which was registered. Later, at a press interview in the hotel, the lead and zinc questions as well as other problems were discussed, although much time was taken up with talk of the indignities which Nixon had endured. Considering the various provocations, Nixon conducted himself admirably.

As with most other points of Nixon's visit, there was considerable conflict of opinion as to the consequences of the entire episode. Some informed persons believed that the manifestations had greatly harmed United States-Peruvian relations. Others contended that the event, even with its distasteful moments (or perhaps because of

[58] *El Comercio*, May 9, 1958, p. 9. *El Comercio*, May 9, 1958, p. 2, tells of Nixon being spit upon by one who was taunting him. In June 1958, *El Mundo*, like many other periodicals and newspapers, commented on Nixon's bravery and poise during the shouting and spitting. A Latin American, in this writer's hearing, referred to Nixon as one who bravely endured the unpleasant manifestation and then played the role of the "wounded butterfly."

[59] *El Comercio*, May 9, 1958, p. 9; and "Nixon in Peru," p. 4.

them) had been the most significant thing in the twentieth century toward bringing about an improvement in relations. The first reaction of almost all the Peruvian press was to criticize the action of the Federation of University Students and to decry the manifestations against the United States and its Vice-President. The expressions ran from merely being ashamed to fear of reprisals and to the repercussions which might follow in United States policy toward Peru, especially if Nixon were elected president of the United States.[60] It was evident early that there was no widespread ill will toward United States citizens as such. Two days after the "Affaire Nixon," Leonard Bernstein was enthusiastically applauded in the Municipal Theater. Of course, the great majority of those attending the concert came from the upper classes, those areas of society where resentment of wealth and power seldom, if ever, flared red-hot.

The student federation seemed to share (and sincerely) in the general expression of regret for the abusive treatment extended Nixon. This is not necessarily inconsistent with the federation's earlier statement. They repudiated the violent manifestations against Nixon, but it was a fact that they had never approved the United States policies of the period and they had not invited Nixon to the university. As far as this writer has been able to determine, neither the student federation at San Marcos nor any official of the university has ever retracted the original motion. By no means should all of the manifestation of hostility be attributed to the students of San Marcos. The activities in the Plaza of San Marcos and in front of the United States Embassy were separate manifestations although some of the same people participated in both. Various publications later were to agree with the protests lodged by the students against the United States, but they did not agree with the tactics used.[61] Twenty persons were detained by court order in a fruitless attempt to place responsibility, and there was an almost universal expression of admiration for the calm, dignified manner in which the Vice-President conducted himself during the greater part of the ordeal. In the press conference, Nixon condemned the moral cowardice of the communists in their demonstration against him.[62] He, like many writers for

[60] El Mundo, June 1958, p. 15.

[61] El Mundo, June 1958, p. 15. E. Ramírez Novoa (see fn. 42 above) defended the student federation on many points and charged Nixon with carrying out his presidential campaign in the Peruvian developments, pp. 25-26.

[62] El Comercio, May 9, 1958, p. 3.

Peruvian publications, assumed that the communists had been active in the affair. *El Comercio*, very critical of the student federation, placed most of the responsibility upon the *Apristas*.[63] The *Apristas*, in turn, blamed the excesses on the communists.[64] Everyone seemed to be in agreement that it was an unfortunate affair. *Semanario Peruano*, often addicted to the Moscow party line, called attention to its April 30 warning and admonition that measures should be taken to prevent any untoward incidents.[65] Many people asked why the police had been conspicuously absent at critical moments. At the same time, they noted that the armed Assault Forces had been at the square in front of the San Marcos University early on the morning of May 8. Recriminations abounded.

Shortly after the "Affaire Nixon," as a left-wing paper called it, the president of the student federation, *Aprista* Orestes Rodríguez, declared that the federation's position had been a clear one. He said that students did not invite Nixon—and no one ordered the gates shut against him.[66] *Ultima Hora* went a step further and said the federation's position was also one which "repudiated" the ". . . imperialist policy of the United States," declared Nixon *"persona non grata,"* and yet it "had not approved any . . . act of violence." [67] After some violence was employed by a few students—at least, alleged to be students, according to most of the Peruvian press—the federation repudiated these actions of violence and lamented the excesses which had occurred.[68]

Because of the wording and because of the arguments, it appears that the anti-Nixon visit motion of the student federation might have been communist-inspired. This may well have been the case, but an analysis of all the principal newspapers and magazines of Lima, 1957-1959, has convinced this writer that the ideological line which separated general expressions of public opinion from the com-

[63] *Ibid.,* May 8, 1958, p. 1. *El Comercio* had long been a bitter opponent of the *Apristas*.

[64] *La Tribuna,* May 9, 1958, p. 1; and May 10, 1958, p. 1. *Caretas,* May 15-30, 1958, p. 9, held that the explanation which tried to place all the blame on the communists was not adequate.

[65] *Semanario Peruano,* IX, No. 7 (May 20, 1958), p. 9.

[66] *Ultima Hora,* May 9, 1958, p. 2.

[67] *Ibid.,* May 9, 1958, p. 10. E. Ramírez Novoa (see fn. 42 above) wrote that Nixon provoked trouble even after he knew that the student federation had passed a motion to let him know that he was not wanted at the university, p. 24.

[68] *La Tribuna,* May 9, 1958, p. 1; and "Nixon in Peru," p. 7.

munist line was a thin and often indistinct one. This is not to infer that most Peruvians were communist-directed or communist in inclination. Rather it is to say that the Peruvian discontent with the United States and its trade policies was based on independent arguments which were quite similar to those of the communists, but that they arose from noncommunist principles or doctrine and had been reached after considerable reflection and freedom of discussion.

Many students and nonstudents logically registered protests against the United States economic preponderance in Peru since the United States was at the same time denying any major obligation towards Peru's economy. The arguments made by such critics of Washington were similar to those that might have been made by people who disliked the Soviets or by those who greatly feared the spread of communism, even though their particular points of view were in close accord with communist ideology concerning United States economic activities in Peru. The majority of Peruvians who held that point of view were not communists (possibly they were anticommunist), but they would have agreed that the communists were correct on certain points.

In all fairness to the students at San Marcos, an impartial observer could see why they would object to opening up the university to anyone who might wish to use it for a political platform of either national or international scope. It should be recognized that the University of San Marcos has long been proud of its independence of the national government. The students would readily admit that on occasion they have been undisciplined and, perhaps, even foolish. But, at the same time, they know that students of their university have been killed by police and by the armed forces of the government of Peru while those very students were defending the constitution or attempting to assert freedom of expression. They have considerable right to be proud of their traditional stand for freedom. It should be remembered that in 1958 most of the students were sympathetic to or outright supporters of *Apra*, although its position was weakened considerably during that year. The party head, Haya de la Torre, had been president of the Federation of Peruvian Students back in 1919 when an earlier period of turmoil over reforms was bloodily contested. In the heat of the discontent with the United States, the federation seemed to have overlooked the very important question: "Was their action conducive to the encouragement of freedom of discussion—or was it the opposite?" Richard Patch, an eyewitness to most of the important events, suggested that Nikita Khrushchev, under similar circumstances, would have been refused permission to present his views at San Marcos.[69] And, who is to say that the students did not have a right to be proud of their traditional stand for freedom? Many times in the past they had insisted on independence for San Marcos, that is independence from the Peruvian government. They knew that that government had in the past often been the object of distrust or dislike by masses of their fellowmen. Only a decade earlier (September 1947) the capital had gone through an emotional upheaval when police killed a student at the nation's largest secondary school.

It is well to keep in mind that the student federation was *Aprista*-dominated in 1957 and early 1958, and that very likely, most students of San Marcos were *Aprista*-inclined. The *Apra* Party had a long anticommunist record prior to May 1958, but there were some signs of a divided ideology as concerned the United States and its economic preponderance in Peru. *Apra* leadership at the national party level had softened its approach toward United States investments in Peru. Haya de la Torre had redefined his definition of "economic imperialism" and its relationship to the United States. He said the United States had changed, but it appeared that he had also softened in his advancing years. Still, there were many *Apristas* in 1958 who maintained that the overwhelming economic power of the United States interests in Peru was, when supported by Washington, an "undesirable economic imperialism." Ten years earlier the Chiclayo, Peru, *Aprista* newspaper had stated: "Wall Street bankers and trusts do represent imperialism." And they are stronger when the ". . . Conservative, rightist, capitalist" Republican Party is in power. "Then . . . imperialism grows." [70] The same writer claimed that anti-imperialism was the defense of natural wealth and of the proper use of the nation's riches. It would appear many young *Apristas* continued to hold that belief in 1958. On the day before the attacks on Nixon, the principal *Aprista* newspaper, *La Tribuna*, had a front-page open letter combining a welcome to Nixon and an attack upon him

[69] "Nixon in Peru," p. 9.

[70] *Hechos*, Chiclayo, Peru, August 21, 1947, p. 1. *Excelsior*, January-February, 1956, p. 5, echoes the charge that the United States became narrowly aggressive under the Republican Party, and that in 1956 "Franklin D. Roosevelt's Good Neighbor Policy had been lost to the Republican Regime" in Washington. E. Ramírez Novoa (see fn. 42 above) was highly critical of John Foster Dulles and his diplomacy, p. 39.

and the United States (more so on the latter). It stated: ". . . your economy is narrow and political . . . and it has hurt us since World War II." "You . . . need to advise your investors to work within our needs." [71] The officers of the *Aprista* student organization wrote a protest letter in which they attacked the United States policies for providing the United States and Peruvian "oligarchies" with a "stranglehold" on the Peruvian economy. In the same letter they stated that they were opposed to "all imperialism."

By early July 1958, influential leaders such as Ortiz de Zevallos, Manuel Seoane, and Bedoya Reyes (later elected Alcalde of Lima) all expressed the belief that Nixon's South American trip would have beneficial results because it had awakened Washington to Latin America's problems and feelings.[72] Possibly the "Affaire Nixon" aroused Lima, as well as Washington, to certain realities. Many Peruvians expressed a basic friendliness toward the United States. The *Apra* Party and its newspaper, *La Tribuna*, have been more circumspect in their criticism of the United States since May 1958. This, of course, could be merely the reciprocal action on *Apra*'s part to the changed economic policies of the United States. The calm, objective reporting that part of the United States press gave the incident was pleasantly received by many in Peru. Novoa, who had been most unhappy with United States policies prior to May 1958, referred in glowing terms to the "clean," fair reporting in the *New York Times*.[73] Many people in Lima seemed to feel that, if nothing else, the visit had provided a window for the United States to look in upon Peru's misery, and at the same time, upon some of the Peruvian feelings toward their northern national "sponsor." Peru's foreign minister, Raúl Porras Barrenechea, was quoted as saying that "Nixon should have knowledge of the life and needs of our people." [74] This, in the long run, may have been the most important result of the "Affaire Nixon."

The Peruvian occurrence, followed by the more dangerous developments at Caracas—where it appears that communists played a more active role—shocked Washington policy makers into reviewing their

[71] *La Tribuna*, May 7, 1958, p. 1.

[72] *El Mundo*, July 1958, p. 18. Bedoya Reyes, cofounder of the Christian Democratic Party, was chosen Alcalde of Lima in a spirited election of December 15, 1963.

[73] E. Ramírez Novoa (see fn. 42 above) may have been favorably impressed with such accounts as the editorial in the *New York Times*, May 10, 1958.

[74] *La Tribuna*, May 9, 1958, p. 1.

approaches south of the border. In some ways it was a turning point. After the Nixon trip, Under-Secretary Douglas Dillon suggested the creation of a development loan bank. Only nine months before Nixon's rude reception the United States secretary of the treasury had refused to consider seriously its establishment. There had been many people in both nations who thought this visit would be just another expedient cliché in the traditional good-will-tour manner of smiling speeches. Things were changing. Like it or not, the "Yankees" were directly involved in complex problems in Lima and Caracas.

Official Washington had lifted its head—what about Lima? As always in Peru, events there moved slowly. Back at University Park and along the halls of San Marcos with its history dating back to the 1540's, the words of Carlos Paz Soldan (1919) seemed to echo and re-echo: "A cyclone of unrest passes over the aged colonial university and beats its weary face and forces it to lift its indifferent eyes to changing reality."

12: REFLECTIONS AND SPECULATION

What general lines of development—with what degree of continuity for both nonofficial and official policies and activities—become apparent as we look back over this study? Where have these lines of development worked for harmonious relations or for nonharmonious relations between the two countries? Questions of this nature are not easily answered. A study as inclusive as this is bound to reveal a complex record with many cross-currents of mixed influences and counterdevelopments. Nevertheless one can find some guidelines for reflection and speculation.

We have been constantly aware of the fact that the United States and Peru represent forces of greatly differing strength—the one, extremely powerful, and the other, relatively weak. Not only has this worked toward a one-sided pressure, but it has also developed the tendency in Peru to let the stronger nation take the responsibility which is normally associated with leadership and strength. At the same time, these conditions tend to encourage the growth of an inferiority complex in the weaker country. After 1930, official United States policy stressed status quo more often than not, most particularly in economic relationships. Possibly it was not a policy of status quo, but neither was it one which encouraged social reform. A great many Peruvians, unhappy with their own government, have come to see the alliance between the domestic minority and the weight of United States interests (both private and public) in Peru as working, in general, to maintain this unsatisfactory "status quoism." And, of course, United States policy changes undertaken since 1959 cannot yet be measured effectively as to their meaning for the Peruvian social system. The study has been quite complex because it is concerned with nonofficial as well as with official matters. And from 1900 to 1960, economic factors (both public and private) preempted first place among United States activities in Peru.

With this word of warning at the outset, it should be recognized that conclusions or reflections drawn from United States policies and activities in Peru will not necessarily shed a bright light on similar policies and activities in other Latin-American nations, and much less so in other parts of the world. This is true because Peru is not Uruguay or Lebanon. Peru is Peru.

On first thought, the casual reader might conclude that the same United States policies in Peru and in Mexico are essentially the same "seed" in similar soil. Many times, however, the seed (policies) will be received in different ways and, at times, even as if it were a very different seed. The crop will not be the same. The historical streams of the distant past and the different cultural patterns of the two nations must determine the flowering. Although Peru and Mexico are of a similar ethnological make-up as to percentages of European and indigenous blood, they are very different in the general racial composition when examined from a cultural point of view. In Peru the Indian and the mestizo have not played as great a role in society. In Mexico, there is much more homogeneity since the mestizo is a very influential cultural factor. Mexico has been strongly independent as a nation since 1917, whereas Peru has been inclined to lean upon "Uncle Sam's" arm and go along where directed whenever real incentives were provided. Of course, Peru has been unhappy when it has found itself poorly led, according to its own interpretation of national needs. Peru has never undergone a profound and sustained social revolution, while most of Mexico's twentieth-century history has been exactly that. Frequently, conservative Peru has been willing to accept leadership from Washington on hemispheric matters, but Mexico, in a more advanced state of nationalism, has not followed that leadership to the same extent. Mexicans, with a much higher percentage of secondary school and college graduates, have more domestic leadership available than do Peruvians. But Peru, with proportionately more abundant natural resources, has received more economic as well as technical aid. Mexico has become, progressively, an independent country with a growing desire to become master of its own household and beholden to no nation. Mexico City has not been interested in military assistance programs whereas Lima, from 1940 to 1960 especially, has held out an open hand for such aid. For several decades, Peru has been growing increasingly dependent upon United States aid, behaving as though it expected it to be forthcoming in the future. It is possible that discontinuation of this assistance at some future time could stir considerable resentment within the country. If one carries comparisons further, it becomes more and more clear that similar United States policies, operating in both countries, will not necessarily have the same results.

Part of the explanation of the outburst against Vice-President Nixon can be found in the fact that university students, as well as others, were beginning to interpret their history. These were past events which they were interpreting, but events which still rankled them. They rankled, in part, because foreign ownership of extractive industries was still great in 1958. They were irritated with the United States even though it had been more than a decade since the United States had intervened in any direct way. Private "Yankee" businesses were beginning to operate in an enlightened manner and to act in a way which would not offend national pride. But the past still merged with the present in the eyes of San Marcos students. Peru had not vindicated itself. It had not erased the stigma as had Mexico. Mexicans could, to some degree, rest in the atmosphere of self-respect and national pride. But the young nationalists of Peru were easily stirred to action. One is prompted, then, to ask if the United States tendency to attempt to follow a general policy for all of Latin America has much meaning when twenty distinctly different nations are involved. Where general hemispheric matters have been in question, Peru and the United States have had little disagreement thus far in the twentieth century. When matters of hemispheric defense arose, there was usually an over-all Latin-American policy outline which helped guide the two governments. The Second World War is a good example of this. Each nation acted as an individual entity and at the same time acted as a member of a region. Manuel Seoane has suggested that Washington should view the Pan-American nations more as a region with the needs of a region. In many matters, however, nations are apt to want to be treated as individual nations. If this can be done in ways which will still encourage long-range, multilateral trade agreements, then the dual role of national and regional approach might be achieved. Other than in the matters of several boundary questions and some economic problems, there has been no noticeable complication between the two types of relationships for the United States and Peru.

Boundary complications are likely to lessen in the future, whereas economic matters will probably increase if the United States does not give more attention to them in a hemispheric context. Consideration of means for moving in the direction of a common market, finding more flexible, and yet common, denominators in monetary matters, and designing long-range combination programs of both hemispheric and national economic development are all imperative if the United States hopes to continue, in any real sense, the dual approach of dealing with the various nations as individual units while at the same time holding out regional goals. If the United States waits for the hemisphere to push it into taking these steps, then the opportunities which accompany leadership and which credit that leadership with good will and foresight will have passed. Over the years, Peruvians have progressively come to the point of saying, "Economic matters shall have first consideration now." This is being said now, more than ever before, because Peruvians now know that a better way of life exists, and they intend to have it, or at least part of it. A new breed of Peruvians is rising. For the first time in history these leaders will not be satisfied with a patchwork of economic aid and military assistance, emanating in the form of half-hearted projects from Washington.

In many respects the unofficial relationships between the two nations have been as significant, over-all, as have been the official. Economic matters loomed large in the 1900-1962 period, since private activities caused important differences of opinion between the peoples involved. Yet those differences have not always appeared on the surface in formal official expressions. In contrast, for the last three decades most of the official diplomatic relationships between the two governments have been harmonious. Very few times has Peru taken a position in opposition to Washington in diplomatic matters of hemispheric or world consequence.

Officially, Peru has expressed a desire to work toward hemispheric economic goals. This was done at the Second Meeting of Foreign Ministers (Havana, July 1940) and at the Ninth Inter-American Conference (Bogotá, 1948) where the Peruvian delegates expressed definite interest in inter-American economic co-operation. Such interest in a closer inter-American commercial and financial program was also expressed in a plan published in Peru's journal of international law.[1] This plan called for a hemispheric clearinghouse of products and a system to stabilize prices and standardize the monetary system. It would appear that official Peru does not want to main-

[1] "Propuestas del Gobierno del Peru Acerca del Futuro Convenio de Co-operación Económica Interamericano," *Revista Peruana de Derecho Internacional*, VII (1947), pp. 243-245; also III (1943), pp. 312-315.

tain as fine a line between public and private commerce and finance as does the United States.

In attempting to evaluate the influences of United States policies within Peru itself, one faces complications, since Peru is a nation which has not, regularly, had a representative government. Since Peru has often had governments which were not freely elected, or even representative, the result has been that these governments have been unpopular (at times, even evoking popular disgust). Over half of the 1900-1960 period was taken up with the rule of three dictators, Leguía, Benavides, and Odría. Not one of these enjoyed popular support although all three spent large sums on public works. The three sought to co-operate with the United States, and the government of the United States was friendly to them. Private United States business interests were lavish in their praise of Leguía and Odría, and the officials in Lima usually reciprocated. But merely because United States policies were pleasing to these three president-dictators does not mean that the policies were acceptable to the majority of Peruvians. Unfortunately, all three regimes left a residue of serious problems and considerable ill will between the two nations and their peoples.

Of the three, Leguía's sixteen years of presidency were vastly more important for over-all relations than were the regimes of the other dictators. His was more of a foundation period so far as United States relations were involved. Peru moved further away from the orbit of British and European trade circles and into the close network of United States commerce. Leguía's second administration, 1919-1930, encompassed the years when the basics of United States official and unofficial economic policies were firmly established. Since that time, Washington and private economic concerns have not varied much from the general pattern conceived and entrenched under Leguía—except for some minor concessions to the growing spirit of Peruvian nationalism. Odría returned to the Leguía tactics of encouraging Washington trade and financial missions, importation easements, and a freer hand in general for foreign interests. Whereas Peru faced serious difficulties immediately after Leguía, there was a short interval following Odría before finances nearly collapsed. The latter benefited from a definite economic stimulant born of the Korean War. Moreover, he did not incur as heavy a debt as did Leguía.

Have United States-Peruvian relations improved as the twentieth century unrolled? If one compares conditions of 1960 with those of 1910, it is easier to demonstrate that relations between the two nations in 1960 were closer than it is to show that they were more harmonious. The increased number and importance of interexchanges have not resulted in improved relations as such. That is to say that borrowing or lending money, buying or selling more goods, or joining the same literary club may merely bring *more* relationships, and not necessarily more *harmonious* relationships. Superficially, relations were "good" during the quarter-century that Peru was governed by Leguía and Odría. But looking ahead in terms of future developments, they were not good.

By 1960 the United States held many areas of interexchange with Peru which had not existed fifty years earlier. This increase ranged from a diversity of business activities to numerous private and public aid projects. If "many relationships" brought congenial relations, then the United States had a better relationship than it had at the beginning of the century. On the hypothesis that increased interexchange provides more opportunity for nations to understand one another, it is often concluded that more harmonious relations necessarily follow. This cannot be proved in the case of Peru, although the extensive official and unofficial aid programs have provided a reservoir in which good will may very well be stored. How that reservoir will be used is, to a great extent, a matter to be decided by domestic Peruvian policies still unfolding, or possibly by decisions toward policy making which have not yet been made. Pedro Beltran, Prado's minister of finance and premier, as well as ambassador to Washington at the close of the Second World War, stated in 1958 that United States-Peruvian relations had been better twenty years earlier.[2] Although this was spoken at a specific time and cannot be taken as proof of his measured judgment on this, still it has great relevancy to our question here. As the private and public agencies from the United States extended their influence in Peru, the Peruvians expected reciprocating benefits. At the same time, they thought that the United States should accept a greater share of responsibility for Peru's economy.

This feeling of increased dependence upon the United States raises another question as to the nature of that responsibility. If private economic interests increase their investments in Peru, whose responsibility should increase? Should it be that of the United States

[2] *New York Times*, October 21, 1958, p. 8.

government or that of the private traders and lenders? If it is both, is it an equal or an unequal growth in responsibility? As the twentieth century has unfolded, the United States government has made itself more and more accountable for the growing involvement in Peru brought on by the expansion of private economic interests.

To this writer, it appears that private economic interests have been more of a liability than an asset in the relations between Washington and Lima. Even while the dollar investors tried to improve their public image in Peru, the economic nationalists of that country persisted in resenting the stereotyped images of the past. While the companies were attempting to make themselves more acceptable in Peru, a tide of national spirit and accompanying antidollar feelings were developing within the maturing Peruvian citizenry which more than canceled out the positive, constructive efforts of the business concerns. It is very possible that, if the United States reduces its responsibility for protection of private interests in Peru, it can then reduce its foreign aid to Peru without having any harmful effects upon United States-Peruvian relations.

In the past the United States government has been expected to shoulder—and has shouldered—most of the responsibility for that growing liability. While cultural relations and both official and unofficial aid programs have, in general, worked for harmonious relations, many of the financial and commercial operations of private citizens or companies have been a deterrent to harmonious relations. Because the United States has officially increased its operations and expenditures in Peru, the relations between the two countries have been relatively agreeable in the twentieth century. The great majority of United States taxpayers might legitimately raise the question as to whether they should pay for extensive aid programs, projects not always efficiently supervised, which are needed to offset both the responsibility and liability incurred by private operations. The question is all the more pertinent when it is noted that private operations greatly benefit only a small minority of United States citizens and directly benefit only a minority of Peruvian citizens.

Private companies have received very valuable assistance from official United States agencies in both Washington and Lima. It is not particularly clear that this aid (to one segment of the United States economic realm) has merited the emphasis it has received, especially if one were to place a high premium on long-term harmonious relations between the two nations. The economic interests of two or three companies (or occasionally a half-dozen) appear to have been in conflict, at various times, with the national interest, national defense, or national security in the broad terms of United States needs. The record does not make it clear that national security or national defense has always received priority of attention over the needs of private mineral interests or other private investments. Problems which demonstrate this conflict of interests have arisen over such matters as the sugar quota, embassy pressure on behalf of copper interests in securing concessions, consideration of the need to summon American warships into Peruvian waters when United States business interests were threatened, the use of missions of the armed forces as well as the sale of armaments to Peru, and difficulties related to the use of surplus agricultural products in Peru. Part of the time, there has been a mutuality of interests between the United States national aims in Peru and private economic interests—but this has not always been the case.

We conclude, then, that increased relationships between nations are not necessarily steps towards closer relations. Also, expanding dollar investments in a foreign nation do not necessarily work for the national security or national interest of the United States. Ever since Leguía "sold the country" to the United States—as his critics charged—or built on United States "dollars and brains"—as his admirers claimed—the government and certain private concerns of the United States have been deeply involved in Peruvian domestic affairs. There is no simple way to distinguish between what has been United States "national interests" and "private interest" in Peru. No one formula is adequate to determine what is "public enterprise" and what is "private enterprise" in many of the relationships between these two nations. A heavy involvement of United States money, publicly or privately, in Peruvian economics, education, and general public welfare became pronounced as early as 1928 when large private loans were made.

United States investors in Peru have claimed a right to high returns by stating that they ran grave risks in Peru, or that they were developing new industries and providing positions for Peruvians when domestic investors would not—or could not—do the same. One immediately recognizes some merit in the observations, but the over-all investment picture in Peru must not be overlooked. For forty-five years there have been good investment conditions which have provided high profits (8 to 30 per cent annual returns for most large United States concerns). And in those forty-five years no major case of expropriation resulted, nor was there even a serious threat of national intervention except for the petroleum industry in the last five years.

Conflict-of-interest charges were brought against individual employees of the United States government when, as in the distribution of food relief, a Washington congressional committee took particular interest. But no serious steps were taken to probe the much greater conflict-of-interest situation that arose when Washington heaped lavish relief upon dictator Manuel Odría—the good friend of private United States investments—after it had been stingy in its support of democratically-oriented José Luis Bustamante y Rivero—a friend of the United States, even if not a special guardian-protector for private United States investments. This writer is forced to conclude that, in the long-range analysis, the United States taxpayers' money was not spent wisely in this context.

Other "conflict-of-interest" cases show up. The Export-Import Bank loan for the purchase of submarines must be considered as such. The loans and grants for Peruvian purchase of arms or maintenance of projects started by United States military missions have been disadvantageous so far as progress toward a more representative government is concerned. Just as Peruvians were moving toward positive social adjustments after both world wars, the United States bolstered Peru's military establishment and institutions. These, in turn, emphasized stability and made it possible for the old order to hold on. Preliminary movements which would be necessary for any effective Alliance for Progress have had to contend with a military system which strengthened the status quo. One part of Uncle Sam's program was out of harmony with another part. When the military took power and prevented the popular candidate from assuming the presidency in 1962, it was evident that United States aid to Peruvian armed forces was being used to the detriment of United States national interests. There had been no real violence during the July elections, when a democratically-inclined candidate and friend of the United States would probably have been elected had the Peruvian army remained neutral.

Rightly or wrongly, after the military coup of July 1962 the generals charged Ambassador James Loeb, Jr., and his wife with having

given support to their long-time rival, Haya de la Torre.[3] It was
generally assumed that Washington broke off relations with the
military government on Loeb's recommendation, and that this led
to the suspension of military aid to Peru as of July 18. The ruling
junta took the position that Loeb was virtually *persona non grata*,
while at the same time the *Peruvian Times* reported that North
American business and industrial enterprises also looked unfavorably
upon him. The investment spokesmen believed that the State Department's "tough" policy toward the military government's *junta*
"not only endangered their interests but was also erroneous." [4] In
any event, Loeb did not return to the embassy in Lima, and by
October 11, 1962, the *junta* could announce that relations were so
improved that the United States had renewed its military aid. The
following year Loeb was appointed ambassador to Guinea.

External as well as internal factors were at work to promote increased United States assistance. These came into play in the period
following the Second World War, when much of Latin America
(and a great part of the rest of the underdeveloped world) was
stirred by forces amounting to a social revolution. Internally, Peru
was not particularly moved by the social revolution, but besides these
internal forces there were some currents of communism and Castroism which provoked agitation. By the time of Nixon's visit in 1958,
and even later, many Peruvians looked to Cuba for ways to go about
curing their own social ailments. The opportunities supposedly
opened up by Cuba were not, at first, thought of as clearly anti-
United States or pro-communism. Whatever else, Castroism represented a change from the disgusting status quo. In 1960 the critic of
Apra, Eudocio Ravines, termed the Cuban Revolution the greatest
emotional upheaval in Latin America since the sixteenth century.[5]
El Mundo magazine earlier printed a criticism of the United States
for not having had the "necessary tact" to prevent the deterioration
of conditions in and relations with Cuba.

We note, then, that, as the twentieth century developed, there
was a variety of forces in action which encouraged Peru to expect
that the United States would take greater responsibility for internal
economic conditions. Combined "Yankee" business concerns were

[3] The *Miami Herald*, August 19, 1962, as reported in the *Peruvian Times*,
August 24, 1962, p. 4.
[4] *Peruvian Times*, August 3, 1962, pp. 1-2.
[5] *El Mundo*, Lima, November 1960, p. 40.

taking more and more natural resources, as well as profits from those resources, out of the country. Peru assumed that its co-operation during two world wars entitled it to greater consideration. The anti-communist and later the anti-Castro attitudes which were adopted by the government in Lima were also expected to draw benefits from the northern nation.

This air of expectancy as regards United States aid appears to have been greater in Peru than in most middle-sized or small nations of Latin America. It has been closely associated with the willingness to transfer certain responsibilities to the northern power. Under Leguía there existed a receptive atmosphere to technical aid and to assistance and direction in education, finances, and welfare matters. Unfortunately, the United States was either not interested or not prepared (possibly both) in doing much at that time. In the period, 1940-1960, when the programs were developed, Peruvians readily accepted most of them almost as if they were entitled by right to such aid. This is not to imply that Peru's recognition of a condition of dependence upon the United States amounts to willing and happy acceptance of this status of dependency.

When Peruvians have flared up against the United States, as on the occasion of Nixon's visit, the cause appears to have been due as much to dissatisfaction with the United States for not taking more responsibility in hard times as to a mere burst of narrow nationalism. Of course, some of both have been evident on such occasions, and ample evidence exists to demonstrate Peruvian resentment of its "inferior position" in economic relationships with the United States.

The traditional pat phrases used by Latin-American extremist critics of the United States, such as "colossus of the North" or "Yankee imperialists," and other, more rabid attacks common to some nations, were not especially obvious to this observer as he viewed Peru's twentieth-century reaction to United States policies. Of course, some such expressions are still common in communist publications. But other complaints of a more reasonable nature have been centered around arguments that the United States has not displayed a real knowledge of, or sincere interest in, Peru's needs. Peruvians, along with their neighbors, after the Second World War asked if there should not have been some sort of Marshall Plan for them at the time that "Uncle Sam" was spending large sums and paying great attention to other distant parts of the globe.

With the forces of world social revolution (a better life meeting

basic needs and fulfilling human dignity for the individual, regardless
of race, nationality, religion, color, or former colonial status) and
with the agitation of communism and Castroism at work, there was
great need for a counterforce. To some extent, counterforces came
in the form of private and public assistance programs and such activity as that of the Cultural Institute. Without these forces, it is
unlikely that private United States business concerns could have
carried on their business-as-usual methods, which, with slight adjustments to Peruvian laws and concessions to nationalism, were basically
the same as those during Leguía's time, some thirty or forty years
earlier. Relations between Peru and the United States would probably have deteriorated if "Yankee" tax money had not moved southward to help smother discontent. At the same time United States
business operations became somewhat more enlightened and related
themselves more directly to Peruvian demands.

It would seem that in various ways the assistance programs have
made real contributions to Peru. The training programs for technicians and professionals have prepared some Peruvians to perform
their tasks more adequately. Even with occasional gross mismanagement, the aid agencies, especially Scipa and Scisp, have made friends
for the United States by helping the Peruvians to help themselves.
Of course, greater efficiency in the projects would have resulted in
more good will with less expense to the "Uncle" up north. Private
aid efforts such as the Summer Institute of Linguistics, the Vicos
Cornell-Peru *hacienda* achievements, and the work of various independent missions have been quite effective in dealing with Peruvian
problems and in working for harmonious relations between the two
nations. At the same time both official and unofficial programs have
attempted to reduce the misery and ignorance at hand and plan for
the years ahead. Just how much potential has been developed is a
question for the future. One can hope, at least, that the average
Peruvian will have been moved in the direction of improved nutri-
tion, more adequate medical care, and a greater share of individual
human dignity. On the surface it appears that some advance has
already been made in these areas. It is another question as to how
lasting those achievements will be. Unless the aid programs are
woven into the basics of Peruvian economy, they are merely stop-gap
measures of little account. The sample survey conducted by this
writer indicated that most Peruvians would prefer that future aid
programs be restricted in some way that would tie them to social

reform projects and at the same time reduce the chances for Peruvian graft.

If the reader has been disappointed by not finding an account of how Peruvian social problems have influenced relations, or how United States policies affected Peru's social system, there is a concise explanation. Not much has happened in this respect. The United States diplomatic corps has had very little communication with the representatives of the great masses of Peruvians. Spokesmen for the Indian population and the low-class coastal workers have seldom come in direct contact with our officials. This writer concluded that aid projects should be designed to "work themselves out of Peru" in a manner which turns affairs and responsibilities back to the nationals. For this to happen, more of the aid activity should be related to building Peru's economy. This will also lessen the need for Peru to lean on the strong "Uncle" up north or to complain if the aid is reduced or cut off at a future date. Washington can begin planning to assume more long-range responsibility for the Peruvian economy, or it can begin planning for the withdrawal of some of the operations —of both a private and public nature—now being carried on in that country.

One noticeable handicap to the entire official aid program—as well as to work in other official activities, and, to some extent, in private operations—has been the short tenure which most United States personnel have had in Peru. Most of the heads of divisions, chiefs, mission directors, executive secretaries, and many embassy officials were constantly undergoing new appointments and adjustments to new appointments. Often the new arrival had only enough time to develop some usage of the language, make some important contacts, and size up his assignment in the light of Peruvian psychology and philosophy before he was sent to another country (possibly Japan or some other distant area of the world). This change of administrative and general personnel was alarmingly evident in embassy cultural activities and such operations where person-to-person associations could be especially helpful, as, for example, in the executive secretary's office of the *Instituto Cultural Peruano-Norteamericano*. Since 1938 the leadership of the Institute has been changed regularly on an average of about every two years. A nation such as Peru, which has traditionally emphasized personal associations, acts and reacts in terms of persons and cannot appreciate our emphasis on organization and institution. Washington official policies have often ignored this factor.

In the sample survey questionnaire answered by Peruvians it was manifest that United States diplomats, businessmen, and aid officials had failed to make significant impressions as individual persons. The question read: "What United States persons (who have lived in Peru some time in the twentieth century) have done the most good toward improving relations between Peru and the United States? . . . Please list three." Ninety-one of 157 responses failed to list even one name. Of the names listed (rarely more than one for each paper) in the other sixty-six responses, names of nonofficial educational workers and Y.M.C.A. personnel dominated the list. One businessman, Elmer J. Faucett, and two diplomats with names consistently misspelled were mentioned in a few cases. It is not impossible to incorporate a more personal relationship approach even as long-range economic or cultural programs are emphasized. It must be granted that, for this to succeed, a real interest in Peru and Peruvians would be a necessary requisite for our personnel. At the same time, United States officials would need to keep a closer supervision on the use of funds. Such a condition calls for more attention from Washington, which in turn will give rise to bothersome details, but these form a necessary part of the responsibility of our self-appointed leadership.

Scanning the horizon behind us, we see that relations between Peru and the United States have been relatively "normal," comparatively void of especially critical matters. There has been little looking ahead beyond the day-to-day, or year-to-year approaches, on the part of either nation. The net effect of such a condition where one nation is super-powerful and not interested in changing the status quo probably leads to this sort of diplomatic holding action. We have observed how numerous factors have brought the two countries into more active relationships. Peru ever more consistently supported Washington on critical issues; especially was this true during the Second World War and following it. The decision to aid the United States in the Second World War was scarcely debated after the one strong popular party began to support the government at Lima on this point. The matter crystallized sometime between 1939 and 1942 with *Apra*'s firm decision to oppose the growth of totalitarianism in Peru and around the world.

The rift, which had threatened under Benavides, passed. The second war, like the first, boosted the United States into an even stronger position relative to Peru's economy. The extensive pattern of private and official assistance programs helped offset the discontent voiced by those who criticized the powerful economic position of the United States. The largest group of moderate Peruvians maintained that the United States had incurred a greater responsibility in their country and that neither private nor public agencies wished to pick up that burden.

A high point in dissatisfaction developed prior to Nixon's visit to Lima in 1958 during a low ebb in the Peruvian economy. Nixon's rude reception served the situation in several ways. Washington's attention was directed to the immediate economic and political difficulties between Lima and the northern nation. It also made clear that a field for further communist exploitation was growing. At the same time, Peruvians were confronted with the question of allegiance or nonallegiance to the over-all pattern linking them to the United States. They saw more clearly than before some of the advantages and disadvantages. Peruvians seemed to be relatively content with the United States "measure of man," but they wanted greater economic returns if they were to continue to adhere to the United States world of trade and international defense notions. A disgruntled segment of the populace was ready to follow communist leadership, but the majority was not ready to break the main ties with Washington.

There are various forces working in Peru to paint a hateful picture of the rich and powerful "Uncle Sam." Some of the principal publications in this category are the following: Rimak (mimeographed bulletin, 1945-?); Democracia y Trabajo (1946-?, not so critical of United States as it was soon after close of the Second World War); Unidad en el Pensamiento y en la Acción (bulletin, 1948-?); La Chispa (Marxist newspaper, issued irregularly, 1948-?); El Proletario (mimeographed bulletin, 1961-); Revolución (newspaper with communist tones, issued irregularly); Semanario Peruano (follows the Moscow party line, 1958-1961); and Libertad (most recent of extreme leftist newspapers). Circulation figures are not available for these publications. If available, the figures would not have much significance for media of this sort are often passed from hand to hand and may reach many readers. These channels of propaganda have exploited the "anti-Yankee" feeling of recent years. It is difficult to evaluate their influence, but one would speculate that, more than anything, it has been the moderate stand of *Apra* (a democratic leftist party) on economic nationalism which has prevented the extreme left from growing more rapidly than it has in the last two decades. Because of *Apra*'s position, Haya de la Torre has received vitriolic criticism from time to time. *Semanario Peruano* (April 10, 1958) said that in 1954 Diego Rivera had assailed Haya as a "dangerous agent of imperialism" and a traitor to the progressive masses of this continent. And *Revolución* (December 1960, No. 2), while lauding Castro's reforms, attacked the United States and *Apra* on questions of foreign investments as well as on Cuban developments. Some communist agitators are inciting the Indian peasants toward violence. If a general blood-letting does take place, economic nationalism will fan the dislike of foreign capital investments. Since foreign capital is identified first with "Yankeeism," justly or unjustly the United States will reap a harvest of hatred. "Anti-Yankeeism" has been growing during the past fifteen years—but the surprising thing about it is that it has not grown even faster.

Developments in Lima, 1958-1963, show that the political forces which are favorable to private United States businessmen and financiers have lost popular support. This tends to demonstrate a continuity in Peru's history since 1919. When the *Apristas* shouted against the dollar, they gained numbers. *Apra*'s diminished prestige in 1963 must be accounted for in part by its willingness to accept dollar investments without strong guarantees to insure Peruvian benefits. A left splinter has broken off in the form of *Apra Rebelde*, and many of the moderate left have become suspicious and aligned themselves with Belaúnde, as was reflected in his election in 1963. Beltrán's political balloons of 1961 and 1962 did not rise high, partly because he was considered to be too soft on foreign investments and foreign influence. Under these circumstances, the fact that he was married to a San Francisco girl was no help to him. Discontented people are not impressed with figures which (however reliable) indicate that Peru needs to attract foreign capital investment. The unhappy are more likely to be most concerned with seeing that outside capital is not in league with the tight, high-interest domestic capital. They prefer an economy which makes real contributions to Peru and to their immediate welfare.

Even if we take a more optimistic approach and conclude that many Peruvians are not unhappy with what they see in the "image" of the man up north, this does not mean that all is well. There is real reason to believe that the policy of the last twenty-three years will encourage the growth of the "charity-type nation" in Peru, if not a downright "beggar nation." United States aid to Peru which sustains United States private investment and holds up a mirror for the image of the United States citizen does not make progress toward building a society or state of mind consistent with "Peru for the Peruvians." As Peruvian nationalism matures, the charity-type nation and its climate of opinion will likely generate an atmosphere of dissatisfaction between the small nation and the giant power.

This study might make it appear that the writer is overly concerned with Peruvian opinion of past United States policies. It is not intended that we should wallow in problems of the past or unduly fret about the "image of the present," but we do need to ask if the former policies will serve national interests in the future. A United States policy or set of policies for Peru should have some real thought for the future and not rest on expediencies and status quo as has so often been the case until recently. Various aspects of the AID programs do look ahead. This much is a constructive start. But it is necessary that the government in Washington learn more about both private and public United States operations in Peru in order that an intelligent policy, designed specifically for that one country, can be programmed. Reluctantly, we have undertaken some domestic governmental planning. When will we consider it in our foreign policy?

United States public and private enterprises would do well to combine their efforts in thinking and planning for the long-range goals in any country where as much is invested as in Peru. The tendency to act too readily and without careful thought and clear design must be curbed or the United States government will continue to spend more and more in Peru and get less and less in return. When assistance is extended to transportation, agriculture, industry, and a group of technicians in isolated spots, it will not make as great a contribution as when designed to fit into a plan for Peru's over-all economic needs. Peruvian public and private enterprise should also be taken into consideration. This may provide a means to influence social reforms as well as economic ones.

The success of any United States plan for future developments will also depend, to a great degree, upon what changes can be wrought in the hearts and minds of Peruvians. Washington's foreign aid programs of the past fifteen years, as well as private United States enterprises, have not moved Peru very far in the direction of assuming its own obligations. If such changes as are mentioned in the next paragraph are not effected, there is great danger that the masses will turn to some schematic program or totalitarian system which promises to mobilize men, money, and machines for the modernizing and revolutionizing of Peru in this decade or the next decade. It is possible that a foreign totalitarian power, by co-ordinating its aid (public and private) and by insisting on over-all harmony for its economic, diplomatic, and military agencies could function more efficiently in Peru than would the United States over a long span of time, say forty or fifty years. Of course the Alliance for Progress is intended to prevent this from happening.

"Pigmy Peru" and "Giant Yankee" have some mutual decisions to make along the following lines. What kind of a market shall exist? How much sharing of marketing responsibility shall we have? Shall a real effort be made to break the crippling hold of large property and/or capital interests so that enterprising new brains can share adequately and justly in Peru's productive potential? What is a fair rate of interest? What tax reform measures can be employed that will bring about a greater degree of equity and still provide the government with funds to finance the needed reforms? How does one develop confidence in representative civilian government, as opposed to military institutions, in this small nation? How can Peruvians build up enough confidence in Peru and its resources so that the nation can face up to its own economic problems?

If the United States, publicly or privately, should take a greater responsibility for certain areas of Peru's economy this can have but limited effect unless there is complementary activity in Latin America. For the acceptance of additional obligation in Washington or New York can significantly benefit Peruvians, in general, only if social reforms are carried out by Peruvians at the same time. To a great degree, reformation must be an obligation of the Peruvians. United States policies, 1900 to 1960, have not usually stimulated social reforms, but now with the changing goals of Alliance for Progress, such changes are encouraged. In the long run this will mean that a great effort will have to come from Lima, not merely from Washington, if real progress is to be made.

It does little good for calm heads to advise young nationalists that they may be, as it were, "kicking a dead dog" when they strike out at "imperialistic Yankee" capital, or that their suspicions are bringing in the past to clutter up and confuse the present. Surely, some of the dollars invested in recent years do not deserve the stigma of past clichés. To the extent that the young Peruvian living a miserable everyday existence dwells on the past, he will tend to use it, or misuse it, in interpretations. In part, some of the past still exists because the domestic oligarchy keeps it that way, even opposing positive reforms suggested by the Alliance for Progress. There are some Peruvians who want gradual reforms, but who fear that the change of a few foundation stones will topple the whole building in one gigantic storm of violence.

Although the intention here is not to analyze the Alliance for Progress in Peru, it is important enough that certain observations should be made. The program of social revolution which is intended is so vast that it will be many years before any definitive study of it can be done. It appears, however, that the social changes proposed by the Alliance will continue to stimulate nationalistic ideas. Nationalistic ideas tend to promote a zeal and a patriotism for nationalizing foreign investments. If that happens, there is danger that it will discourage the entrance of new foreign capital which is needed to help attain various of the objectives of the Punta del Este Charter. On the other hand, a growing national spirit will probably force new capital, both domestic and foreign, to adapt itself more closely to national needs by taking socially desirable forms of investment which should ultimately be compatible with the objectives of the Alliance for Progress.

An example of this is the entrance of United States capital into new ventures such as housing construction. The Agency for International Development (AID) loaned money to Apollo International of Pittsburgh and at the time of this writing that concern had completed one hundred homes for the market. More of such construction is under way by Apollo and the International Basic Economy Corporation. The construction is termed "low-cost." At 123,500 soles (about $4,500) this is not "low-cost" for the majority of Peruvians, but it does bring capital into a field where it is much needed, and where it should work to improve housing conditions in general.[6] It also appears that established monetary and financial agencies of the United States, as well as international offices, are being induced

[6] *Hispanic American Report*, XVII (March 1964), p. 63. Also see *Andean Air Mail and Peruvian Times*, Lima, August 16, 1963, p. 6.

to lower the interest rates on money loaned to Peru.[7] This could prove to be very important in a social and political context, as well as in the economic.

Peruvian response to the Alliance for Progress would seem to have been quite positive up to date. This does not mean that the vast majority of Peruvians have experienced any appreciable change in their well-being. It may be that a more favorable view of the United States as a nation and of foreign investments is developing, but one cannot even demonstrate this at the present time. Many of the underprivileged masses remain skeptical or even suspicious of the "rich Uncle" up north. An unfortunate and atypical incident—distorted in some newspapers—took place in March 1964 when nine Peace Corps volunteers (possibly performing in an admirable manner) were driven, by threat of violence, from the Vicos community.[8] This was the area where United States citizens had made such positive contributions over a period of thirteen years. It would be easy to overemphasize the negative aspects of this unfortunate and isolated incident, and yet it points up one of the greatest problems confronting the Alliance for Progress. It demonstrates the need for the Alliance to develop in the Peruvians the belief that, to a great extent, the Alliance program is *their* program. Agrarian reform and agricultural development, promotion of industry, basic education reform, housing and urban development and other proposals will ultimately depend upon the Peruvians. Teodoro Moscoso put it this way: "What is still lacking . . . is a sense of national involvement with the purposes and ideals of the Alliance. . . ."[9] Success for the program depends on the degree to which greater national

[7] *Report of National Advisory Council on International Monetary and Financial Problems* (referred to the Committee on Banking and Currency and ordered to be printed) (Washington, June 25, 1963), p. 35; and a later report (July 23, 1963), p. 23.

[8] Richard W. Patch, "Vicos and the Peace Corps," *American Universities Field Staff* (New York-Lima, March 1964), pp. 1-8. See also *La Prensa*, Lima, March 13, 1964. Patch reports that Paul Doughty, a Cornell anthropologist associated with the Vicos community project, has started to prepare an account of the Peace Corps incident.

[9] From address, "The Latin American View of the Alliance for Progress," delivered by Teodoro Moscoso, U.S. co-ordinator of the Alliance for Progress, at the World Affairs Conference, Marquette University, Milwaukee, Wisconsin, September 29, 1962, and printed in *U.S. Policy in Latin America* (ed. Grant S. McClellan), The Reference Shelf, XXXV, No. 1 (New York, The H. W. Wilson Company, 1963), p. 222.

production is translated directly into a higher standard of living for the masses.

Peruvians have pointed out that a stronger Peruvian economy could benefit the United States as well as Peru, even if this does not at first appear to be the case. They contend that if the United States buyers of their raw-material exports paid higher prices, the increased Peruvian purchasing power would be reflected in larger purchases of United States products, and that in this way both sides would benefit. (See Chapter 10 for the statement of Luis Alberto Sánchez.) Just how this would work on a long-term basis depends, to some degree, upon various factors which are not operative at the moment. But Sánchez is not alone in holding this point of view, the foreign ministers of Mexico and Brazil having been outspoken on the same matter. Higher prices paid by United States purchasers of Peru's raw materials would tend to improve relations between the two countries in these respects: (1) less of the handout or charity-type aid would be needed from Washington; (2) Peruvians would be encouraged to take more pride in their own economy and depend less upon the help from north of the border; (3) the foreign exchange gained by Peru would enable that nation to buy more manufactured articles from the United States producers; (4) if any part of the higher prices for raw materials were passed on to the various laboring groups concerned, this would tend to raise wages in other areas of the Peruvian economy as well as elevate the standard of living in general; and (5) as has been pointed out, the United States would expand its consumer market.

Pedro Beltran sounded a warning note in 1956, one which may have helped prepare the way for a critical examination of the old methods of extending aid. "If a nation relies on handouts in order to live, then no matter how convenient such help may appear to be, its future is doomed." [10] It will be more and more difficult for such a nation to get on its feet and make its own way. "It has no sure and independent source of income. Instead it lives by what it receives for political considerations," which are uncertain. It ends by "making no effort to develop its own resources or be self-supporting." As long as this condition prevails, "such a country will never come of age," but will continue to be dependent with little hope for the future.

Some Peruvian intellectuals have been prompted to speculate

[10] Pedro G. Beltran, "Foreign Loans and Politics in Latin America," *Foreign Affairs* (January 1956), p. 300.

about the nature of Washington's aid program as they stand on the pivot between further support for United States world and hemisphere policies or turning away from them. Vague but deep questions still stir them. Does the United States see values in the Peruvian social system which it wants to preserve? Is there any real interest in the cultural pattern? Or is the northern power willing to give more handouts merely to keep Peru in the geographic-economic bloc which it is hoped will check the advance of communists or the forces of some sort of Castroism? Most Peruvians seem to hope (but not knowing if the hopes are justified) that the United States government and its people hold respect for some of the main features of their Peruvian cultural pattern. But, if the United States purports to be leading, "just where does it propose to go?" And in recent years some of the United States citizens working with the Alliance for Progress have started asking, "And if we did try to lead, would they follow?" Just possibly the need is neither for leaders nor followers, but, rather, for more co-operative effort guided by the older and more advanced nation. Even after 140 years, the words of Simón Bolívar still pique the minds of the curious: "Oh, that the United States would only do something with Peru, which has chosen it in mockery as a guarantor!"

APPENDIX

The Federation of University Students of San Marcos, in its motion passed May 5 declared Vice-President Nixon unwelcome. The complete motion follows.

"Considering:

"1. That there has been announced the visit to Peru of Mr. Richard Nixon, Vice-President of the United States of North America;

"2. That confronting this situation, the reform students as a consequence of our essentially anti-imperialist position wish to remember some acts and attitudes which are definitely American and which fully reveal their imperialist character before the world;

"3. That in a continental view the 'Good Neighbor' and 'defense of democracy' policies of the Government of North America are false and insincere because of that country's easy understanding with military dictators: Odría, Pérez Jiménez, Trujillo, Somoza, Rojas Pinilla, Stroessner, Batista, etc., which have harassed popular democratic movements;

"4. That the United States, and specifically the Department of State, obeying the interests of the great capitalists of Wall Street, recognized and applauded the coup of Adría [sic], and encouraged the criminal devaluation of our currency with the euphemism 'free exchange' which perpetuated the anti-Peruvian tyranny;

"5. That the President of the United States of North America, General Eisenhower, decorated Odría, in spite of his being a genocide and a vulgar ruler-by-force who placed outside the law the popular parties of Peru, and who persecuted, imprisoned, and assassinated leaders who fought for the liberty of our people.

"6. That the North American imperialism forced Peruvian legislative reforms, such as the Mineral Code, which permitted them, in ominous conditions, to take power over the iron of Marcona and Toquepala and the national petroleum wealth. And that even today we are threatened with new tariffs upon our exports: copper, lead, zinc—as they have already done with tuna; and with dumping, or unfair competition, of our raw materials such as cotton;

"7. That the United States and Odría agreed to a military pact which meant the gift of arms to a tyrant, as they are today helping Batista, and the submission of our people, and which, in addition to being a sacrifice of our national economy, places our youth in the danger of becoming flesh for the cannons of imperialism. Because by means of these pacts they have imposed upon our countries the unfriendly and discriminatory tactic of giving or denying arms to this or the other government, inflaming rivalries and risking internal conflicts; and insinuating its intentions to establish atomic bases in our America in its measureless warlike eagerness which the Indo-American people have already rejected;

"8. That still present in the minds of all is the insolent aggression perpetuated by the imperialists of the United States on our sister republic of Guatemala, where the United Fruit Company was adversely affected by the agrarian reform, and by the gallant and patriotic stance of the democratic governments such as those of Dr. Juan José Arévalo and Jacobo Arbenz, and by the strict economic control placed over the North American monopolies. These interests mobilized their influence and pressed the government of Washington to intervene and provoke a fratricidal war which crushed the popular revolution of Guatemala, demonstrating before continental opinion that the much vaunted democracy which the United States pretends to defend was neither nationally nor continentally defended, but was rather trampled upon and bloodied with the arms of military pacts and the dollar loans of the American treasury;

"9. That economically, while the United States scatters thousands of millions of dollars to finance its European colonial allies, it systematically denies tenths of this amount to develop technical help for Indo-America in its eagerness to arrest the development of our continent and maintain us in an underdeveloped position as simple producers of raw materials and for the satisfaction of its mercantilist appetite. For these reasons, defending despotic regimes, the great imperialist capitalists make themselves the proprietors of our natural riches, fixing a price which strangles and impoverishes our people, and impeding trade with other countries of the world, as was done in the epoch of colonial Spain;

"10. That the aid given by the government of the United States to the great colonial powers such as England, France, and Holland, against the peoples who fight for their independence, violates the profound nationalist sentiment and conviction of our brother countries, and they are seen as even further wounded by the example of Puerto Rico, which is today a North American colony with its nationalist leaders such as the patriot, Dr. Pedro Albizú Campos, suffering persecution, prison, and exile, for the crime of fighting for the emancipation of their fatherland;

"11. That the United States has apportioned economic and military assistance to the Dictator Batista in Cuba, who at this very moment continues with impunity to bloody the glorious land of San Martín, in full view and with the approbation of our international organizations such as the Organization of American States and the United Nations;

"12. That this maneuver of deception and the protestation of good faith, inevitable and inherent characteristic of the development of imperialism, has extended itself among all the peoples of Indo-America who are wearied by the hard lessons learned in the past two World Wars and their respective consequences. On both occasions the handsome promises formulated before and during the conflicts vanished, and there reappeared the bitter reality of a large country, powerful and armed, which blocks our political and economic progress, which stimulates intrigues threatening the unity of Indo-America, which attacks with acerbity the popular regimes which do not prostrate themselves, which imposes a monopoly of commerce assuring the low price of its imports and the high price of its exports;

"13. That all of these irrefutable facts, apart from others beyond this list, make up the typical aspects of the imperialism of the government of the United States of North America, of whose aggressive activities in our America there remains evident the deeply graven tracks in Haiti, Nicaragua, Santo Domingo, Cuba, Panama, Puerto Rico, Honduras, and our never-forgotten sister republic of Guatemala;

"We agree:

"1. To ratify the anti-imperialist position of the students of San Marcos in particular and the students of Peru in general, and to express our fraternal salute to North American students and to the North American people, whose democratic virtues we recognize, and who have been so often sacrificed in imperialist wars;

"2. To declare *non grata* the presence in Peru of the Vice-President of the United States of North America, Mr. Richard Nixon, because he embodies the plutocratic and imperialist interest of the North American government;

"3. That the visit of Mr. Richard Nixon to our University is without the approval of any student organization.
"Lima, May 5, 1958."

The above is taken from Richard W. Patch's "Nixon in Peru," American Universities Field Staff, *New York-Lima, May 20, 1958.*

BIBLIOGRAPHICAL NOTE

Although there are several general accounts of United States relations with Latin America, there is almost nothing which treats exclusively with Peruvian-United States relations. On the over-all subject, United States and Peru in the twentieth century, there has been no monograph done in either English or Spanish, and no significant article in English deals comprehensively with bilateral relations.

One explanation as to why so little was written is that there was no particular incident dramatic enough to attract attention until Vice-President Nixon's visit to Lima in 1958. There was neither a Baltimore Affair, as with Chile, nor a Veracruz occupation, as in Mexico. Nor did a United States diplomat in Lima or a Peruvian diplomat in Washington ever publish more than a smattering on his experiences. It is noted also that the four dictators, Leguía, Sánchez Cerro, Benavides, and Odría, forbade full disclosure during the third of a century that they governed. Therefore Peruvians could not write from the official record and United States citizens did not publish appreciably in the field.

This account is based on the sources cited in the notes. Each chapter documents deserving authors, records, associations, or agencies. The publishers are recognized in all cases of English titles. As this was not always possible for Spanish titles, only the author, title, place, and date are listed. It would be misleading to single out one or two sources and designate them as having been "the most important." Although practically the same research methods were used in both national capitals, the documents in Lima were not as helpful or as complete as those in Washington. Interviews, a survey, and secondary accounts had to carry more of the weight for Peruvian matters than was the case for the United States. The official *memorias* (records) of the cabinet members at Lima, although fragmentary, are of considerable assistance. Even with its great inadequacy as to twentieth-century documents and manuscripts, the National Library in Lima has a useful collection of newspapers and periodicals.

For the Washington perspective up to the time of the Second

World War, the *Papers Relating to the Foreign Relations of the United States*, published under the auspices of the United States Department of State, constitute the best single source. As to the period since 1942, one must depend more upon a diversity of official reports, periodicals, newspapers, and personal observations.

INDEX

237

Previous volumes in the
International Studies Series

Empire by Treaty: Britain and the Middle East in the Twentieth Century. M. A. Fitzsimons

The USSR and the UN's Economic and Social Activities. Harold Karan Jacobson.

Chile and the United States: 1880-1962. Fredrick B. Pike.

Death in the Forest: The Katyn Forest Massacre. J. K. Zawodny.

East Central Europe and the World: Developments in the Post-Stalin Era. Stephen D. Kertesz, ed.

Soviet Policy Towards International Control of Atomic Energy. Joseph L. Nogee.

American Diplomacy in a New Era. Stephen D. Kertesz, ed.

Diplomacy in a Changing World. Stephen D. Kertesz and M. A. Fitzsimons, eds.

The Russian Revolution and Religion, 1917-1925. Edited and translated by Boleslaw Szczesniak.

Soviet Policy Toward the Baltic States, 1918-1940. Albert N. Tarulis.

Introduction to Modern Politics. Ferdinand Hermens.

Freedom and Reform in Latin America. Fredrick B. Pike, ed.

What America Stands For. Stephen D. Kertesz and M. A. Fitzsimons, eds.

The Representative Republic. Ferdinand Hermens.

Theoretical Aspects of International Relations. William T. R. Fox, ed.

Catholicism, Nationalism, and Democracy in Argentina. John J. Kennedy.

Christian Democracy in Western Europe, 1820-1953. Michael P. Fogarty.

Why Democracies Fail: A Critical Evaluation of the Causes for Modern Dictatorships. Norman L. Stamps.

The Fate of East Central Europe. Stephen D. Kertesz, ed.

German Protestants Face the Social Question. William O. Shanahan.

Soviet Imperialism: Its Origins and Tactics. Waldemar Gurian, ed.

The Foreign Policy of the British Labour Government, 1945-1951. M. A. Fitzsimons.

Diplomacy in a Whirlpool: Hungary between Nazi Germany and Soviet Russia. Stephen D. Kertesz.

Christian Democracy in Italy and France. Mario Einaudi and François Goguel.

Bolshevism: An Introduction to Soviet Communism. Waldemar Gurian.